Chattahoochee River
User's Guide

WATERFALL,
CHATTAHOOCHEE NATIONAL FOREST
IN WHITE COUNTY

Chattahoochee River User's Guide   Joe Cook

GEORGIA RIVER NETWORK GUIDEBOOKS

Published in Cooperation with Chattahoochee Riverkeeper

The University of Georgia Press   Athens & London

A Wormsloe
FOUNDATION
nature book

© 2014 by the University of Georgia Press
Athens, Georgia 30602
www.ugapress.org
Designed by Omega Clay
Set in Quadraat serif and sans by Omega Clay
Manufactured by Everbest for Four Colour Print Group
Printed in China
The paper in this book meets the guidelines for permanence and durability of the Committee on Production Guidelines for Book Longevity of the Council on Library Resources.
Most University of Georgia Press titles are available from popular e-book vendors.

18 17 16 15 14 P 5 4 3 2 1
Library of Congress Cataloging-in-Publication Data
Cook, Joe, 1966–
Chattahoochee River user's guide / Joe Cook.
pages cm. — (Georgia river network guidebooks)
"Published in cooperation with Chattahoochee Riverkeeper."
ISBN 13: 978-0-8203-4679-3 (pbk.)
ISBN 10: 0-8203-4679-9 (paperback)
1. Boats and boating—Chattahoochee River—Guidebooks.
2. Outdoor recreation—Chattahoochee River—Guidebooks.
3. Chattahoochee River—Guidebooks. I. Title.
GV776.G42C473 2014
797.109758—dc23   2013049758
British Library Cataloging-in-Publication Data available

Contents

Acknowledgments

Telling the story of the Chattahoochee's 434 miles is a daunting task and would not have been possible without the previous research and assistance of many others.

We thank the Historic Chattahoochee Commission for their years of commitment to documenting the historic sites and culture of the Chattahoochee Valley. I leaned heavily on books commissioned and/or published by the commission for information about the Lower Chattahoochee. Those books include Lynn Willoughby's *Flowing through Time: A History of the Lower Chattahoochee River* and *Fair to Middlin': The Antebellum Cotton Trade of the Apalachicola/Chattahoochee River Valley* and Edward Mueller's *Perilous Journeys: A History of Steamboating on the Chattahoochee, Apalachicola and Flint Rivers*. Additional important resources included Fred Brown and Sherri Smith's *The Riverkeeper's Guide to the Chattahoochee*, Matt Gedney's *Living on the Unicoi Road*, the Heard County Historical Society's *Chattahoochee River Stories in Heard County*, and Suzanne Wielander's *A Canoeing and Kayaking Guide to Georgia*.

Others lending their expertise and knowledge of the river include Dave Gale of Wildwood Outfitters, Jerry Hightower of the Chattahoochee River National Recreation Area, Charlotte Gillis of the National Park Service, Jason Ulseth and the staff of Chattahoochee Riverkeeper, and Georgia Department of Natural Resource staff members: fisheries biologists Brett Albanese, Patrick O'Rouke, and Brent Hess; and aquatic zoologist Jason Wisniewski.

Chattahoochee Riverkeeper Sally Bethea deserves special mention, not only for her support and assistance in this book project, but for her leadership in protecting the Chattahoochee and Georgia's other rivers since 1994.

Master mapmaker and geographic information system specialist Andy Carroll created beautiful, informative, and accurate maps of each mile of the river, sorting through reams of information and multiple revisions to complete this book.

Thanks also to April Ingle and the staff and board of Georgia River Network (GRN), including Dorinda Dallmeyer, who first envisioned a series of guidebooks to Georgia's rivers. The GRN staff has a vision for Georgia's rivers in which easy access to our rivers is the norm, not the exception. For that, all river users—and river user wannabes—are grateful.

Finally, a special thanks to all those individuals who assisted with shuttles, paddle trips, and other ventures so I could learn and write more about this great river, including Peter Morgan, Doc Stephens, April Ingle, Mike McCarthy, my daughter Ramsey Cook, and my wife Leanne Hand Cook.

Generous support of Georgia River Networks is provided by

Hennessey Land Rover Centres

Turner Foundation, Inc.

The Mildred Miller Fort Foundation

Map Legend

★ **Point of Interest**

◎ **Shoal/Rapid**

⊠ **Fish Weir**

⊗ **Water Intake/Discharge**

• **River Mile Marker**

■ **River Gauge**

⛺ **Campground**

⚓ **Marina**

⊙ **Outfitter**

▰ **Take Out/Launch Site**

▰ **Public Land**

The map on the next page provides an overview of the length of the river, detailing sections covered on individual maps included in this book. The symbols included in the legend are used on individual maps throughout the guide.

Chattahoochee River User's Guide

HIKING THE HEADWATERS,
CHATTAHOOCHEE NATIONAL FOREST
IN WHITE COUNTY

Introduction

The Chattahoochee River begins its life 3,600 feet high in the North Georgia Mountains as a tiny trickle on the flank of Jacks Knob in far southeast Union County. Salamanders and crayfish call this place home; the water issuing forth from the ground is pure and bone-chilling cold. Occasionally, hikers on the Appalachian Trail stop to fill a canteen. Here, the Chattahoochee is a baby—unblemished, innocent, and unaware of what it is to become.

By the time it mingles with the Flint River in Seminole County of Southwest Georgia to become Florida's Apalachicola River, the Chattahoochee has wound longer than any other Georgia river—434 miles—and grown into the state's most important, most celebrated, and most fought-over body of water.

Quenching the thirst of nearly 40 percent of the state's citizens and carrying away the waste of those same citizens, the Chattahoochee is a workhorse. From tiny Nora Mill Dam in the headwaters, where its water powers century-old millstones, to the Alabama Power Co. Farley Nuclear Power Plant, where that same water cools nuclear reactors, it is used, abused, reused, and subdued.

And, all the while, this workhorse maintains its proud beauty.

Spilling out of the Chattahoochee National Forest, it descends 2,000 feet over waterfalls and rapids in its first 10 miles. From there it spreads some 1,500 feet of descent over its next 424 miles. It cuts a bucolic path through the Nacoochee Valley and the fabled "hills of Habersham," and then jumps rapids to the backwaters of Lake Sidney Lanier—a fittingly named reservoir honoring the Georgia poet who penned "Song of the Chattahoochee"—a celebration of the river's answer to the call of duty in service to man.

Below Buford Dam, it flows through a misty landscape to Atlanta, following an ancient geological fault line that in places renders the flanks of the river into soaring rock cliffs and faces and creates in its tributaries beautiful shoal-filled streams.

Passing by the big city, it continues southwest where, despite years of pollution, it remains a peaceful and inviting stream that alternates between playful shoals and long stretches of flatwater. At West Point along the Georgia-Alabama state line it is dammed again, and in the next 38 miles downstream to Columbus is dammed six more times as it drops 300 feet in elevation, descending out of the piedmont, across the fall line, and into the Coastal Plain. While much of the old river channel lies beneath the numerous lakes formed by these dams, the rugged beauty of this transitional area between the state's geological regions remains.

1

Beyond Columbus, the river winds 150 miles through the high Coastal Plain. Dammed three more times along its route, the river spreads into Lakes Walter F. George, George W. Andrews, and Seminole. Between the dams it meets high bluffs, slips past beautiful sandbars, and is fed by crystal-clear springs. Finally joining the Flint River at Lake Seminole, it leaves Georgia as the Apalachicola River, which flows another 106 miles to Apalachicola Bay, Florida's most productive estuary.

Like all rivers originating in the southern Appalachians, it gives life to an incredible variety of aquatic animals, including 104 fish species, 24 species of aquatic turtles, 37 species of salamanders and sirens, about 30 species of frogs and toads, and, historically, as many as 45 species of freshwater mussels. In fact, the rivers of the southeastern United States contain the richest diversity of aquatic fauna of any temperate area in the world, harboring 493 fish species—an amazing 62 percent of the total species of fish found in the United States.

CHATTAHOOCHEE SPRING, UNION COUNTY

Since humans began dwelling in this region, this ribbon of life has woven itself into the culture of the river's people. That relationship is revealed during any journey on it. The story is told through ancient structures that still remain: in historic accounts of river crossings, ferries, and bridges; in the annals of biologists who have tracked the rise and fall of the river's fish and mussels; and in relics rescued before floodwaters from the river's dams forever concealed that history.

On the Upper Chattahoochee, Native American fish dams bisect the river. These rock structures were employed to catch fish, a staple in the diet of the region's original inhabitants, and many date back 1,000 years or more. Likewise, the secrets of these ancient civilizations lay buried in places like the Rood Creek Indian Mounds on the banks of the river in South Georgia's Stewart County.

As the frontier pushed west, the Chattahoochee served as a boundary between Native Americans and early Georgians, like Thomas Powers in Cobb County, who established ferries into Indian territory and whose names are still attached to roads and bridges.

During the summer of 1864, the river was a strategic prize to be fought for and won as the Union Army pushed to capture Atlanta during the Civil War. For a few brief days in the midst of this fighting, both the Union and Confederate armies laid down their guns to bathe in the river together—such was the allure of its cool water.

Throughout the 1800s and 1900s, the river was aggressively harnessed. The first dam across the river went up in 1824 in the Nacoochee Valley; the dam building didn't stop until 1974 with the completion of West Point Dam. With 13 dams, the

Chattahoochee is Georgia's most altered river. In fact, of its 436 miles, nearly 200 lie on manmade still water behind dams.

Today, the river would be largely unrecognizable to the likes of Benjamin Hawkins, the U.S. Indian agent who lived among the Creek Indians in the late 1700s, and who first recorded the word "Chattahoochee" to mean "flowered rock." Likewise, one wonders how the famed botanist-explorer William Bartram would describe the river today—would he still consider the water "clear, cool and salubrious," as he described it in the 1770s?

Indeed, the changes wrought on the Chattahoochee in the last two centuries are both miraculous and tragic.

We have engineered facilities—from hydroelectric dams to nuclear power plants—that with the help of the Chattahoochee, light hundreds of thousands of homes annually. We have learned how to take raw sewage and transform it into water suitable for drinking—we've even devised plans to turn that sewage into energy sources. Most recently, efforts to restore the river's historic rapids and shoals at Columbus have prompted the removal of two 150-year-old dams. The river, and often our need to preserve it, have inspired innovation and progress.

But, what is progress for some may well be destruction for others. A river that once had the greatest assemblage of mussels of any eastern Gulf Coast river now hardly supports any mussels in its mainstem. Lovers of flowing rivers, the mussels disappeared as the dams rose. Likewise, migratory fish like Alabama shad,

BUCK SHOALS RAPID, HABERSHAM COUNTY

WATERFALL,
CHATTAHOOCHEE NATIONAL FOREST
IN WHITE COUNTY

gulf sturgeon, and striped bass all ran into walls on their historic upriver runs and exclaimed, "Dam!"

Pollution has also exacted a toll. Polychlorinated biphenyls (PCBs) and mercury have made many of the river's fish unfit to eat. Dirt and sediment from land development and farms have killed aquatic insects—the base of the aquatic food chain— and destroyed spawning grounds of fish. Spills from sewage plants and hot-water discharges from power plants have resulted in massive fish kills.

These threats to the health of the river and the animals and people that depend on it are compounded by what is probably the river's greatest threat in the 21st century—our own seemingly unquenchable thirst.

In 1990, when Metro Atlanta communities petitioned the U.S. Army Corps of Engineers to use more water from Lake Lanier and the Chattahoochee for water supply, the states of Alabama and Florida filed suit to prevent this reallocation and to preserve flows to downstream communities. In 2013, those lawsuits had still not been settled and uncertainty over future water supplies spawned all manner of "solutions" to meeting the region's water needs—everything from damming tributary streams and filling them with water pumped from the river itself to piping water 100 miles from the Tennessee River.

Metro Atlanta, it has been said, does not have a water problem, instead it has a people problem: too many people in the wrong place. Unlike other Georgia cities that grew up along major rivers during the age of river navigation (Savannah, Augusta,

NEAR NEW FERRY, HEARD COUNTY

SHOALS NEAR WHITE CREEK, WHITE COUNTY

Columbus), Atlanta was founded on a ridgeline where railroads met—miles from the Chattahoochee. The only other major metropolitan area in the United States to sit at a higher elevation than Atlanta is Denver, Colorado. In fact, no other major metro area in the nation must depend on a smaller watershed for its primary water source. A populace of more than 4 million people sits just 80 miles from the spring that starts the river. Despite receiving an average of more than 50 inches of rainfall each year, Atlanta has more in common with cities in arid locales like Phoenix and Los Angeles, where large populations stress limited water supplies.

While water conservation efforts have gained ground (the region reduced per capita water use by more than 20 percent from 2000 to 2009), much still remains to be done. In 2012, the nonprofit river protection organization Chattahoochee River-keeper estimated that the metro region that currently demands about 500 million gallons a day (MGD) could save 140 MGD by implementing a series of commonsense water efficiency measures.

How Metro Atlanta responds to the challenges of meeting the water needs of its populace will likely determine the health of its primary source of drinking water, not to mention the future of those downstream communities also linked to the river.

In 1877, when Sidney Lanier penned "Song of the Chattahoochee," the river was celebrated in terms of what it accomplished on behalf of humankind:

But oh, not the hills of Habersham,
And oh, not the valleys of Hall
Avail: I am fain for to water the plain.
Downward the voices of Duty call—
Downward, to toil and be mixed with the main,
The dry fields burn, and the mills are to turn,
And a myriad flowers mortally yearn . . .

Nearly 150 years later, the tables are turned. After centuries of serving man, the river and its future now hinge on what humankind will do for this river.

For all the river's troubles, it remains a place of undying beauty and a respite for those it quenches—between Lake Lanier and the Chattahoochee River National Recreation Area alone, the river hosts 10 million visitors annually.

This book is an invitation to this place. Our hope is that in exploring and understanding the Chattahoochee, you, the reader, will return to it often and return its gifts by caring for and keeping it for future generations.

Safety

Every year, people drown on the Chattahoochee or in one of its lakes. Like all rivers, the Chattahoochee is not without its dangers. Rivers are unforgiving of our carelessness. Being properly prepared for your excursion and abiding by safe boating practices (including state boating laws) will reduce your risk of mistakes and keep you coming back to the river time after time.

Wear Your Life Jacket

This is the No. 1 rule of boating safety. PFDs—personal flotation devices—are known as "life jackets" for a reason: they save lives. Wear a PFD or run the risk of being DOA. Georgia state law requires that all vessels have at least one U.S. Coast Guard–approved Type I, II, III, or V PFD for each person on board. However, Type V PFDs are acceptable only when worn and securely fastened. Children under the age of 10 must wear a life jacket at all times on a moving vessel.

Though state law doesn't require it, wearing your life jacket at all times is the best practice.

Know Your Boat

Whether you are in a canoe, kayak, paddleboard, or motorized boat, know how to operate your vessel. Canoe and kayaking classes are taught by numerous organizations. The Georgia Canoeing Association (http://www.gapaddle.com/) teaches regular classes on paddling and boating safety. The Georgia Department of Natural Resources (http://www.georgiawildlife.com/boating/safety) also provides extensive information on safety practices in motorized vessels.

Know the River and Prepare for Your Trip

If you are reading this, you've taken the first step toward a safe river trip—learning about the section of river that you plan to travel and its unique dangers. For example, the Duncan Bridge section includes Class ii–iii rapids, the Columbus section includes Class ii–iv rapids, and the Langdale-Riverview, Goat Rock, and Columbus sections all include lowhead dams where water flows over open spillways. At these dams, the waterfall on the backside of the dam creates powerful hydraulics that can trap and drown boaters. Furthermore, hydropower releases from Buford Dam at Lake Lanier and the river's other dams cause sudden and dramatic changes in water levels and flow velocity. Always check dam-water release schedules and river flow gauges using the information provided in each chapter. Do not attempt river sections that are beyond your skill levels. Leave your trip itinerary with someone else who can notify authorities if you don't return as planned. Remember, what you take on the trip is all you have to survive and rescue yourself. Carry appropriate food, water, clothes, and rescue equipment. While no section of the Chattahoochee is far from "civilization," expect the unexpected and plan accordingly.

Wear the Right Clothes

Wear the appropriate clothes to protect from sun, heat, rain, and cold. Cold water is especially dangerous, as extended contact with cold and wet can lead to hypothermia and even death. During cool weather, dress in layers using clothing made of synthetic fabrics such as polypropylene, nylon, neoprene, and polyester fleece. Always bring extra clothing protected in a waterproof container. When temperatures are below 60 degrees Fahrenheit or combined air and water temperatures are below 120 degrees Fahrenheit, wear a wet suit or dry suit. Waterproof shoes, socks, and gloves are also recommended. Always wear secure-fitting river shoes to protect your feet. Helmets should always be worn when paddling whitewater.

Watch for Other Boaters

This safety practice is especially important on the river's lakes and on whitewater sections. The river's lakes experience heavy motorized-boat traffic. Paddlers should stay close to shores and avoid main channels whenever possible. Waves created by motorboats are best navigated by turning the bow (nose) of the boat into the wave rather than taking the wave broadside. When paddling at night, a white light must be shown toward oncoming traffic. On whitewater sections (and in other locations where navigational hazards exist), paddlers should confirm that downstream boaters are clear of the rapid or obstacle before proceeding.

- ☐ A Spare Paddle . . . because paddles break and motors die
- ☐ Hat or Helmet . . . hat for sun protection and/or warmth and a helmet whenever paddling whitewater
- ☐ Whistle or Signaling Device . . . three sharp blows on a whistle are a universal distress signal
- ☐ Throw Bags (ropes) and Other Rescue Gear . . . especially important in whitewater
- ☐ "River" Knife . . . a safely and easily accessible knife can save a life when entangled in rope or other hazards
- ☐ Extra Clothing in Dry Bag . . . dry clothes keep you warm; wet clothes, not so much
- ☐ Bilge Pump or Bailer
- ☐ Sunscreen
- ☐ Compass and Map
- ☐ First-Aid Kit
- ☐ Matches
- ☐ Small-Boat Repair Kit with Duct Tape

Boating Etiquette

Practice No-Trace Travel

Practicing no-trace travel is simple: just remember to leave your route so that those who come behind would never know that someone passed before them. Never litter and always pack out trash (including the trash of those less considerate).

Conduct all toilet activity at least 200 feet from any body of water. Bury your waste in a cathole 6–8 inches deep or pack it out. Be conscious of private property and do not conduct your toilet activity in someone's backyard.

Additionally . . .

- Avoid building campfires, except in established fire rings or in emergencies.
- Minimize impacts to shore when launching, portaging, scouting, or taking out.
- Examine, but do not touch, cultural or historic structures and artifacts.
- Leave rocks, plants, and other natural objects as you find them.
- Do not disturb wildlife.

Respect Others

The Chattahoochee is traveled by many, and many people make their homes along it. Always be respectful of other river users and riverfront property owners. Poor behavior by some river users can adversely impact other users through increased

NORA MILL DAM, WHITE COUNTY

regulation and fees, limitations on access, and damage to the environment. The vast majority of property along the Chattahoochee is privately owned. Islands within the river are also private property. While Georgia law allows boaters the right of passage on navigable streams, the law does not extend the right to travel on private property. Remain in the river channel, except in cases where you know public land exists or where you have confirmed that property owners allow boaters access.

Additionally . . .

- Know and obey all rules and regulations.
- Be courteous and polite when communicating with others.
- Avoid interfering with the recreational activities of others.
- Never engage in loud, lewd, or inappropriate behavior.
- Take care to avoid paddling near areas of heightened security.
- Control pets or leave them at home.

A Note on Parking at Launch Sites and Take Outs

While many popular launch and take out sites have designated parking areas or pull-offs on rights-of-way, some river-access locations identified in this guide do not have adequate parking. Care should be taken when parking vehicles and unloading boats. Avoid parking on roadsides wherever possible.

How to Use This Book

A variety of circumstances can drastically alter river conditions. The conditions described in this book should be used as a general guide, and all information contained within this book is for reference only and shall be used solely at the user's discretion.

Each chapter presents a portion of the river that can generally be paddled in a canoe, kayak, or other nonmotorized vessel within a single day and provides essential information about the estimated length of the run (both in hours and miles), the water levels necessary to attempt the journey, the location where the current water level may be found, and directions to launch and take out sites. Where alternative launch and take out sites are available, they are noted. The largest portion of each chapter presents, by mile and GPS coordinates, points of interest along the river. Chapters covering lakes use river mile markers to provide a location along the river's original channel where a feature is located, but GPS coordinates provide the exact location. In many instances, a boat ramp or park may be located at a certain mile marker, but a mile or more from the main channel. The maps provided are intended for use as a reference while on the river. For that reason, all maps are oriented from upstream to downstream rather than from north to south, and they show for reference only the most important roads. Drivers should use, in conjunction with the written directions to launch and take out sites, a road atlas and/or GPS.

FLY FISHERMAN
— IN CHATTAHOOCHEE NATIONAL FOREST
IN WHITE COUNTY

A Chattahoochee River Fishing Primer

As Georgia's longest river and one that passes through three distinct geological regions, the Chattahoochee is home to a diverse fishery. From brook trout in the Chattahoochee National Forest of North Georgia to catfish and bass on Lake Seminole in Southwest Georgia, this river that is home to 104 fish species has a bit to offer every angler.

Trout Water
(Headwaters and Nacoochee maps)

The Chattahoochee's headwaters support a native population of brook trout in the Chattahoochee National Forest upstream of Chattahoochee River Campground, while brown and rainbow trout are stocked in the river below this location. The sections upstream of Ga. 75A bridge are open to fishing only during trout season; downstream to Lake Lanier, the waters are open to year-round trout fishing.

Sections of the Chattahoochee within the national forest are particularly popular, but fishing trips in the headwaters should be undertaken with care due to the remoteness of the river and rugged terrain. Trout can be caught using a variety of live or dead bait or artificial lures. For flycasters, caddis and mayfly patterns as well as streamers produce well. If the water is muddy, fishing deep, slow, big, and gaudy is the way to go. If the water is running clear, small bright-colored flies cast to the shadows yield the best results.

The trout fishery is strong well into the Nacoochee Valley and beyond the mouth of Sautee Creek. While trout can be found downstream of Ga. 255, shoal-loving bass species become the dominant sport fish.

Upper Chattahoochee Bass
(Duncan Bridge, Belton Bridge, and Lula maps)

From Ga. 255 through the backwaters of Lake Lanier, bass become the dominant predator. In the whitewater sections of the river, shoal bass are abundant while in the slower-moving water, luck can be had landing spotted bass. As the river nears Lake Lanier, the spring spawning runs of striped and white bass upriver from the lake can produce large stringers of fish.

Shoal bass, conditioned to life in fast-moving water, are among the Chattahoochee anglers' favorites. Hook into one and you'll think you've caught a much larger fish. They're best caught by wading the shoals as you would in pursuit of trout, using buzzbaits, flukes, and spinners.

In the slower-moving water of the Upper Chattahoochee, spotted bass lurk in the eddies created by boulders and wood, waiting to ambush prey in the current. Use smaller, but similar, lures to those you'd use to land largemouth bass, including jerkbaits, spinners, plastic worms, and tube jigs.

In the Belton Bridge and Lula sections, spring is the right time to be on the river. When water temperatures rise (about the time dogwoods start blooming), white bass begin running upstream to spawn, followed shortly by striped bass. They can be caught in the lake's backwaters and on up into the shoals above Belton Bridge using live shad or artificial lures that imitate shad. Landing striped bass in the 20-to-40-pound range is common during this spring ritual. The Georgia Department of Natural Resources also stocks walleye in Lake Lanier, and these fish make their own runs upriver between February and April.

Lake Lanier
(Lake Lanier maps)

Lake Lanier offers a host of target species from catfish and sunfish to the lake's biggest predator—striped bass.

The lake's upper end of the Chattahoochee arm holds the largest concentration of largemouth bass throughout the year, but to be successful finding (and catching) them it pays to make note of temperatures. In the spring, bass move to shallow water to spawn. In the winter and summer, you'll find them in deeper water and in the fall, they roam all habitats looking for a meal of shad or herring. Always, they prefer areas with structure—tree stumps, standing timber, or rock outcroppings.

Striped bass follow a similar pattern. They are caught easily on artificial lures near the surface in the spring, but once the hot weather hits they retreat in schools to deep water, making high-resolution electronic fish finders essential to locating them. Herring, shad, or trout are good live baits.

Lanier also holds a multitude of crappie that can be caught using live minnows and crappie jigs cast near underwater structures including submerged trees, bridge abutments and docks with submerged brush.

To land catfish on Lanier, use night crawlers and chicken livers; sunfish are best caught using red wigglers or crickets; and carp can be had, especially in the spring in shallow water, using catfish baits, dough balls, or corn.

Tailwater Fishing
(Tailwaters, Jones Bridge, Morgan Falls, and Palisades maps)

Thanks to the cold, clear water coming from Buford Dam since 1956 and a state stocking program, what was once a warm-water fishery is now a haven for trout and the anglers that pursue them. Stocked rainbow trout, and naturally producing brown trout, lure anglers to this 48-mile run of river that stretches from the dam to Peachtree Creek in Atlanta. In fact, the state record brown trout (18 lb., 6 oz.) was caught here, and Trout Unlimited, a national trout conservation organization, has named the Chattahoochee to its top 100 trout streams list. In addition to the robust trout fishery, below Morgan Falls Dam, stocked striped bass and shoal bass are a viable pursuit.

State trout fishing regulations vary on this stretch of river. From Buford Dam to Sope Creek, trout fishing is permitted only during trout season (May 15–Oct. 31), and between Ga. 20 and Medlock Bridge only artificial lures are permitted. The river from Sope Creek to U.S. 41 is managed as a delayed harvest stream in which trout may be caught and released from November 1 to May 14 using artificial lures only with a single hook per lure. These rules do not apply during trout season.

Recommended flies include caddis, mayfly, and attractor dry-fly patterns and Wooly Buggers. From Buford Dam to Peachtree Creek the river alternates between short stretches of shoals and flatwater, offering opportunities for both wading and float trips.

The striped and shoal bass fishery heats up in the summer when the shoalies move to shallow, swift-moving water and when the stripers congregate between Morgan Falls Dam and Cochran Shoals seeking cold-water refuges. Rod and reel anglers should have luck with shoal bass using spinner baits. Fly fishermen can try streamers that imitate baitfish or crayfish. Live baits, cut baits, and artificial lures imitating shad are best bets for the Chattahoochee's stripers.

Middle Chattahoochee

(Buzzard Roost, Chattahoochee Hill Country, Whitesburg, McIntosh, and Hilly Mill maps)

During the first half of the 20th century, the Chattahoochee below Atlanta was the haunt of many a commercial fisherman, but pollution from the big city caused a precipitous decline in the fishery during the latter half of the 1900s. During the past two decades, significant strides have been made in properly treating all of Metro Atlanta's sewage, and as a result, the river between Atlanta and Lake West Point is once again an inviting place for boaters and anglers. All sport fish can be found throughout the 70-mile stretch from Atlanta to Franklin, but hot fishing spots are concentrated in the shoals of Heard County above Franklin: Daniel and Bushhead Shoals.

That's where striped and hybrid bass tend to congregate in March and April as they make their spring spawning run from Lake West Point, where the Georgia Department of Natural Resources stocks the fish. Stripers over 20 pounds are regularly caught here. As the summer wears on, stripers will continue moving upstream to Atlanta and beyond. Live shad is the preferred bait, but artificial lures imitating the bass's favorite food also work well.

Catfish are also caught in large numbers in this run of the river, with flathead and blue catfish topping the list. Fish over 10 pounds are common.

Lake West Point
(Lake West Point Backwaters and Lake West Point maps)

In the late 1980s, less than two decades after the creation of Lake West Point, scientists warned of extreme eutrophication (an accumulation of organic nutrients in water that can lead to algae blooms and fish kills) in the lake—long before what would be considered normal for a lake of its size. Newspaper headlines told of a lake polluted by Metro Atlanta's failing sewage treatment systems, and anglers largely abandoned West Point. With improved treatment of the big city sewage, West Point has regained its thriving fishery and still supports multiple commercial fishing guides. Bass—largemouth, hybrid, stripers, and spots—are the main draw, but catfish and crappie also attract anglers from around the state.

Spotted bass are the most populous bass on West Point, and though they lack the size of the largemouths, they are aggressive predators and more apt to attack a lure than largemouths. Big fish up to 20 inches can be had in the springtime in the shallow water of protected coves and creek mouths using worms, jigs, crankbaits, and spinners. As the summer wears on and the fish retreat to deeper water, you'll need to

TROUT FISHING NEAR MULBERRY CREEK, COBB COUNTY

fish deeper. And, always be on the lookout for logs and stumps where the bass like to hide. Largemouths on West Point follow a similar pattern, with the best fishing generally in April and May.

Hybrids and stripers are also abundant on West Point due to the state's stocking program, and the early spring is the time to catch them. As noted above about the Middle Chattahoochee, these fish congregate around Daniel and Bushhead Shoals during their spring spawning run, and large fish can be caught regularly, using live shad and artificial lures imitating the bait fish.

In the remainder of the year, hybrids and stripers can be caught throughout the lake. A tested method for locating the fish is to watch for seagulls. Where there is a flock of seagulls feeding, there are likely big bass feeding on the same fish.

For catfish anglers, there are also plenty to be had. Channel cats fill the lake and targeting these fish in the spring on the Chattahoochee around Franklin can produce excellent results. Flathead catfish are becoming more abundant in the lake and river, with 20-pound-plus specimens landed regularly. Stink bait, cut bait, and night crawlers all work well with West Point cats.

West Point crappie are large and abundant. Trolling with jigs in the upper portions of the river's tributaries produce the best results.

Fall Line
(Langdale/Riverview, Bartletts Ferry, Goat Rock, and Columbus maps)

Between West Point and Columbus, six dams create a series of small lakes with just a few miles of free-flowing river remaining. The lakes—Bartletts Ferry, Goat Rock, and Oliver—provide good fishing for all sport fish, but catfish, crappie, and bream top the list. In the spring, hybrid and striped bass also garner attention below the Riverview and Bartletts Ferry Dams. With the removal of two historic dams in downtown Columbus, two miles of free-flowing river has been restored, providing habitat for shoal bass.

Catfish over 10 pounds are regularly caught on this section of the river. Fish on the bottom in deep water, such as along the river's old channel. Live bait, night crawlers, stink bait, and cut bait are all effective. Night fishing during the summer can prove very productive.

Through the spring months, crappie and bream keep anglers occupied. Crappie fishing is best from February through April. Trolling live minnow or jigs is effective in the main river channel and along the shoreline where structure exists. On Lake Harding formed by Bartletts Ferry Dam, most crappie caught are in the range of 10–15 inches, and the average 8-incher is about a pound. The bream fishery heats up as the crappies slow down with the peak months running April through June. Work sheltered coves and sloughs with crickets and worms to catch a stringer of fish ranging in size from a quarter pound to more than a pound.

Also in the spring, look to the base of Riverview and Bartletts Ferry Dams, where striped and hybrid bass have their spawning runs blocked and monster fish can be had. The same is true for the shoals at Columbus, where migrating bass from Lake Walter F. George reach the upstream limits of their spring run. Those same shoals are home to shoal bass that can be taken using spinners or other artificial lures that mimic bait fish or crayfish.

Lake Eufaula
(Fort Benning, Riverbend, Rood Creek, and Lake Eufaula maps)

The fishery downstream from Columbus, including Lake Eufaula (Walter F. George), is the unofficial bass capital of the world and in 2012 was included in *Bassmaster* magazine's list of the top 100 bass fishing lakes. While largemouth bass are the lake's calling card, fishing is also excellent for stripers and hybrids, catfish, and panfish.

Peak largemouth bass season is from March through May, when the fish can be found in shallow water and enticed with shallow running crankbaits, plastic worms, lizards, tube baits, and jigs. Hydrilla, an invasive aquatic plant, is abundant in some portions of the lake, and fishing it can be productive using rattle baits served up on the surface. The best bass are to be had off the main channel of the river in creeks such as Cowikee, Grass, Rood, and Pataula.

Stripers and hybrids are stocked in the lake regularly, and the hybrid fishery is especially robust in the winter and early spring. Trolling over sand flats in 10–15 feet of water with live shad should bring in a stringer-full.

Catfish, especially in the river and in the upper end of Lake Eufaula, are abundant and large. Blood baits and worms work well for average-sized catfish, but the trophies are usually taken on cut shad and bream.

Spring and summer is the time for bream on Lake Eufaula. Crickets and worms fished in the shallow ends of coves, creeks, and sloughs are most effective, and the fishing tends to peak around the full moon, as this prompts the fish to move to bedding areas.

The crappie fishery is also excellent during the early spring. Bridges, piers, and mouths of creeks are the usual hot spots. The fish can be best caught using minnows or jigs fished in 12–16 feet of water. During the spawning season (March–May), they can also be had in shallow water.

Between the Lakes
(Fort Gaines, Coheelee, and Alaga maps)

Home to the state record blue catfish (80 pounds, 4 ounces), the run of river from Walter F. George Dam to the backwater of Lake Seminole is a hotbed for catfish anglers.

The tailraces of Walter F. George and George W. Andrews Dams are especially productive—and are the sites of two state record catches. Fish larger than 10 pounds are common, and blue catfish larger than 40 pounds are available. Worms and blood baits are effective; for larger fish, cut shad and live bream are recommended. Find the deep holes and you're apt to find a monster.

These tailrace areas are also popular spots for landing hybrid and striped bass during their spring spawning runs (February–May).

Lake Seminole
(Lake Seminole map)

Largemouth bass fishing is king on Lake Seminole. Like Lake Eufaula, Seminole was included in *Bassmaster* magazine's top 100 bass fishing lakes in 2012; the magazine has also recognized the lake as one of 35 historically significant lakes because of its importance in promoting the sport of bass fishing.

Because of the expansive hydrilla beds and other aquatic plants, anglers must learn to tease the big bass out of this cover (and contend with nettlesome hydrilla gnats!). Lipless crankbaits, plastic worms, spinnerbaits, and top-water lures cast into and along the edges of the hydrilla stands will produce steady strikes of 2-pounders, with many fish 6 pounds and above. The bass fishing is best from January through May, with bedding fish found during March and April. Though the fishing drops off during the summer months, good fish can still be had working the edges of lake's aquatic vegetation.

If you're looking for panfish, Seminole is also renowned for its redear sunfish. During the spring and early summer, these fish can be found on spawning beds in shallow backwater sloughs off the mainstem of the Chattahoochee. The fishing continues to be strong into the late summer. Red wigglers and crickets are the preferred bait.

For more detailed and updated fishing reports on the Chattahoochee, visit the Georgia Department of Natural Resources webpage http://www.georgiawildlife .com/fishing/opportunities.

A word of caution about fish caught in the Chattahoochee: the Georgia Department of Natural Resources issues fish consumption guidelines for specific species caught in various sections of the Chattahoochee due to elevated levels of mercury and PCBs, contaminants that can cause a variety of health problems in humans who consume these fish. Generally, the largest predatory fish contain the highest levels of contaminants. It is best to take photos of the large fish and release them. Smaller fish are generally safer to eat. Consult the fish consumption guidelines at the Georgia Department of Natural Resources webpage http://www.gaepd.org/Documents/fish_guide .html.

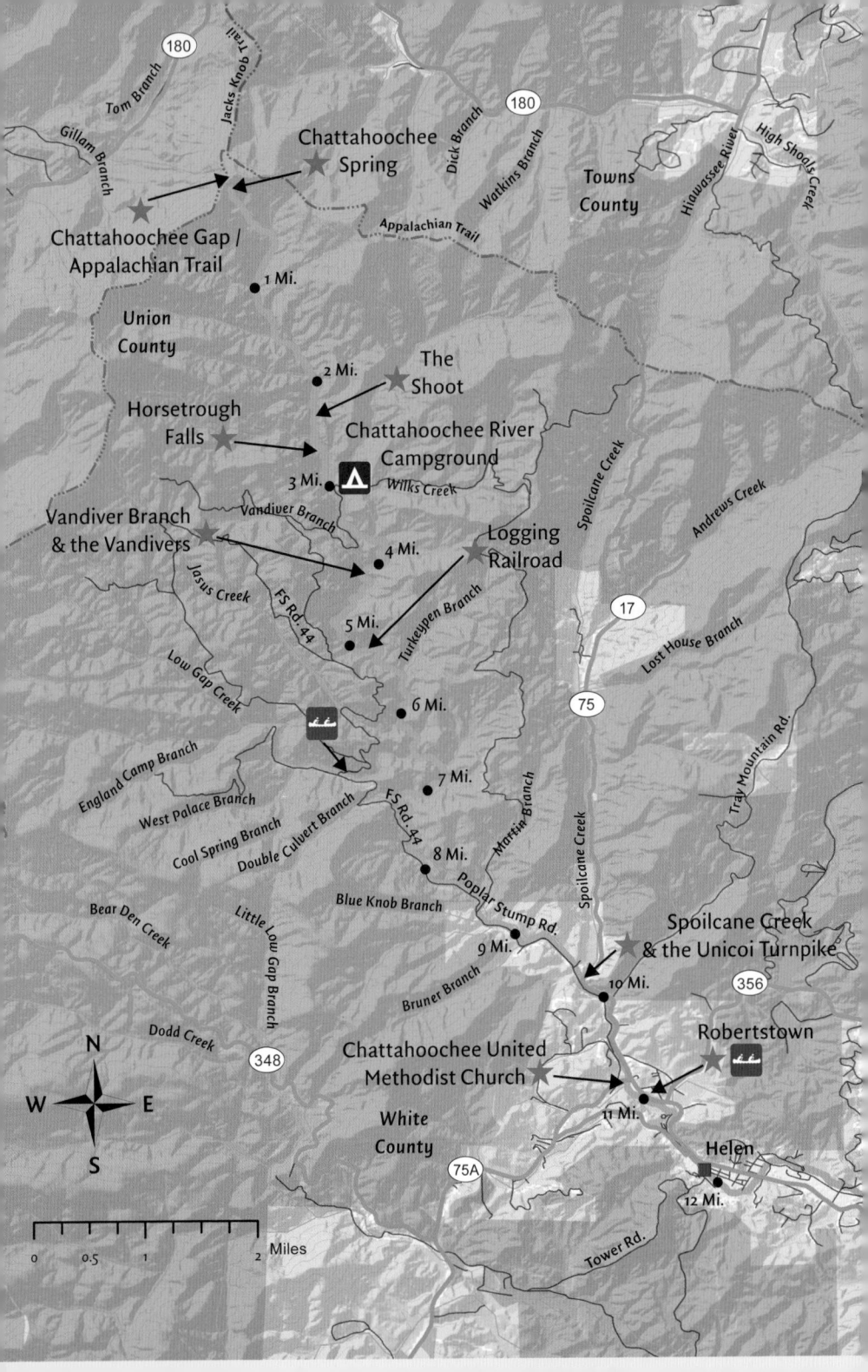

Headwaters

Length 11 miles (Chattahoochee Gap to Robertstown; 13.5 miles if accessing from Ga. 180 and Jacks Knob Trail)

Class This section is accessed by foot travel only; however, the section from Low Gap Creek to Robertstown with Class III–IV rapids can be paddled by boaters with whitewater experience when water levels permit. Sections above Low Gap Creek include rapids and falls that approach the limits of navigability.

Time 8–10 hours on foot

Minimum Level The Low Gap Creek to Robertstown section can only be run after heavy rain events. Levels below 200 cubic feet per second at the Helen gauge render this section impassable.

River Gauge The nearest river gauge is downstream at Helen: http://waterdata .usgs.gov/ga/nwis/uv?site_no=02330450.

Trailhead The Jacks Knob trailhead for accessing Chattahoochee Gap/Appalachian Trail and Chattahoochee Spring is at the intersection of Ga. 180 and Brasstown Bald Road.

DIRECTIONS From Helen proceed 12.5 miles north on Ga. 75. Turn left onto Ga. 180 and proceed 5.3 miles to the intersection with Brasstown Bald Road. Parking is in the clearing at the crossroads. The trail to Jacks Knob and Chattahoochee Gap leads from the southeast side of the highway. In the opposite direction, the trail leads to the top of Brasstown Bald.

Alternative Trailhead The Chattahoochee can also be accessed from U.S. Forest Service (FS) Road 44 (Poplar Stump Rd.), which leads to the FS's Chattahoochee River Campground. The campground is a good spot to begin a hike downriver to Robertstown.

Launch Site The launch site is where FS Road 44 crosses Low Gap Creek. When flows allow, paddlers can float Low Gap Creek to its confluence with the river. Otherwise, boats must be carried along the creek to the river.

DIRECTIONS TO ALTERNATIVE TRAILHEAD AND LOW GAP CREEK LAUNCH SITE From the intersection of Ga. 75 and Ga. 75A in Robertstown, travel west 0.1 mile on Ga. 75A to Poplar Stump Road. Turn right onto Poplar Stump Road, which becomes FS Road 44. At 4.3 miles, cross Low Gap Creek. Limited roadside parking is available here. To reach the Chattahoochee River Campground, continue on FS Road 44 an additional 5.2 miles. Parking is available at the campground.

Take Out Site The take out site is a small roadside picnic area 0.2 mile downstream of the Ga. 75A bridge on river left. Multiple pull-offs along FS Road 44 between Ga. 75A and the Chattahoochee River Campground provide access to the river.

DIRECTIONS From the intersection of Ga. 75 and Ga. 75A in Robertstown, travel south 0.2 mile on Ga. 75. The picnic area is on the right, adjacent to the river.

Description For lovers of Georgia rivers, this is holy ground—the birthing suite of Georgia's longest and most important river. Starting as a tiny spring on the flank of Jacks Knob at an elevation of about 3,600 feet, the river drops more than 2,000 feet as it spills from the Chattahoochee National Forest to Robertstown. Its journey through the forest is tortured, and many a hiker has described a walk along its route as tortuous. Rugged terrain, frequent tributaries, and numerous waterfalls and smaller cascades make this a journey not for the faint of heart. An abandoned and overgrown logging railroad parallels the river, offering some level treadway and a glimpse into the region's past. Those who venture into this terrain are rewarded with breathtaking beauty. The 11-mile route is best split into two hikes—one from Jacks Gap trailhead to Chattahoochee River Campground; the second from Chattahoochee River Campground to Robertstown (or locations along FS Road 44, which parallels the river). The river below its confluence with Low Gap Creek is navigable by experienced whitewater paddlers.

Points of Interest

MILE 0 (34.823965, -83.796297) Chattahoochee Gap / Appalachian Trail. A weathered wood sign at Chattahoochee Gap points the way to water and Chattahoochee Spring for Appalachian Trail hikers. This site along the Tennessee Valley Divide is the starting point for many a long journey. From this location, it is 46 miles to the trail's southern terminus at Springer Mountain, and more than 2,100 miles to Mount Katahdin in Maine. Rain falling on the north side of the ridge takes a journey of more than 1,600 miles down Town Creek and then the Notteley, Hiawassee, Tennessee, Ohio, and Mississippi Rivers to reach the Gulf of Mexico. Rain falling on the south side of the ridge instead follows the Chattahoochee and Apalachicola Rivers some 540 miles to the Gulf of Mexico and ends up just 250 miles east of the mouth of the Mississippi River.

MILE 0.1 (34.822838, -83.795825) Chattahoochee Spring. Members of the Georgia Appalachian Trail Club, who maintain this section of the famous footpath, claimed to be the first to "discover" this spring in 1932. Two years later they would fight the federal government to prevent the construction of a road through Chattahoochee Gap. The club's letters to the U.S. Forest Service proved successful, and the service halted the project because of its conflict with the Appalachian

Trail. Remnants of the abandoned road project are still visible leading from the southeast corner of Chattahoochee Gap.

MILE 2.5 (34.793627, -83.785353) The Shoot. This small, picturesque waterfall is a harbinger of things to come farther downstream, as the river spills over increasingly larger falls on its run out of the Blue Ridge.

MILE 2.6 (34.792041, -83.785096) Horsetrough Falls. The creek meeting the river on the right here leads to these falls, which cascade about 50 feet. The source of this water is Horsetrough Mountain, a 4,000-foot peak to the west.

MILE 3 (34.786226, -83.783379) Chattahoochee River Campground. This U.S. Forest Service–maintained campground provides campsites, flush toilets, and hand-pumped water. User fees apply. Open March through October. 706-754-6221.

MILE 4.1 (34.776330, -83.778594) Vandiver Branch & the Vandivers. What appears today as a vast wilderness was, around 1900, home to several families that lived a hardscrabble existence, ranging livestock in the forests, raising crops in the limited bottomland, and shooting wild game. The Vandiver family, for whom this tributary was named, was one of those families. George and Lula Vandiver arrived here in 1900 and lived in a log cabin with their seven children, two of whom were born here. Their community was large enough to support a one-room schoolhouse, with the various families taking turns boarding the teacher.

ANGLER, CHATTAHOOCHEE NATIONAL FOREST IN WHITE COUNTY

HORSETROUGH FALLS,
CHATTAHOOCHEE NATIONAL FOREST
IN WHITE COUNTY

MILE 5.2 (34.766193, -83.778457) Logging Railroad. Paralleling the river from Robertstown to the Chattahoochee River Campground are the remains of a narrow-gauge logging railroad that dates to around 1913, when the Byrd-Matthews Lumber Company set up a sawmill in present-day Helen. The railroad brought massive logs—some of which measured 25 feet in circumference—from the river's headwaters to the sawmill. Along the river's banks, the bed is still clearly visible in some locations; in others, abandoned rail can still be seen. The railroad operated for less than 20 years, being abandoned sometime in the early 1930s once the accessible timber had been stripped from the land. What was left bears no resemblance to the dense forest you see today.

MILE 9.8 (34.725572, -83.751600) Spoilcane Creek & the Unicoi Turnpike. The creek entering on river left was followed by one of the first "roads" built across the Blue Ridge in Georgia. The Unicoi Turnpike, little more than an improved footpath in 1819, connected coastal Georgia with Tennessee. The original road crossed various streams, including Spoilcane, 28 times before it reached the Tennessee Valley Divide 10 miles above this location. The arduous journey up the mountain required numerous stops for livestock, and it is believed that this creek received its name because of the overgrazing of river cane along its banks.

MILE 10.8 (34.712893, -83.745973) Chattahoochee United Methodist Church. From the Ga. 75A bridge, it's 0.1 mile west to this church, which is notable for those interned in its cemetery and for its role in the 1951 film *I'd Climb the Highest Mountain*. Starring Susan Hayward and William Lundigan, much of it was filmed in White County, with some scenes shot at this church. The film, based on the novel by Georgian Corra Harris, tells the story of a circuit-riding minister and his city-born wife on their first assignment in North Georgia. Buried at the cemetery are some of the Chattahoochee headwaters' original dwellers, including George and Lula Vandiver.

MILE 11 (34.710406, -83.743141) Robertstown. A roadside picnic area provides access to the river. Robertstown is named for Charles Roberts, a young and wealthy Englishman who came to the area seeking gold and who bought property along the river in the 1890s. While he developed his gold-mining business, he also established a winery, greenhouses, and a general store. His endeavors in gold were a bust, and he later moved to Atlanta, where he died at age 44 in 1907. At this picnic area, a historic marker commemorates Sidney Lanier's poem "Song of the Chattahoochee." Lanier is believed to have been visiting White County when he penned the famous verse.

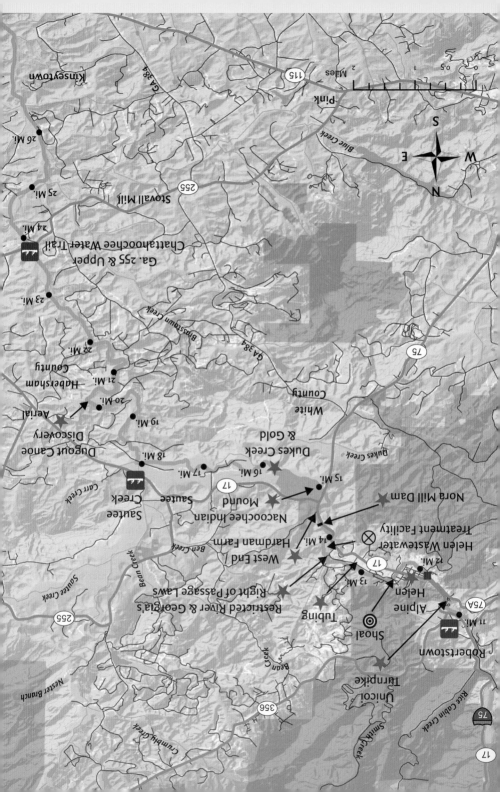

Nacoochee

Length 13 miles (Robertstown to Ga. 255)

Class 1

Time 6–8 hours

Minimum Level This section is heavily dependent on rainfall. Levels above 100 cubic feet per second at the river gauge in Helen should be adequate.

River Gauge The nearest river gauge is at Helen: http://waterdata.usgs.gov/ga/nwis/uv?site_no=02330450.

Launch Site(s) The launch site is a small roadside picnic area 0.2 mile downstream from the Ga. 75A bridge on river left. This launch site provides access to 2.5 miles of river through Helen to the Helen Tubing & Waterpark take out. From there to the Ga. 75 bridge south of Helen (about 1.5 miles), access to the river is restricted by Unicoi Outfitters, which leases property for trout fishing. The lower section of the river is accessible from Sautee Creek to Ga. 255. Parking is available along the right-of-way on Ga. 17 at the Sautee Creek Bridge. Wildwood Outfitters (706-865-4451) also maintains a private parking area and launch site on Sautee Creek.

DIRECTIONS TO ROBERTSTOWN LAUNCH SITE From the intersection of Ga. 75 and Ga. 75A in Robertstown, travel south on Ga. 75 for 0.2 mile. The picnic area is on the right, adjacent to the river.

DIRECTIONS TO SAUTEE CREEK LAUNCH SITE From the intersection of Ga. 75 and Ga. 17 south of Helen, travel east on Ga. 17 for 2.8 miles to the bridge over Sautee Creek. Parking is on the right-of-way.

Take Out Sites Paddlers exploring the river through Helen may, during the off-season, sometimes use the private landings maintained by the tubing vendors in Helen (contact the vendors first; see the Outfitters section for contact information). During the peak summer season, the volume of tubers and low water levels make this a section to avoid in canoes and kayaks. The take out site for the lower section is at Ga. 255, where parking is limited and there are no developed access points. A steep trail leads from the river beneath the bridge to the road.

DIRECTIONS TO GA. 255 TAKE OUT SITE From the picnic area on Ga. 75, travel south 3 miles through Helen. Turn left onto Ga. 17 and proceed 7.3 miles. Turn right onto Ga. 255 and proceed 1.4 miles to the bridge over the river.

Description Crowded with tubers on summer days and access restricted in other areas, the first 4 miles of this section rarely see canoes or kayaks. However, from Sautee Creek to Ga. 255, the river is accessible and gently winds through a beautiful wooded landscape where riverfront homes occasionally interrupt the views. From Robertstown to Ga. 255 the history is rich—including the uniquely transformed logging town of Helen, century-old Nora Mill, and the bucolic Nacoochee Valley—and a journey along the river's path is a trip into the region's deep cultural roots.

Outfitters Two businesses in Helen provide tube rentals for 1- to 3-hour float trips through town.

Cool River Tubing Company, 590 Edelweiss Strasse, Helen, Ga. 30545, 706-878-2665, www.coolrivertubing.com

Helen Tubing & Waterpark, 9917 Hwy. 75, North Helen, Ga. 30545, 706-878-1082, www.helentubing.com

Wildwood Outfitters provides boat rentals and shuttles from Sautee Creek to Ga. 255: 26 Megan Dr., Cleveland, Ga. 30528, 706-865-4451, www.wildwoodoutfitters.com

Points of Interest

MILE 11.4 (34.707248, -83.740587) Unicoi Turnpike. Ga. 75, which parallels the river here, was the first "road" connecting the headwaters of the Savannah River system to the east with points west of the Blue Ridge in North Carolina and Tennessee. Completed in 1819, the road was authorized to be 20 feet wide and cleared of rocks and stumps. In practice, the rocks and stumps, rather than being cleared, forced rerouting of the road. Tolls for passage on the road were authorized by the Georgia General Assembly, and when it opened, a traveler in a wagon with a team of livestock paid $1 for the privilege of following the challenging road up the mountain to Unicoi Gap. Unicoi is a Cherokee word for "white," and it is believed that the name became attached to the road because it was the "white man's road."

MILE 12.4 (34.700960, -83.729322) Alpine Helen. The ersatz Alpine village surrounding the Chattahoochee here hosts some 2 million visitors each year—an amazing feat for a town that in 1968 was a sleepy North Georgia hamlet left over from the lumber boom of the early 1900s. In 1910, the Byrd-Matthews Lumber Company set up shop along the river here, and by 1917 the sawmill was pumping out 70,000 board feet of lumber each day (the equivalent of 16 logging trucks). The town was named in honor of a daughter of one of the sawmill managers, and it boomed until the timber ran out. In 1931, the sawmill closed. A few years later the railroad servicing the sawmill was dismantled, and Helen became

something of a ghost town. In 1969, Helen's business leaders looked to local artist John Kollock to give the town's buildings a new look—something to attract tourists visiting the mountains and nearby Unicoi State Park. Kollock, who had become familiar with Bavarian architecture while stationed in Germany during a stint in the army, produced a small watercolor sketch of an Alpine village. Helen's leaders ran with it, and the rest is history. Today, the town is one of Georgia's top tourist destinations. In 2011, tourists spent $53 million in White County and supported 530 jobs.

MILE 12.5 (34.701251, -83.728983) Shoal. The only significant shoal in the river's run through Helen is just downstream of the Main Street bridge.

MILE 13.1 (34.699707, -83.719183) Tubing. On river right is the take out for Cool River Tubing. Helen Tubing & Waterpark has a take out just downstream. From May through September, these two vendors put tens of thousands of people down the river. On any given summer Saturday, more than 1,000 people make the 2-mile float. In 2006, in an effort to manage the crowds and the litter that comes with them, the city of Helen began banning all coolers and beverage containers (including cups, bottles, and cans) from the river.

MILE 13.6 (34.698375, -83.711576) Restricted River & Georgia's Right of Passage Laws. The Brucken Strasse Bridge marks the last road crossing in Helen. Downstream access to the river is restricted by Unicoi Outfitters, a local trout-fishing service, which leases property along a 1.5-mile section of the river. Here, as on certain other Georgia rivers and streams, an 1863 law is being used to prohibit passage by boaters. That law says that an owner of land on both sides of a "nonnavigable stream" owns the stream and therefore can restrict access. Navigable streams, according to the law, are those "capable of transporting boats loaded with freight in the regular course of trade either for a whole or a part of the year. The mere transporting of timber or the transporting of wood in small boats shall not make a stream navigable." Thus, many Georgia streams, including the Chattahoochee at this location, have been deemed nonnavigable, and access has been restricted. While Georgia law has not been kind to canoeists and kayakers, federal regulations offer hope. U.S. Army Corps of Engineers regulations state that the "presence of recreational craft may indicate that a waterbody is capable of bearing some forms of commerce." It remains to be seen whether Georgia's law written before the advent of "recreational use" of rivers and streams will stand the test of time. For now, boaters attempting to paddle from here to the river's Ga. 75 bridge downstream of Nora Mill are subject to prosecution.

MILE 13.8 (34.695314, -83.711759) Helen Wastewater Treatment Facility. On river right here is the Alpine village's wastewater treatment plant.

MILE 14.3 (34.690010, -83.711166) Nora Mill Dam. This location is said to be the site of the first dam built on the Chattahoochee—in 1824—a structure that powered John Brown's gristmill and sawmill. In 1876 John Martin purchased the property and constructed the existing mill building, using Brown's original dam. In 1902 Dr. Lamartine G. Hardman, governor of Georgia from 1927 to 1931, bought the mill and named it Nora Mill in memory of his sister Nora. The mill remained in the family until 1998. Still in operation today, the four-story building produces grits and cornmeal, and the proprietors, Rich and Joann Tarpley, offer a host of other products. The wooden dam has been rebuilt numerous times since 1824.

MILE 14.5 (34.687108, -83.710399) West End / Hardman Farm. On river left at the Ga. 75 bridge sits West End, a home built by James Nichols in 1869. In 1903 Dr. Lamartine G. Hardman purchased the property. Hardman, who would serve as Georgia's governor from 1927 to 1931, farmed the land and passed it on to his children. In 2002, with assistance from the Hardman family, the Trust for Public Land, and others, the state acquired the property to transform it into a state historic site. Restoration efforts—including the installation of solar panels—are expected to bring the historic home up to LEED certification standards. More than 100 years before these space-age restorations, visitors to the place sang its praises. In his 1892 *Health Resorts of the South*, George Chapin wrote, "Captain Nichols has gathered around him everything that makes life pleasant, a large farm, well stocked rich fields, trained hounds, and plenty of game, fish ponds, a choice library, billiard room, gas, pure spring water throughout, green house, (and) fountains." In addition to the main house, the site includes 19 historic outbuildings.

NEAR GA. 255, HABERSHAM COUNTY

MILE 15 (34.681391, -83.710517) Nacoochee Indian Mound. On river left is this
iconic structure of the Nacoochee Valley. The Indian mound has been at this
location for perhaps more than 1,000 years, the gazebo on top since the late
1800s, when James Nichols, the builder of West End, erected it. It is possible that
those who built this mound also built a structure at its pinnacle. Excavations
of the mound in 1915 revealed 75 human burials, many accompanied by high-
status items such as copper axes, effigy vases, and conch shell beads and cups.
Burial mounds like this are common along rivers because of the importance

of water to ceremonial rites. Ethnologist James Mooney, who lived among and studied the Cherokee in the late 1800s, explained: "Ceremonial bathing formed an important part of the proceedings connected with their sacred dances, such as the green-corn dance and the medicine dance, where the whole body of performers came out of the town house to the water, and, after certain ablutions, returned thereto. It was necessary, therefore, that the building be near a stream. As the level areas in the narrow mountain valleys are often overflowed, it is quite probable that in order to place these sacred houses above the floods, they were, as stated in tradition, located on artificial mounds." It is believed that Cherokee Indians occupied this site as late as the mid-1700s.

MILE 15.8 (34.677028, -83.699450) Dukes Creek & Gold. This tributary on river right was the epicenter of Georgia's gold rush in 1828. That year John Witheroods of North Carolina and a slave of Major Frank Logan of Loudsville, Georgia, separately discovered gold in the creek, setting off a quest for the precious metal that climaxed in the 1830s and was revived in the late 1800s with the advent of new mining techniques—including hydraulic "giants," in which water from high elevations was piped through hoses to blast away earth. The method left scars on the landscape of the Nacoochee Valley that still remain. Lesser known than the "giants" were river dredges, which dug sand and gravel off the river bottoms. In 1905 the U.S. Mint reported that a dredge operating on the Chattahoochee in the Nacoochee Valley had been "a steady producer."

MILE 18 (34.676411, -83.668036) Sautee Creek. Less than a half mile upstream on this creek is the Ga. 17 launch site.

MILE 20.1 (34.662226, -83.656170) Dugout Canoe Discovery. In 1974 near the mouth of Mauldin Mill Creek, canoe and fishing guide Delbert Greear of Helen found a dugout canoe. The 24-foot-long and 2-foot-wide vessel had been hewn from yellow pine. It was traced to Cherokee origins and is now on display at the Museum of the Cherokee Indian in Cherokee, North Carolina.

MILE 23.8 (34.627573, -83.642003) Ga. 255 & Upper Chattahoochee Water Trail. This undeveloped access point is the first take out site along the Upper Chattahoochee River Water Trail—a 36-mile route stretching from the Nacoochee Valley to Lake Lanier. In 2009 Chattahoochee Riverkeeper worked with the National Park Service's Rivers, Trails and Conservation Assistance Program to conduct a feasibility study and present the results to the Georgia Department of Natural Resources. The study identified access points that need improvement, like this one, as well as potential access points, including three state-owned properties between here and Lake Lanier. In 2012, the U.S. Department of the Interior named the 48 miles of the Chattahoochee between Buford Dam and Atlanta as one of the nation's first National Water Trails, helping to build momentum for the Upper Chattahoochee trail and others across the state.

Duncan Bridge

Length 8 miles (Ga. 255 to Duncan Bridge)

Class II–III

Time 4–7 hours

Minimum Level Levels above 200 cubic feet per second (cfs) at the river gauge at Duncan Bridge should be adequate to float this section. Levels above 1,500 cfs require appropriate whitewater paddling skills.

River Gauge The nearest river gauge is at Duncan Bridge, the take out site for this section: http://waterdata.usgs.gov/ga/nwis/uv?site_no=02331600.

Launch Site The launch site is at Ga. 255, where roadside parking is limited and there are no developed access points. A steep trail leads to the river beneath the bridge.

DIRECTIONS From the intersection of Ga. 17/115 and Ga. 385 in Clarkesville, travel west 1.9 miles on Ga. 17/115. At 1.9 miles, turn right onto Ga. 17 and proceed 3.9 miles. Turn left onto Ga. 255 and proceed 1.4 miles to the bridge over the river.

Take Out Site The take out site is just upstream of Duncan Bridge on river right at Wildwood Outfitters, which leases property from the Georgia Department of Natural Resources. The take out site provides parking, restrooms, water, and an outfitter store. User fees apply for parking and shuttles provided by Wildwood Outfitters.

DIRECTIONS From the Ga. 255 launch site, proceed west 2.7 miles. Turn left onto Ga. 384 (Duncan Bridge Rd.) and proceed 6.4 miles. Turn left onto Megan Drive. The entrance to the outfitter is on the immediate right.

Alternative Take Out Site To create a 4-mile trip, paddlers and floaters can take out at the Ga. 115 boat launch. This take out eliminates the final 4 miles of this section, which include the Chattahoochee's most challenging whitewater.

DIRECTIONS TO GA. 115 TAKE OUT SITE From the Ga. 255 launch site, proceed west 2.7 miles. Turn left onto Ga. 384 (Duncan Bridge Rd.) and proceed 3.1 miles. Turn left onto Ga. 115 and travel 1.6 miles. Turn right onto Mineral Springs Trail. Parking for the boat launch is on the right.

Description This 8-mile section is considered the Chattahoochee's whitewater run, drawing more than 10,000 paddlers each year. The first 4 miles are highlighted by Smith Island Rapid, a strong Class II. Below Ga. 115 the pace quickens with a series of Class II–III rapids, including Buck Shoals, Three Ledges, and Horseshoe. Beautiful and scenic throughout, this is the place where novice whitewater paddlers come to cut their teeth before moving on to bigger water.

Outfitters Wildwood Outfitters provides boat rentals and shuttles from Ga. 255 to Duncan Bridge. The outfitter also has a contract with the Georgia Department of Natural Resources to manage camping at Buck Shoals State Park. Reservations for on-river campsites in the state park must be made through the outfitter (user fees apply). Wildwood Outfitters, 26 Megan Dr., Cleveland, Ga. 30528, 706-865-4451, www.wildwoodoutfitters.com.

Points of Interest

MILE 24.2 (34.625002, -83.640645) Chicken Houses & Phosphorus. On river left are several chicken houses—a ubiquitous sight in the Chattahoochee watershed of North Georgia where Gainesville, just downstream, is considered the Chicken Capital of the World. Broilers are the state's largest single agricultural commodity, accounting for 45 percent of the state's agricultural economy. Annually, Georgia's poultry farmers produce more than a billion broilers; those broilers, in turn, generate 3 billion pounds of manure each year. That manure, when spread on pastures as is common practice, contributes to nutrient-rich stormwater that courses into the river and collects in Lake Lanier, contributing to algae growth. In 2003, Georgia implemented new rules regulating the handling and disposal of chicken manure, but in 2008 high nutrient levels were still entering Lake Lanier downstream, contributing to violations of clean-water standards.

MILE 26.4 (34.598145, -83.642394) Riverfront Development. In the early 1970s, there was hardly a home along the banks of the river in White and Habersham Counties; 40 years later, the row of houses on river right is commonplace. Second-home and retirement-home construction in North Georgia is big business, and riverfront parcels bring top dollar. State laws protect a 50-foot vegetated buffer along trout streams like the Chattahoochee, but the cumulative impacts of the transformation of forest and field to house and asphalt is difficult to mitigate. Studies suggest that when as little as 10 percent of the land draining to a river is covered by manmade surfaces, the health of the river begins to decline.

MILE 26.7 (34.594303, -83.640731) Smith Island Rapid. The route through this Class II rapid is to the left of the island. At the head of the island, stay far left. After reaching the first pool, move right across the river toward the island to run the main chute. A large pool and eddy allows for recovery below the rapid. Smith Island is notorious for incidents in the 1980s in which the owner of the island fired weapons at paddlers to prevent them from stopping to scout the rapid. Today, the island remains private property but under different ownership. No similar incidents have been documented since that time. Navigating right of the island leads to a significant ledge that is navigable only during high water.

MILE 27.7 (34.579191, -83.638333) Shoals.

MILE 27.8 (34.578243, -83.637314) Shoals.

MILE 27.9 (34.577038, -83.635919) Shoals.

MILE 28.1 (34.575163, -83.634552) Sidney Lanier Bridge Launch Site & Shoals. Beneath the Ga. 115 bridge is a small shoal, and on river left is a Georgia Department of Natural Resources boat launch. The bridge is named in honor of Macon native Sidney Lanier, the poet who penned "Song of the Chattahoochee." Though Lanier only lived to age 39 (dying in 1881 from complications from tuberculosis he contracted while a Confederate prisoner of war in Maryland), he lived a remarkable and varied life. After returning from the war, he taught school, worked as an organist, served as a school principal, practiced law, and then attained the first flautist position with the Peabody Orchestra in Baltimore. He finished his career as a faculty member at Johns Hopkins University. Of course, he also wrote some of Georgia's most beloved poems, selling them to magazines to support his wife and three children. Today, in addition to this bridge, his name is attached to an elementary school, technical college, lake . . . and another bridge—the state's longest suspension bridge—in Brunswick.

MOUNTAIN LAUREL NEAR AMYS CREEK, HABERSHAM COUNTY

MILE 28.3 (34.574036, -83.633961) Shoals.

MILE 28.7 (34.570392, -83.634058) Buck Shoals. For the next 0.6 mile the river runs through Buck Shoals, a series of Class I–II rapids that require much technical maneuvering. At high flows, some waves can exceed 4 feet and the rapids rank as Class III.

MILE 29.3 (34.563408, -83.628812) Canoe Eater Rock. This infamous rock sits in the middle of the last drop in Buck Shoals and earned its name from the canoe paint that covers its surface and the many vessels it has capsized. To avoid this obstacle, steer to the right as you make the final drop.

MILE 29.4 (34.563149, -83.628758) Buck Shoals State Park. The sandy beach on river right at the end of Buck Shoals marks this state park. The 580 acres and nearly 2 miles of riverfront was secured by the Nature Conservancy in the 1990s and transferred to state ownership in 2000. Since then, the Georgia Department of Natural Resources has been slowly developing a management plan for the park. In 2011, the state began allowing permitted overnight camping at riverfront sites through Wildwood Outfitters; paddlers may camp overnight for a nominal fee after first securing a permit from the outfitter (706-865-4451). Camping is primitive, with only portable toilets. The park is only accessible by boat.

SMITH ISLAND RAPID, HABERSHAM COUNTY

MILE 29.5 (34.562159, -83.627854) Greater Jumprocks & Chattahoochee Fish Diversity. Swimming in the swirling water of these shoals is one of the Chattahoochee's endemic fish species—the greater jumprock, a fish that is found in the Chattahoochee and Flint river basins and nowhere else in the world. A member of the carp family, it has a sucker-like mouth, grows up to 17 inches long, and thrives in swift-moving riffles like these. You'll sometimes find them spawning here in May and June. The river is home to 42 native fish species, as well as eight introduced species. The rivers of the southeast United States contain the richest diversity of aquatic fauna of any temperate area in the world, harboring 493 fish species (62 percent of those found in the United States).

MILE 29.7 (34.560117, -83.624314) Three Ledges Rapid & Whitewater Lexicon. As the name suggests, this Class II rapid is a series of three ledges with calmer water separating each. The first ledge is navigated on river left, the second requires a ferry back to the center of the channel and the final (and largest of the three) is best run on river left. Making the entry into the third ledge is critical as a strong hydraulic created by this fall can hold boats and paddlers. Spend enough time at this ledge and you'll likely hear paddlers using some odd lingo. Here's a primer:

> A *hole or hydraulic* is a river feature where water drops over a rock or ledge into deeper water. This causes water on the surface to be drawn back toward the rock or ledge. This can be a potentially hazardous feature but for advanced paddlers is a feature used for playboating. A *suckhole* is a VERY powerful hydraulic. A *pillow* is the water that builds up on the upstream side of an obstruction. A *boof* is a maneuver in which a kayaker uses his paddle, rock or water feature to lift the bow of the kayak over a drop. And, finally, an *eddy* is a river feature formed when an obstacle creates a calm pool on its downstream side. Being able to "catch" or stop in these calm pools is one of the keystones of whitewater paddling.

MILE 30.3 (34.554967, -83.617061) Washboard Rapid. This appropriately named rapid takes you over a series of small shelves.

MILE 30.8 (34.548577, -83.617705) Horseshoe Rapid. A Class II rapid at normal flows, at higher flows it becomes Class III. The route begins on river right. Paddle to river left around the large rock in the center of the river and then make a sweeping right turn to the pool at the bottom. Once you reach the pool, a strong draw to the left takes you over another pair of ledges that are favorite spots for surfing.

MILE 31 (34.547039, -83.616514) Soque River. Pronounced *So Qwee*, this is the northernmost tributary of the Chattahoochee. With its headwaters situated along the northeast flank of Tray Mountain, it spends its entire 29-mile course in Habersham County. Its upper stretches are a trout fishing hot spot, in large part because of private management of the fishery. In 2004, the state record rainbow trout was caught on the Soque—a 17-pound, 8-ounce monster.

HORSESHOE RAPID, HABERSHAM COUNTY

HORSESHOE RAPID, HABERSHAM COUNTY

MILE 31.2 (34.545926, -83.617275) Waterfall. This unnamed tributary meets the river in dramatic fashion and is worthy of inspection. It drains portions of Pea Ridge and is dammed about a quarter mile from the river.

MILE 31.5 (34.543502, -83.621360) Johnny's Ford. This is the site of a historic crossing of the river by early white settlers. It later became a ferry and operated until the advent of bridges across the river. A rusted relic on river left is part of the ferry apparatus.

MILE 31.6 (34.543329, -83.619012) Shoals.

MILE 31.8 (34.541825, -83.616481) City of Baldwin Water Intake. This structure on river left pumps water to the city of 3,200 residents about 6 miles to the east. Baldwin residents have the distinction of being the northernmost community to depend on the Chattahoochee for its water supply. They are not alone. Downstream, more than 4 million more Georgians rely on the river for their drinking water. Baldwin can take up to 4 million gallons a day (MGD); for comparison, Metro Atlanta uses an average of 450 MGD.

MILE 32.2 (34.540407, -83.620290) Iron Bridge. This is the original site of Duncan Bridge Road and the only remaining iron bridge upstream of Buford Dam.

MILE 32.4 (34.54079195, -83.622527) Wildwood Outfitters. A part of the Chattahoochee's landscape since 1972, Wildwood Outfitters had humble beginnings. The Gale family started the business by driving from their home in Atlanta to Helen one summer Saturday, hauling a trailer full of canoes to "test the waters" and see if they could rent the boats. That day, not long after the release of the movie *Deliverance*, they rented every vessel in their fleet, and they have been riding the wave of paddlesports popularity ever since. The outfitter provides shuttles, guide services, and canoe, kayak, and raft rentals.

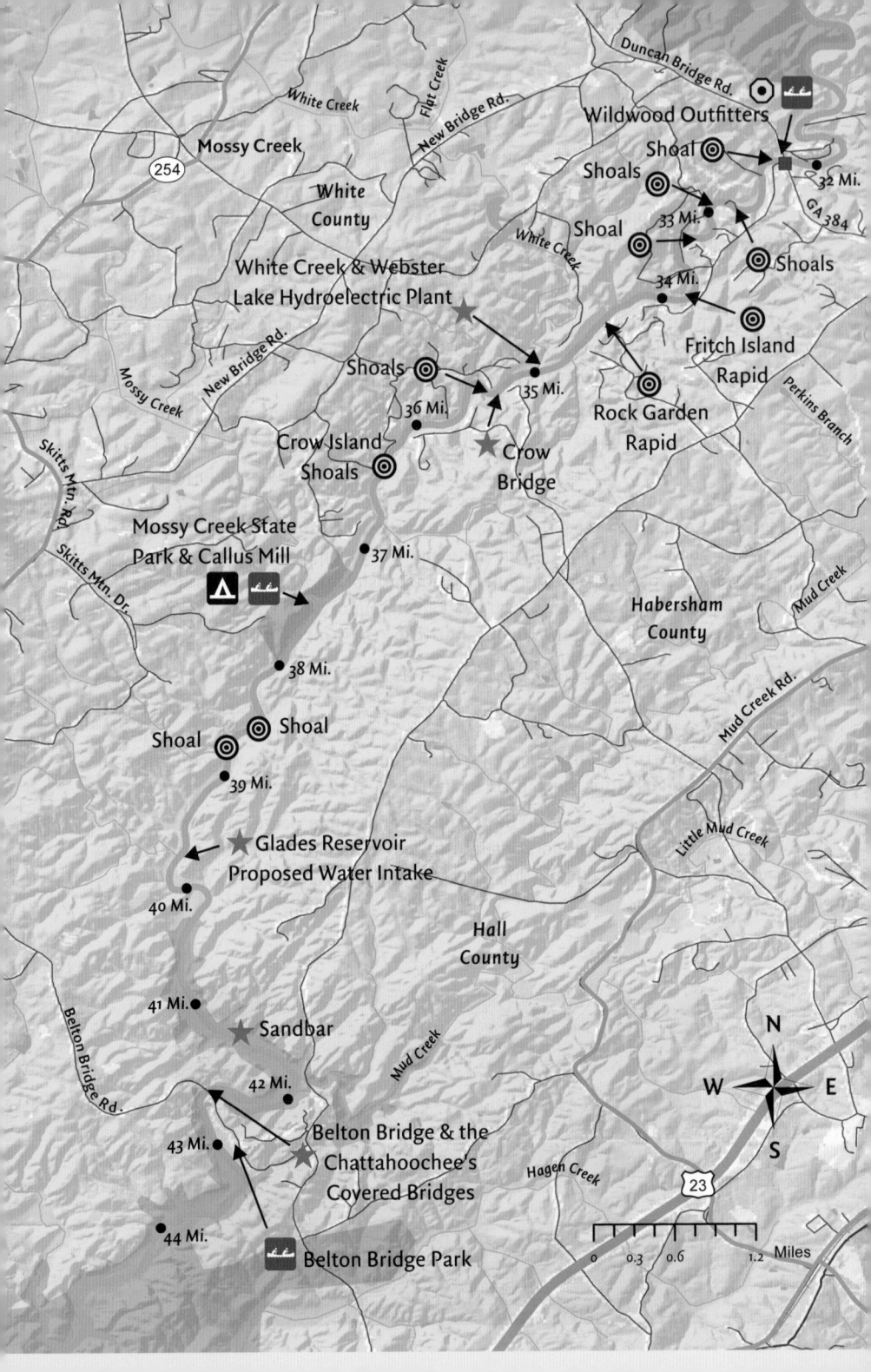

Belton Bridge

Length 11 miles (Duncan Bridge to Belton Bridge)

Class 1

Time 4–7 hours

Minimum Level Levels above 200 cubic feet per second at the river gauge at Duncan Bridge should be adequate to float this section.

River Gauge The nearest river gauge is at Duncan Bridge, the launch site for this section: http://waterdata.usgs.gov/ga/nwis/uv?site_no=02331600.

Launch Site The launch site is just upstream of Duncan Bridge, adjacent to Wildwood Outfitters, which leases property from the Georgia Department of Natural Resources. The site provides parking, restrooms, water, and an outfitter store. User fees apply for parking and shuttles provided by Wildwood Outfitters.

DIRECTIONS From the intersection of U.S. 23 and Ga. 384 (Duncan Bridge Rd.) near Baldwin, travel north 4.2 miles on Ga. 384 to the river. Cross the bridge and turn right onto Megan Drive, and then immediately turn right again into Wildwood Outfitters.

Take Out Site The take out site is 0.6 mile downstream of Belton Bridge on river left. Belton Bridge Park provides parking and a boat ramp.

DIRECTIONS From Megan Drive, turn left onto Ga. 385 and proceed 1.4 miles. Turn right onto Pea Ridge Road and travel 7.8 miles. Turn right onto Belton Bridge Road and proceed 0.9 mile to the Belton Bridge Park entrance on the left.

Alternative Take Out Site A 5-mile paddle can be created by utilizing the Georgia Department of Natural Resources access point on Mossy Creek.

DIRECTIONS TO MOSSY CREEK TAKE OUT From Megan Drive, turn right onto Ga. 385 and proceed 1.2 miles to New Bridge Road. Turn left and travel 5 miles on New Bridge Road to Skitts Mountain Road. Turn left onto Skitts Mountain Road and proceed 0.4 mile. Turn left onto Skitts Mountain Drive and travel 0.6 mile. Turn left onto Rattler Drive and proceed 1.6 miles to the parking area by Mossy Creek.

Description The last gasp for the Upper Chattahoochee's whitewater, this 10-mile run offers numerous playful Class 1 and borderline Class 11 shoals and serves as an alternative to the Duncan Bridge section when water levels are low. Two tributaries, White and Mossy Creeks, spill off the river's west flank over a series of waterfalls and shoals, and thanks to preservation as a state park, Mossy's beautiful falls are accessible via a short paddle or walk from the creek's mouth. Below Mossy, the shoals give way to slow-moving water as the effects of Buford Dam some 40 miles downstream are felt. This section of the river is also a flashpoint for water supply planning in Georgia—just upstream of Belton Bridge, a massive water withdrawal from the river is proposed to fill a controversial reservoir that prompted a national river advocacy group to name the Chattahoochee one of the nation's "most endangered" rivers.

Outfitters Wildwood Outfitters provides boat rentals and shuttles from Ga. 255 to Belton Bridge. The outfitter also has a contract with the GADNR to manage camping at Mossy Creek State Park. Reservations for on-river campsites in the state park must be made through the outfitter (user fees apply). 26 Megan Dr., Cleveland, Ga. 30528, 706-865-4451, www.wildwoodoutfitters.com.

Points of Interest

MILE 32.1 (34.540769, -83.624091) Shoal.

MILE 32.6 (34.536050, -83.627650) Shoals.

MILE 32.9 (34.535124, -83.631006) Shoals.

MILE 33.3 (34.532859, -83.632360) Shoal.

MILE 33.8 (34.527046, -83.633685) Fritch Island Rapid. A pair of islands mark this Class 1 rapid that is best run on far river right. A series of shoals begin at the head of the island and culminate in a significant ledge just downstream of the island.

MILE 34.3 (34.523506, -83.643526) Rock Garden Rapid. A large rock garden on river left constricts the flow here and creates a fun chute with nice waves on river right.

MILE 34.9 (34.519322, -83.649422) White Creek & Webster Lake Hydroelectric Plant. On river right White Creek spills into the Chattahoochee. Its route from Webster Lake, about 2 miles upstream, flows over several falls and shoals. The geography on this flank of the river has long lent itself to harnessing water power—from the 1800s to the present. The dam at Webster Lake was operated as a private hydropower plant into the 21st century.

MILE 35.2 (34.517338, -83.653391) Crow Bridge. Standing sentinel in the middle of the river is an abutment for Crow Bridge (sometimes also referred to as Kings Bridge). Prior to the bridge, a ferry known as Head's Ferry operated near here. The ferry was eventually replaced by this bridge. In 1888, the rural post office of Head's Ferry was established just east of this location. Crow Bridge, and Crow Island 1.2 miles downstream, likely derive their names from the Crow family that settled in this area during the 1800s. J. A. Crow was postmaster in Head's Ferry.

MILE 35.3 (34.517132, -83.654880) Shoals.

MILE 36.3 (34.509474, -83.665880) Crow Island Shoals. This set of Class I shoals extends downriver 0.4 mile to the end of Crow Island, a small island on river left. The most significant rapids are adjacent and just downstream of the island.

MILE 37.5 (34.495398, -83.672735) Mossy Creek State Park & Callus Mill. A Georgia Department of Natural Resources boat launch is at the mouth of Mossy Creek on river right. Secured with assistance from the Nature Conservancy and the Trust for Public Land, this state park encompasses more than 120 acres and a half mile of river frontage. Its acquisition was part of an effort started by the organizations in 1995 with the goal of protecting important river frontage from Helen to Columbus. More than $140 million was raised to this end, including more than $50 million in private contributions. In the late 1990s, the state spent $14 million to purchase this parcel and three others in the Upper Chattahoochee corridor. Though development of the parks has been slow, Mossy Creek is part of an Upper Chattahoochee Water Trail stretching from Sautee Creek to Lake Lanier that is being promoted by Wildwood Outfitters, Chattahoochee River-keeper, the Trust for Public Land, the U.S. National Park Service, and others. The boat launch provides access to a parking area, and the pasture on the north bank of the creek can be used for camping. Mossy Creek itself is a beautiful stream filled with waterfalls, some of which are within sight of the creek's mouth. The circa-1800s Callus Mill is still farther upstream, outside the state park. The creek is a favorite of whitewater paddlers because of its 2.5 miles of Class II–IV rapids ending at the creek's mouth.

MILE 38.6 (34.482505, -83.680020) Shoal.

MILE 38.8 (34.480612, -83.682745) Shoal.

MILE 39.7 (34.466271, -83.687134) Glades Reservoir Proposed Water Intake. This is the location of a proposed raw-water withdrawal that would help fill Glades Reservoir—a controversial "pump storage" water supply project proposed for construction about 4 miles south of here on Flat Creek. Because the creek alone can't provide enough water for the project, water would be pumped from here to the reservoir, stored and then released as needed to the creek to flow downstream to Lake Lanier, where it would be withdrawn from already existing pumps operated by the city of Gainesville. Proponents of the project say that the reservoir would provide additional water storage for the region; opponents call it a boondoggle, suggesting that a less environmentally damaging solution would be to simply store the same water in Lake Lanier, letting the river carry to the lake the same water that the $130+ million project would. In 2012, this reservoir proposal prompted American Rivers, a national river advocacy organization, to name the Chattahoochee the third most endangered river in the country. This is not the first overengineered solution to a perceived economic development need

on the Chattahoochee. In 1895, the authors of a State Department of Agriculture Report titled "Georgia: Her Resources and Possibilities," wrote that "near Belton, the stream is wide, and there is a long shoal, which could be utilized to furnish water for a canal to secure navigation by a cross route from the Mississippi to the Atlantic." Not surprisingly, this "possibility" is today little more than an odd note on the pages of a yellowing state document. Glades Reservoir has the potential to be remembered similarly.

MILE 41.3 (34.451418, -83.683314) Sandbar. As the river nears Lake Lanier, sandbars like this one on river left become more prevalent. River sandbars form on the inside of bends where the water slows, allowing suspended particles to fall out of the water column. Heavier sand falls out first, and as the river nears Lake Lanier, the river bottom becomes less sandy . . . and more muddy. That's because as the river slows, lightweight suspended particles remain in the water column longest, leaving the riverbed on the lake's backwaters covered in thick silt.

MILE 42.5 (34.445508, -83.684993) Belton Bridge & the Chattahoochee's Covered Bridges. Beginning in 1900, a covered bridge spanned the river here. That era ended in 1962, when the bridge was destroyed in a fire. From the 1830s to 1880, virtually all of the bridges built across the Chattahoochee were of the covered variety—designed to protect the bridge's base from the elements. That changed in the late 1800s with the advent of steel bridges. Belton and Keith Bridge (1903) downstream were among the last covered bridges constructed across the river.

MILE 43.1 (34.437190, -83.681289) Belton Bridge Park. A boat ramp on river left here leads to a paved parking area. "Notorious" and "infamous" are words often associated with this secluded park. The park once extended from here upstream to the bridge, but in 2010, following a homicide, the U.S. Army Corps of Engineers closed off its most remote sections. A den of drug use and other criminal activity, the park has been the site of five murders in 30 years. The bodies of two of those victims were found in the river.

CROW BRIDGE,
WHITE COUNTY

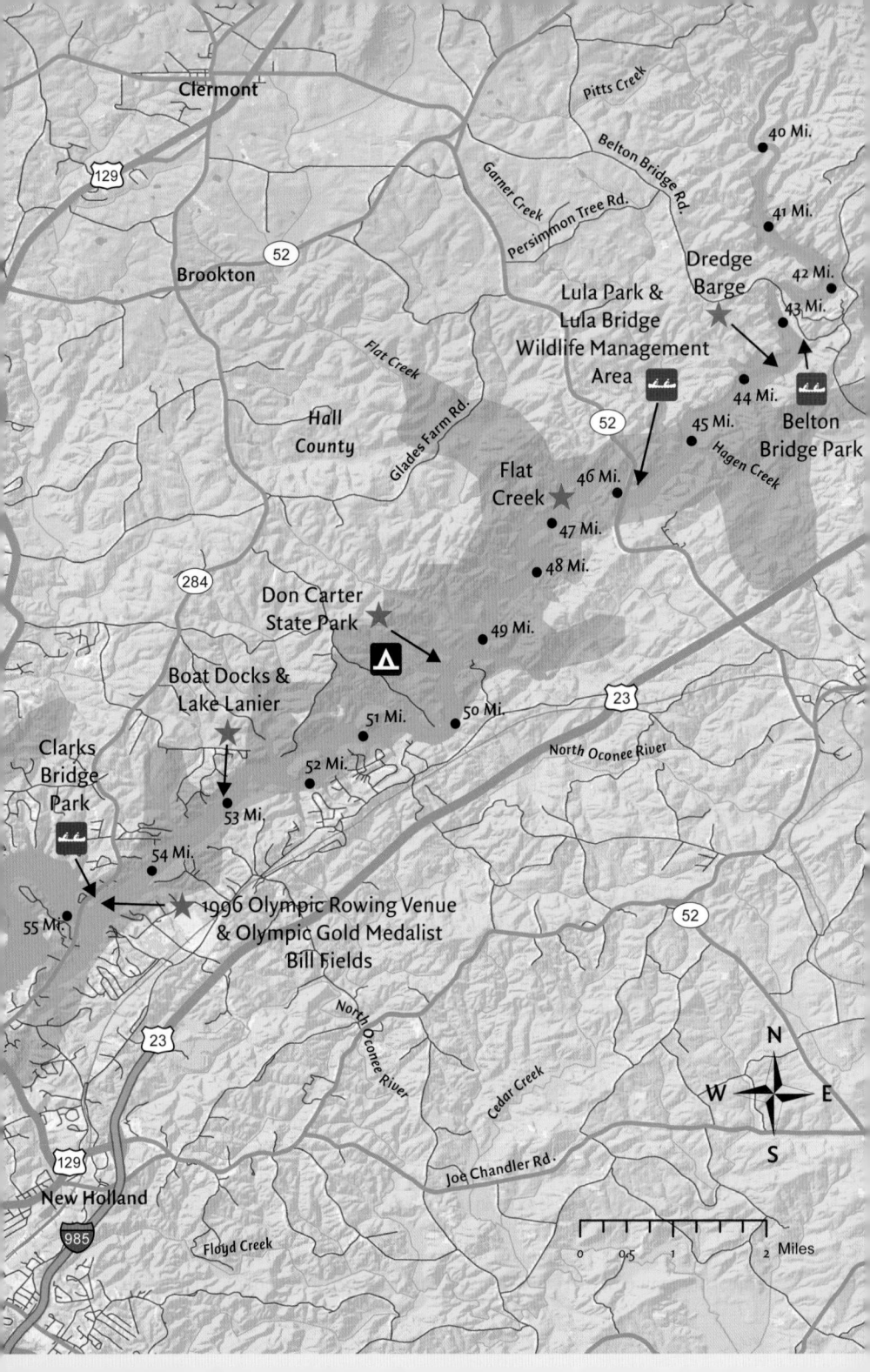

Lula

Length 12 miles (Belton Bridge to Clarks Bridge)

Class 1

Time 5–8 hours

Minimum Level This 11-mile stretch through Lake Lanier's backwaters is navigable year-round. Information about Lake Lanier water levels is available at http://water.sam.usace.army.mil/acfframe.htm. Lake levels can change dramatically depending on rainfall, but generally fluctuate 7 feet, from 1,064 to 1,071 feet above mean sea level, with the highest levels occurring in the summer months and the lowest levels during the fall and winter.

River Gauge The nearest river gauge is upstream at Duncan Bridge: http://waterdata.usgs.gov/ga/nwis/uv?site_no=02331600.

Launch Site The launch site is at Belton Bridge Park, which is 0.6 mile east of Belton Bridge and has a parking area and boat ramp.

DIRECTIONS From the intersection of U.S. 23 and Belton Bridge Road near Lula, travel west on Belton Bridge Road 2.3 miles to the intersection of Pea Ridge Road and Belton Bridge Road. Turn left onto Belton Bridge Road and proceed 0.4 mile to Belton Bridge Park on the left.

Take Out Site The boat ramp at Clarks Bridge Park is just upstream from Clarks Bridge on the north side of Lake Lanier. The park, home of the 1996 Olympic canoe, kayak, and rowing venue, offers parking, restrooms, water, and picnic areas. A 3-mile trip can be made by utilizing the take out at Lula Bridge.

DIRECTIONS From Belton Bridge Park, turn left onto Belton Bridge Road and proceed 2.6 miles. Turn left onto Persimmon Tree Road and travel 1.8 miles. Turn left onto Ga. 52 (Lula Rd.) and proceed 0.3 mile. Turn right onto Glades Farm Road and proceed 3.9 miles to the fork in the road. Bear left at the fork onto Ga. 284 (Clarks Bridge Rd.). On Ga. 284, proceed 4.9 miles to the entrance of Clarks Bridge Park on the left.

Alternative Take Out Sites To create a 3-mile trip, boaters can take out at Lula Bridge or, for a 6-mile trip, at Don Carter State Park, a full-service park with camping, rental cabins, beach, boat ramps, and recreational trails.

DIRECTIONS TO LULA BRIDGE From Belton Bridge Park, turn left onto Belton Bridge Road and proceed 2.6 miles. Turn left onto Persimmon Tree Road and travel

1.8 miles. Turn left onto Ga. 52 (Lula Rd.) and proceed 2.9 miles to Lula Bridge Park on the left.

DIRECTIONS TO DON CARTER STATE PARK From Belton Bridge Park, turn left onto Belton Bridge Road and proceed 2.6 miles. Turn left onto Persimmon Tree Road and travel 1.8 miles. Turn left onto Ga. 52 (Lula Rd.) and proceed 0.3 mile. Turn right onto Glades Farm Road and travel 3.9 miles to the fork in the road. Bear left at the fork onto Ga. 284 (Clarks Bridge Rd.) and proceed 0.5 mile. Turn left onto Browning Bridge Road and travel 1.9 miles to the park entrance on the left.

Description This is where the free-flowing Chattahoochee dies. The river's current slows and then disappears as it spreads across the lowlands in the backwaters of Lake Lanier. From here to Apalachicola Bay, the U.S. Army Corps of Engineers controls the river and Mother Nature is relegated to backseat-driver status. Nevertheless, this 11-mile run offers up some of Lake Lanier's most secluded water, with much of the shoreline protected as the Lula Bridge Wildlife Management Area and Don Carter State Park. Downstream of these areas is a taste of the real Lanier as docks and homes line the shore approaching Clarks Bridge. Lake levels can vary dramatically depending on rainfall and releases from Buford Dam.

Outfitters Lanier Canoe and Kayak Club at Clarks Bridge Park offers canoe and kayak rentals on weekends from May to September: 3105 Clarks Bridge Rd., Gainesville, Ga., 770-287-7888, www.lckc.org.

Points of Interest

MILE 43.7 (34.432830, -83.68518) Dredge Barge. On river right is a dredging operation; the dredge barge and associated equipment may be visible in the river. This operation removes sand and gravel from the river bottom, maintaining flood and water supply storage in Lake Lanier and maintaining a navigational channel on these upper reaches of the lake. The sand and gravel are used in many ways, but especially as ingredients in concrete. Every 100,000 tons of sand removed here represents 15 million gallons of storage capacity in the lake. River advocates have long suggested dredging Lanier to provide more storage, rather than damming streams to build expensive new reservoirs.

MILE 45.8 (34.413537, -83.708591) Lula Park & Lula Bridge Wildlife Management Area. This parking area and boat ramp is on river right just upstream from Lula Bridge. The access point is part of the 513-acre wildlife management area (WMA) that stretches along the banks of the river from just above Belton Bridge to Don Carter State Park. The Georgia Department of Natural Resources manages more than 90 WMAs that encompass more than 1 million acres of land. It is said that a WMA is within an hour's drive of every resident in the state.

MILE 46.5 (34.415281, -83.715908) Flat Creek. Upstream 0.8 mile on this creek is the site of the proposed Glades Reservoir Dam, which would impound an 850-acre water supply reservoir. The reservoir would hold water from Flat Creek as well as water pumped from a site on the Chattahoochee just upstream of Belton Bridge Road (see Belton Bridge section). The dam would be designed to regulate flows into Lake Lanier where the city of Gainesville already has a withdrawal for public supply. Opponents of the project suggest that a less expensive and less environmentally damaging alternative would be to let the Chattahoochee and Flat Creek carry the water to the lake and simply store more water in Lake Lanier itself. The poorly named Flat Creek, which flows over some precipitous falls and shoals, has long been ex-

LULA BRIDGE WILDLIFE
MANAGEMENT AREA,
HALL COUNTY

ploited by humans. At the mouth of the creek (now under Lanier's backwaters) once sat Clark's Mill, a gristmill operated by Jesse Clark, and about 5 miles upstream on the property surrounding Glade Shoals, in the mid-1800s an extensive mining operation was established that also included a cotton gin, sawmill, and gristmill powered by the water of Flat Creek.

MILE 49.5 (34.387918, -83.735842) Don Carter State Park. This 1,800-acre park protects 6 miles of river and lakefront property and was secured through the Nature Conservancy and the Trust for Public Land's Chattahoochee River Greenway initiative. The Georgia Department of Natural Resources (GADNR) opened the park in 2013. It features cabins, RV and tent camping, a beach, picnic areas, docks, and trails. The park is named in honor of a Gainesville realtor who served 29 years on the GADNR board that oversees the state agency charged with maintaining the state's parks.

MILE 53 (34.368119, -83.771054) Boat Docks & Lake Lanier. On river right is a line of docks and homes—a ubiquitous sight on the heavily developed lake. Though only 47 percent of the lake's 692 miles of shoreline are zoned for docks, it seems that they are everywhere. A 2003 study completed by the U.S. Army Corps of Engineers concluded that the lake had a carrying capacity of 10,615 docks; by 2012 virtually all the available dock permits had been claimed, thus driving up property values of lots with floating access.

PADDLING NEAR LULA BRIDGE, HALL COUNTY

LULA BRIDGE WILDLIFE MANAGEMENT AREA, HALL COUNTY

MILE 54.7 (34.352106, -83.790753) 1996 Olympic Rowing Venue & Olympic Gold Medalist Bill Fields. On the west bank of the river stands the timing tower for the 1996 Olympic canoe, kayak, and rowing venue. That year, this site hosted hundreds of athletes from around the world. Today the facility still holds regular events, including some international competitions, organized by the Lanier Canoe and Kayak Club and the Lake Lanier Rowing Club. The venue is within sight of the home of the late Bill Fields, a Georgia native who in 1952 won gold at the Helsinki Olympics as a member of the U.S. eight-man crew team. A graduate of the U.S. Naval Academy, he retired from the navy with the rank of commander and returned to Gainesville, where he coached a high school crew team. Before his death in 1992, he consulted with the Atlanta Olympic Organizing Committee and played a role in bringing the rowing venue to Lanier.

MILE 54.8 (34.351433, -83.793263) Clarks Bridge Park. This park providing boat ramp, parking, restrooms, and water sits on high ground above a historic crossing of the river originally settled in 1819 by William Clark. His son Sevier stayed on the land and in the 1830s built with his wife, Elizabeth Ingram Clark, a home that still stands on the north side of the park. It is one of Hall County's oldest homes. Elizabeth should probably be given much of the credit for the continuation of the Clark name at this location. When her husband died in 1842, she was left to care for nine children (including a 3-week-old baby). Undaunted, she continued to manage the family's 2,000 acres, slaves, and a ferry across the river. In 1860, she orchestrated the construction of a toll bridge across the river here.

LAKE LANIER NEAR LULA BRIDGE, HALL COUNTY

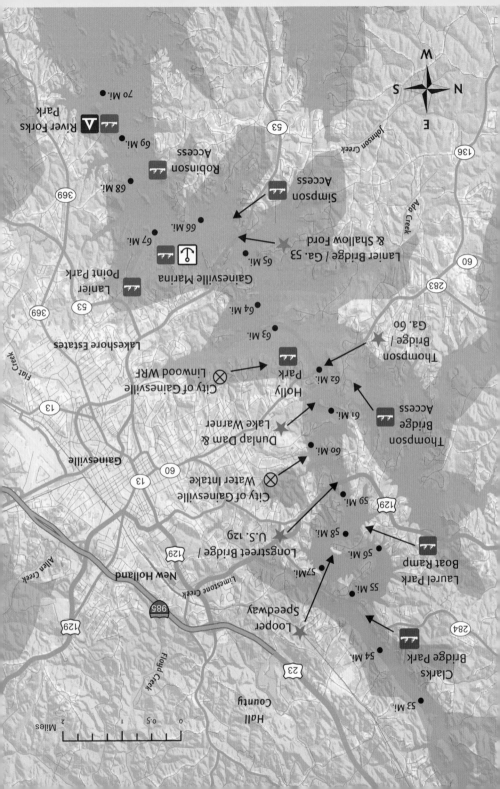

Lake Lanier

Length 26 miles (Clarks Bridge to Buford Dam). In this chapter, Lake Lanier is divided into three maps with corresponding descriptions of points of interest. For ease of reference, points of interest are identified as being on river left or right where appropriate. Points of interest are located by river mile and GPS coordinates. The river mile provides a general location along the river's original channel where a feature is located, while GPS coordinates provide exact location. In many instances, a boat ramp or park may be located near a specific mile marker but a mile or more from the main channel.

Class 1

Time 12+ hours

Minimum Level The lake is navigable year-round. Information about Lake Lanier water levels is available at http://water.sam.usace.army.mil/acfframe.htm. Lake levels can change dramatically depending on rainfall but generally fluctuate 7 feet from 1,064 to 1,071 feet above mean sea level, with the highest levels occurring in the summer months and the lowest levels during the fall and winter.

River Gauge The nearest river gauge is upstream at Duncan Bridge: http://waterdata.usgs.gov/ga/nwis/uv?site_no=02331600.

Launch Site The launch site is at Clarks Bridge Park on the northeast side of Clarks Bridge. The park, home of the 1996 Olympic canoe, kayak, and rowing venue, offers a boat ramp, parking, restrooms, water, and picnic areas.

DIRECTIONS From the U.S. 23 and Ga. 369 interchange in Gainesville, travel west on Ga. 369 (Jesse Jewell Pkwy.) for 0.6 mile. Turn right onto U.S. 129 (Limestone Pkwy.) and proceed 1.5 miles. Turn right onto Clarks Bridge Road (Ga. 284) and proceed 1.7 miles to the Clarks Bridge Park on the right.

Take Out Site There are multiple access points on the U.S. Army Corps of Engineers–operated Lake Lanier. Lake users can create many trips utilizing Corps campgrounds and boat ramps as well as local parks. On the mainstem of the river and just off the mainstem, you'll find at least 30 boat landings in the 26 miles from Clarks Bridge to Buford Dam. User fees are required at some locations; campsites also require fees. For those through-paddling, it is possible to portage around Buford Dam by taking out on the east side of the dam, carrying across Buford Dam Road, and sliding your vessel down the grassy bank on the back side of the dam.

Description The 26 miles of river from Clarks Bridge Road to Buford Dam are Atlanta's water playground. Just 30 minutes from the big city, Lake Lanier hosts more than 7 million visitors each year. With more than 13,000 homes dotting its 692 miles of shoreline, 10,000 docks crowding its banks, and 10 private marinas and an 1,100-acre resort vying for the patronage of lake visitors, the lake can be extremely busy on summer weekends. But with 38,000 acres of water, 124 islands, and countless coves, it offers almost endless exploration opportunities for canoeists, kayakers, and paddleboarders. Caution should be used, however, for the lake is the domain of powerboats, which are numerous. Powerboats are available for rent at many of the lake's marinas.

Outfitters Six establishments provide canoe, kayak, or powerboat rentals. Facilities that do not offer rentals are listed in the main body of this chapter.

Lanier Canoe and Kayak Club at Clarks Bridge Park offers canoe and kayak rentals on weekends from May to September in the area around Clarks Bridge Park: 3105 Clarks Bridge Rd., Gainesville, Ga. 30506, 770-287-7888, www.lckc.org

Gainesville Marina, on the mainstem of the river just downstream of Ga. 53, provides boat launches, docks, boat gas, repairs and service, a store, and pontoon boat rentals: 2145 Old Dawsonville Hwy., Gainesville, Ga. 30501, 770-536-2171, www.gainesvillemarina.com

Port Royale Marina on the west bank of the mainstem of the river just downstream from Browns Bridge Road provides boat launches, docks, boat gas, repairs and service, a store, boat and personal watercraft rentals, and a restaurant: 9200 Lan Mar Rd., Gainesville, Ga. 30506, 770-887-5715, www.bestinboating.com/port_royale

Aqualand Marina lies on the east bank of the mainstem of the river about 4 miles downstream of Browns Bridge Road. This marina provides boat launches, docks, boat gas, repairs and service, a store, boat and personal watercraft rentals, and a restaurant: 6800 Lights Ferry Rd., Flowery Branch, Ga. 30542, 770-967-6811, www.aqualandmarina.com

Holiday Marina is off the mainstem on the river on the east bank of the lake up Flowery Branch about 5 miles upstream from Buford Dam. This marina provides boat launches, docks, boat gas, repairs and service, a store, boat and personal watercraft rentals, and a restaurant: 6900 Lanier Islands Pkwy., Buford, Ga. 30518, 770-945-7201, www.holidaylakelanier.com

Lake Lanier Islands Resort, on a large peninsula on the east side of the lake along the mainstem of the river about two miles upstream from Buford Dam, offers an array of amenities and activities from golf and horseback riding to a waterpark and zip-line tours. The facility provides boat launches, docks, boat gas, a store; boat, personal watercraft, kayak, and stand-up paddleboard rentals; lodging, camping, cabin rentals, and several restaurants. User fees apply. 7000 Lanier Islands Pkwy., Buford, Ga. 30518, 770-945-8787, www.lakelanierislands.com

Points of Interest

MILE 56.8 (34.346027, -83.805290) Looper Speedway. Among the structures submerged during the creation of the lake was this dirt-track speedway located in bottomlands on the west bank of the Chattahoochee. For a decade after the track opened in 1947, it hosted local racers and thousands of spectators at Saturday night races. Among the winners at the track was Dawsonville racing legend Gober Soseby, a two-time NASCAR race winner. According to one frequent visitor to the track, "Gainesville drivers were only interested in three things: drinking moonshine, fighting and then, maybe, getting around to racing." During extreme drought, the top of the grandstands at the raceway become visible along the banks of Laurel Park on river right.

MILE 58.4 (34.355026, -83.813873) Laurel Park Boat Ramp. This ramp on river right provides access to Laurel Park, a Hall County park that is primarily a softball-tennis complex with restrooms, water, picnic areas, and other amenities.

MILE 59.1 (34.348565, -83.822765) Longstreet Bridge / U.S. 129. This bridge is named in honor of Confederate general James Longstreet, the right-hand man of General Robert E. Lee. After the war, Longstreet became a controversial figure in the South for supporting the peaceful rejoining of the Union. In postwar Louisiana, he led the state militia (which included many black men) against a mob that was fighting to overthrow the state government to prevent the state's return to the Union. In the fighting Longstreet was wounded, captured, and held prisoner.

SUNSET AT HOLLY PARK, HALL COUNTY

In 1875, he moved to Gainesville, where he continued to advocate for reconciliation with the North as well as for civil rights for former slaves—an unpopular stance in the reconstruction South. Fires that destroyed his home and damaged the hotel he owned were deemed to be suspicious. He died in 1904.

MILE 59.9 (34.340309, -83.830916) City of Gainesville Water Intake. On river left, the city of Gainesville pumps an average of 18 million gallons a day (MGD) from the lake to meet the needs of the city's nearly 50,000 water customers. Lanier also supplies water to the surrounding cities of Cumming and Buford as well as to Forsyth and Gwinnett Counties. Together, with Gainesville, these entities can pump up to 214 MGD from the lake.

MILE 61.2 (34.341443, -83.840553) Dunlap Dam & Lake Warner. Some 70 feet below the water surface here is Dunlap Dam. Completed in 1908, this dam is 370 feet long and 32 feet high. It supplied the city of Gainesville with electricity and powered the city's streetcars. Lake Warner, the reservoir created by the dam, was the Lanier of its day. Streetcars ran from downtown Gainesville to the shores of the lake, where the Gainesville Electric Railway Company developed Chattahoochee Park, a resort with boating, picnicking, dancing, and other amusements for streetcar patrons.

MILE 61.4 (34.352409, -83.845859) Thompson Bridge Access. The slough at river right here leads up the Little River and 1 mile to this boat ramp and parking area.

MILE 62 (34.34271, -83.849737) Thompson Bridge / Ga. 60.

MILE 62.5 (34.333337, -83.853409) Holly Park. A boat ramp on river left provides access to this city of Gainesville park with parking, restrooms, water, and picnic pavilions.

MILE 62.8 (34.328880, -83.855287) City of Gainesville Linwood WRF. This sewage treatment plant, or water reclamation facility (WRF), on river left discharges about 2.5 million gallons a day (MGD) to the lake. The discharge pipe is below the lake's surface. The city's largest treatment facility on Flat Creek, a Lanier tributary, handles about 6 MGD. Gainesville is the northernmost city to discharge its wastewater into the mainstem of the river. Gwinnett County, however, is the largest discharger of treated wastewater to the lake. It is permitted to discharge up to 40 MGD—a reminder that even in Atlanta's water playground, you're always swimming in someone else's waste.

MILE 65.2 (34.322456, -83.880188) Lanier Bridge / Ga. 53 & Shallow Ford. Just upstream from this bridge, a large island (now under the surface of Lake Lanier) split the river at a place once known as Shallow Ford, a historic crossing of the river for travelers between Gainesville and Dahlonega. The place was described in 1895 by the Georgia Department of Agriculture as a mile-long set of shoals that dropped a total of 6 feet. It is also the likely site of this incident recorded in the *Gainesville Eagle* in 1894: "A gentleman living near Shallow Ford captured a beaver this week, brought it to town and disposed of it at Brown & Welchel's Market. Beaver meat has an excellent reputation. Someone on seeing the animal dressed and hanging in the market exclaimed, 'Golly, that cat was killed while it was scared. Look at its tail.'"

MILE 65.5 (34.315784, -83.878536) Gainesville Marina. On river left is this private marina that provides boat launches, docks, boat gas, repairs and service, a store, and pontoon boat rentals.

MILE 65.5 (34.319501, -83.891421) Simpson Access. Directly opposite Gainesville Marina on river right is this public boat ramp with picnic areas and restrooms.

MILE 66.9 (34.296650, -83.871026) Lanier Point Park. The cove on river left leads 0.8 mile to a boat ramp that provides access to this city of Gainesville park. Primarily an athletic field complex, the park offers restrooms, water, a picnic area, and walking trails.

MILE 68.1 (34.30303, -83.897118) Robinson Access. This boat ramp on river right provides parking, restrooms, water, and picnic areas.

MILE 69.5 (34.287875, -83.906924) River Forks Park. A boat ramp in the cove on river left 0.4 mile off the river channel provides access to this Hall County park with campsites, restrooms with showers, water, picnic areas, and a swimming area. User fees apply. 770-531-3952.

MILE 70.5 (34.289227, -83.921998) Oberbys Shoal. Lying beneath about 80 feet of water here is a rapid that would race the hearts of today's paddlers. In 1895, it was described as a shoal that dropped nearly 7 feet over a span of just 0.1 mile.

MILE 70.5 (34.306315, -83.930751) Duckett Mill Park. This U.S. Army Corps of Engineers campground is 1.6 miles up the Chestatee River and provides a boat ramp, parking, RV and tent campsites, restrooms with showers, water, and a swimming area. User fees apply. 770-532-9802.

MILE 70.7 (34.286474, -83.925936) Chestatee River. Here the Chattahoochee and Chestatee Rivers join. Originating along the flanks of Blood Mountain as Dicks, Blood Mountain, and Frogtown Creeks, the Chestatee flows some 50 miles before mixing with the Chattahoochee. The name Chestatee is believed to be a Cherokee Indian word that translates as "pine torch place" or "place of lights."

MILE 70.8 (34.284701, -83.926580) Keith Bridge. About 40 feet below the water surface here are the remains of Keith Bridge. Built in 1903, this is said to have been the last covered bridge constructed in Hall County. It was destroyed by fire in 1953, four years before the water of Lake Lanier would have swallowed it. It was predated by a ferry that operated here just downstream from the confluence of the Chattahoochee and Chestatee Rivers. Remnants of the old Keith Bridge Road are still visible on the island immediately to the southwest.

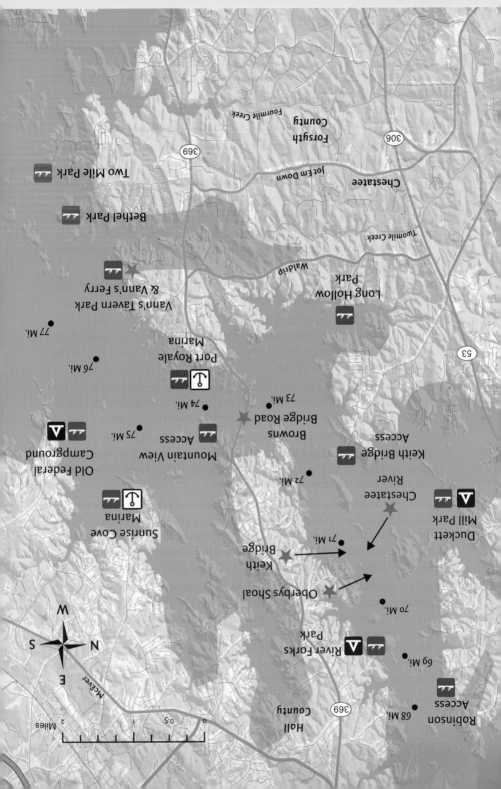

MILE 71.9 (34.282689, -83.943488) Keith Bridge Access. Located on river right just beyond the point of the large island here, this boat ramp provides access to parking, restrooms, water, a swimming area, and picnic areas.

MILE 73 (34.281490, -83.971912) Long Hollow Park. Located 1.2 miles up the cove on river right, this boat ramp provides access to parking, restrooms, water, a swimming area, and picnic areas.

MILE 73.4 (34.261885, -83.951395) Browns Bridge Road. This is the site of the oldest bridge crossing of the river in Hall County. In 1839, the Georgia legislature authorized Minor W. Brown to build a bridge at this site, allowing him to charge 50 cents for a two-horse wagon to cross. Below the bridge were what became known as Brown Mill Shoals, a series of rapids that dropped 16 feet over a distance of 1.6 miles. By the 1860s, a gristmill was operating here and, later, a sawmill.

MILE 74.1 (34.252800, -83.953257) Port Royale Marina. Located on river right, this marina provides boat launches, docks, boat gas, repairs and service, a store, boat and personal watercraft rentals, and a restaurant.

MILE 74.2 (34.255194, -83.944331) Mountain View Access. Located 0.6 mile north of the island on river left, this boat ramp provides access to parking, restrooms, water, and picnic areas.

MILE 75.1 (34.237053, -83.936228) Sunrise Cove Marina. Tucked into a cove on river left 1.2 miles off the river channel, this marina provides boat launches, docks, boat gas, and a store: 5725 Flat Creek Rd., Gainesville, Ga. 30504, 770-536-8599, www.sunrisecovemarina.com.

MILE 75.6 (34.222759, -83.950526) Old Federal Campground. Located on river left, this boat ramp provides access to this U.S. Army Corps of Engineers campground with RV and tent campsites, restrooms with showers, water, and picnic and swimming areas. The campground is named for its proximity to the Old Federal Road, a road into Cherokee territory designated in 1805. 770-967-6757.

MILE 77 (34.234581, -83.981045) Vann's Tavern Park & Vann's Ferry. Located on river right, this boat ramp provides access to parking, restrooms, and water. It was once the site of Vann's Tavern, a stopover on the Federal Road operated by the Cherokee, James Vann, the son of a Scottish trader and Cherokee woman. Influential in his day, Vann used his power and position to secure one of his greatest coups—the rights to operate a ferry and tavern along the Federal Road at the Chattahoochee. Along with his large plantation near present-day Chatsworth, this privilege helped make him one of the wealthiest men in Georgia. Prone to drink and become violent, he was also reviled by many, and in 1809 he was shot and killed by an unknown assailant at one of the Federal Road taverns. His son, Joseph Vann, inherited his father's wealth and his palatial home, but in 1834, the Georgia Guard evicted the younger Vann for violating a Georgia law that prohibited a Cherokee from hiring a white man. Vann filed a lawsuit against the state and was eventually awarded $19,605. The two-story Vann's Tavern constructed of logs in 1805 was rescued from Lanier's water in 1956 and moved to the New Echota State Historic Park in Calhoun.

MILE 78 (34.204899, -83.968516) Aqualand Marina & Lights Ferry. Located on river left is this marina with boat launches, docks, boat gas, repairs and service, store, boat and personal watercraft rentals, and a restaurant. Lights Ferry, a river crossing that dates to the 1820s, was on the river here. It retains the name of its first owner and operator, Obadiah Light, one of Hall County's earliest residents. The remains of Lights Ferry Bridge now lie beneath Lanier's water.

MILE 78.5 (34.226682, -83.990963) Bethel Park. Located on river right north of Three Sisters Islands, a boat ramp here provides access to parking, restrooms, and water. Navigate to the north side of the islands to reach this ramp.

MILE 79 (34.221145, -84.001437) Two Mile Park. Located on river right just north of Three Sisters Islands, a boat ramp provides access to parking, restrooms, and water. Navigate to the north side of the islands to reach this ramp.

MILE 79 (34.208532, -83.994930) Three Sisters Islands. These islands paralleling the west bank are some of the lake's 124 islands. Lanier's islands are popular destinations for boaters, and while the U.S. Army Corps of Engineers recognizes some with "official" names like Gaines Ferry and Flat Creek, the unofficial names are more colorful and some have stuck, among them King of Spain, Robinson Crusoe's, Naked Man's, and Pirate's Adventure. While the Corps allows day use of the islands, overnight camping is prohibited.

MILE 79.4 (34.186059, -83.979084) Van Pugh Park & Gaines Ferry. Located on river left, this boat ramp provides access to this U.S. Army Corps of Engineers campground with parking, restrooms with showers, water, RV and tent campsites, and picnic and swimming areas. User fees apply. 770-945-9531. The road leading to this park is Gaines Ferry, named for a historic crossing of the river established here in the 1840s.

MILE 80 (34.172692, -83.997639) Holiday Marina & Aquamarina Lazy Days. Located alongside each other on river left in the cove between Van Pugh Park and Lake Lanier Islands Resort, these two marinas provide boat launches, docks, boat gas, repairs and service, and stores. Holiday Marina also provides boat and personal watercraft rentals and a restaurant.

MILE 82 (34.180379, -84.027584) Lake Lanier Islands Resort. These islands on river left encompass more than 1,000 acres of state-owned land that is operated by the private Lake Lanier Islands Management. The resort includes a hotel and conference center, rental cottages, campsites, golf, tennis, horseback riding, boat rentals, a marina, multiple restaurants, zip-line tours, and a waterpark . . . but only one boat ramp—on the south side of the islands 3 miles off the mainstem of the river. Entry fee and user fees apply.

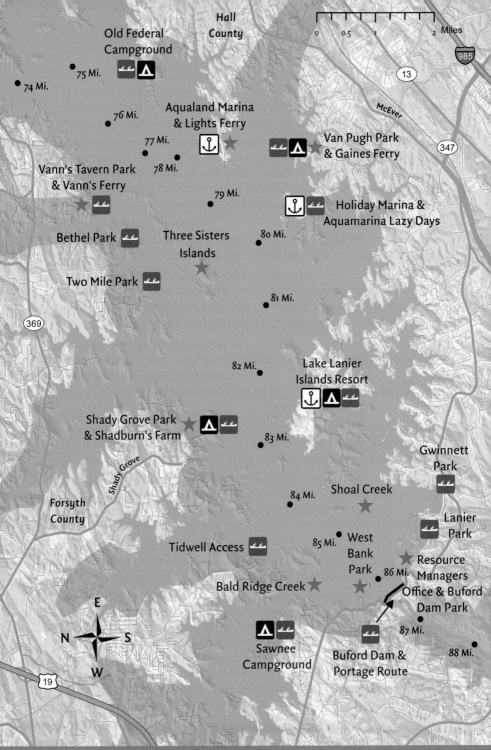

Hall County

Old Federal Campground

74 Mi.
75 Mi.
76 Mi.
77 Mi.
78 Mi.
79 Mi.
80 Mi.
81 Mi.
82 Mi.
83 Mi.
84 Mi.
85 Mi.
86 Mi.
87 Mi.
88 Mi.

Aqualand Marina & Lights Ferry

Van Pugh Park & Gaines Ferry

McEver

Vann's Tavern Park & Vann's Ferry

Holiday Marina & Aquamarina Lazy Days

Bethel Park

Three Sisters Islands

Two Mile Park

Lake Lanier Islands Resort

Shady Grove Park & Shadburn's Farm

Shady Grove

Gwinnett Park

Forsyth County

Lanier Park

Shoal Creek

Tidwell Access

West Bank Park

Resource Managers Office & Buford Dam Park

Bald Ridge Creek

E
N — S
W

Sawnee Campground

Buford Dam & Portage Route

0   0.5   1   2 Miles

985

13

347

369

19

LAKE LANIER

MILE 82.5 (34.202792, -84.036558) Shady Grove Park & Shadburn's Farm. Located on river right, this Forsyth County campground provides a boat ramp (on the backside of the point facing Buford Dam), parking, RV and tent campsites, restrooms with showers, water, and swimming and picnic areas. User fees apply. 770-205-6849. The bottomland between this park and the old channel of the river is often referenced as the "beginning" of the Lanier project. In 1948, the federal government purchased the first piece of land for the lake—a 100-acre farm owned by 81-year-old Henry Shadburn, who received $4,100.

MILE 84 (34.194468, -84.063788) Tidwell Access. Located on river right, this U.S. Army Corps of Engineers park provides a boat ramp, parking, restrooms, and water. User fees apply.

MILE 85 (34.166814, -84.060768) Shoal Creek. This cove extending eastward from Buford Dam leads 2.5 miles to the U.S. Army Corps of Engineers Shoal Creek Campground (770-945-9541) and Lanier Harbor Marina (2066 Pine Tree Dr., Buford, Ga. 30518, 770-945-2884, www.lanierharbor.com).

MILE 85.3 (34.177108, -84.070461) Bald Ridge Creek. This cove on river right leads 3 miles to Habersham and Bald Ridge marinas, the U.S. Army Corps of Engineers Bald Ridge Campground (770-889-1591), Lanier Beach Park, and the city of Cumming's Mary Alice Park.

Habersham Marina, 2200 Habersham Marina Rd., Cumming, Ga. 30041, 770-887-5432, www.habershammarina.com

Bald Ridge Marina, 1850 Bald Ridge Marina Rd., Cumming, Ga. 30041, 770-887-5309, www.baldridgemarina.com

MILE 85.3 (34.177335, -84.073621) Sawnee Campground. Located just west of Buford Dam at the mouth of Bald Ridge Cove, this U.S. Army Corps of Engineers campground provides RV and tent campsites, restrooms with showers, water, and a swimming area. User fees apply. 770-887-0592.

MILE 85.9 (34.167737, -84.070799) West Bank Park. Located adjacent to Buford Dam, this U.S. Army Corps of Engineers park provides restrooms with water and swimming and picnic areas.

MILE 86 (34.159925, -84.066089) Resource Managers Office & Buford Dam Park. Located just east of the dam is this U.S. Army Corps of Engineers office and day-use area. Inside the office are numerous interesting exhibits about the history of the Corps and the creation of Lake Lanier. The park surrounding the office provides parking, restrooms, water, and swimming and picnic areas.

MILE 86 (34.151379, -84.058094) Lanier Park. Located 1.1 miles east of the dam in a small cove just beyond the Resource Managers Office & Buford Dam Park, this boat ramp provides access to parking, restrooms, water, and a swimming area.

MILE 86 (34.149588, -84.050047) Gwinnett Park. Located 1.5 miles east of the dam in a small cove just beyond Buford Park is this boat ramp and parking area.

MILE 86.2 (34.158822, -84.072240) Buford Dam & Portage Route. At the east side of the earthen Buford Dam, it is possible to carry a canoe or kayak up the steep, riprap bank, across Buford Dam Road and then down the grassy backside of the dam to launch in the river. Constructed from 1950 to 1956 at a cost of $44 million, Buford Dam is 2,360 feet long and 192 feet high. In front of the dam, the water depth at full pool is 157 feet. If you dropped the Statue of Liberty off in front of the dam, she'd be completely swallowed. To say that this structure has transformed the region would be an understatement. While reshaping the landscape and economy of the area since 1957, since 1990 the dam has also been the epicenter of water disputes between Georgia, Alabama, and Florida. Releases from the dam affect the production of hydropower, the storage of drinking water supplies, and flows to the downstream communities and states. Only 6 percent of the river's drainage area is captured in Lake Lanier, but because of its size and depth the lake holds 63 percent of the storage capacity in the river system. Thus, in 1990 when Metro Atlanta communities petitioned the U.S. Army Corps of Engineers to allocate more of Lanier's storage for water

BROWNS BRIDGE, HALL COUNTY

supply instead of releasing it downriver, the action set off a storm of lawsuits that decades later had still not been resolved. When groundbreaking ceremonies for the project took place in 1950, it's doubtful anyone could have envisioned such controversy. Atlanta mayor William B. Hartsfield said in front of the 3,500 optimistic onlookers who attended the ground breaking that the occasion marked "the beginning of a new era in the industrial development of North Georgia." The excitement was felt at the local level too. Cumming mayor Roy Otwell had roadside signs made that read: "The Best City in Georgia by a Dam Site." Yet there was much flotsam left in the wake of this progress. The lake displaced 700 families, and six churches, 15 businesses, and 20 cemeteries were relocated or destroyed.

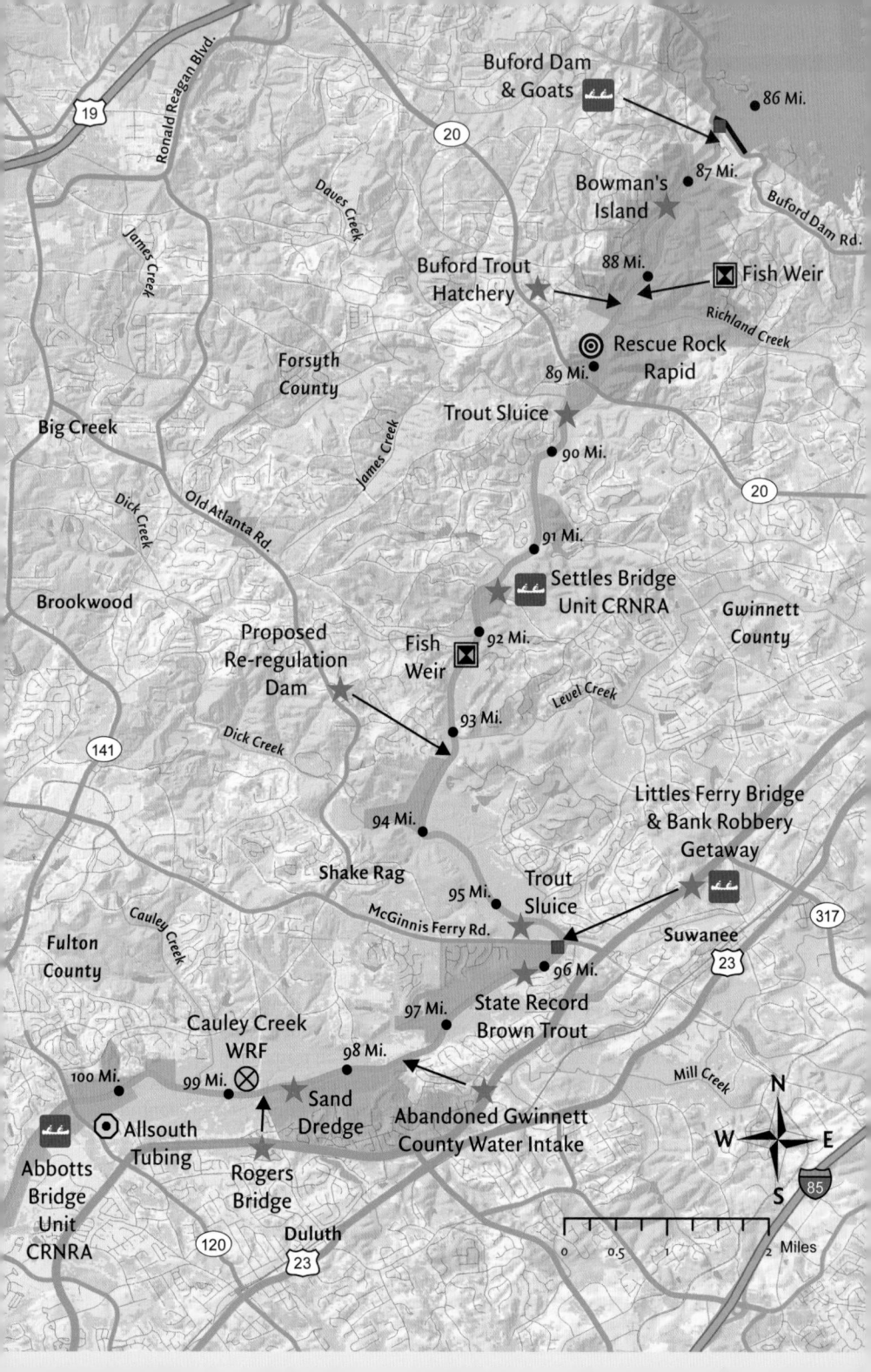

Tailwaters

Length 14 miles (Buford Dam to Abbotts Bridge)

Class I–II

Time 6–8 hours

Minimum Level The river here can be run year-round, but releases from Buford Dam can create unsafe conditions. Boaters and anglers should use extreme caution when traveling this section. Hydropower releases from Buford Dam cause dramatic rises in water levels and flow velocity. Release schedules are issued by the U.S. Army Corps of Engineers daily and can be retrieved at http://water.sam.usace.army.mil/todaySched.htm or by calling 770-945-1466. The Chattahoochee River National Recreation Area records on average two deaths each year on the river, and many such deaths are the result of river users being unaware and unprepared for the powerful releases from Buford Dam.

River Gauge The nearest river gauge is at Buford Dam: http://waterdata.usgs.gov/ga/nwis/uv?site_no=02334430.

Launch Site The launch is off Buford Dam Road east of Cumming. This developed launch site is on the west bank of the river below Buford Dam. Amenities include parking area, boat ramp, and restrooms.

DIRECTIONS From the Ga. 400/Ga. 20 interchange in Cumming (exit 14 on Ga. 400), travel east on Ga. 20 for 1.8 miles. Turn left onto Samples Road and proceed 2.2 miles. Turn right onto Buford Dam Road and travel 1.6 miles to Little Mill Road on the right and the entrance to the Buford Dam Lower Pool area. Proceed 0.7 mile to the parking area. The site can also be accessed from the east and I-985.

Take Out Site The take out is on river left just downstream of Abbotts Bridge Road. This site is part of the Chattahoochee River National Recreation Area. Amenities include parking area, boat ramp, public restrooms, picnic tables, and picnic shelter. User fees apply.

DIRECTIONS From the intersection of Little Mill and Buford Dam Roads, turn left onto Buford Dam Road and proceed 1.6 miles. Turn left onto Samples Road and proceed 2.2 miles to Ga. 20. Continue across Ga. 20 as Samples Road becomes Trammel Road. Continue for 2.4 miles. Turn right on Windemere Parkway. Proceed for 2.1 miles. Turn left onto Old Atlanta Road and proceed 4.5 miles. Continue across McGinnis Ferry Road where Old Atlanta Road becomes Bell Road. Continue 2.2 miles to Boles Road. Continue straight on Boles Road 1 mile. Turn left onto Abbotts

Bridge Road (Ga. 120) and proceed 0.5 mile. Turn right into the entrance to the Chattahoochee River National Recreation Area on the right.

Alternative Take Out Sites To create a 5-mile trip, paddlers and floaters can take out at the Settles Bridge Unit of the Chattahoochee River National Recreation Area. This unit provides parking and a canoe-kayak launch. An 8-mile trip can be made by taking out at a public boat ramp at the McGinnis Ferry Unit of the Chattahoochee River National Recreation Area. This unit provides parking and a boat ramp.

DIRECTIONS TO SETTLES BRIDGE UNIT CRNRA From the intersection of Little Mill and Buford Dam Roads, turn right onto Buford Dam Road and proceed 1.6 miles. Turn right onto Suwanee Dam Road and travel 3.8 miles. Turn right onto Johnson Road and proceed 1.1 miles. Turn right onto Settles Bridge Road and travel 0.9 mile to the parking area.

DIRECTIONS TO MCGINNIS FERRY UNIT CRNRA From the intersections of Little Mill and Buford Dam Roads, turn left and proceed 1.6 miles. Turn left onto Samples Road and travel 2.2 miles. Continue across Ga. 20 as Samples Road becomes Trammel Road. Continue for 2.4 miles. Turn right onto Windemere Parkway and proceed for 2.1 miles. Turn left onto Old Atlanta Road and travel 4.5 miles. Turn left onto McGinnis Ferry Road and proceed 2 miles to the entrance to the boat ramp on the left.

Description This section of the river flows through several units of the Chattahoochee River National Recreation Area, which encompasses some 10,000 acres along the river between Buford Dam and Atlanta. The water flowing from Buford Dam and the bottom of Lake Lanier remains about 50 degrees Fahrenheit year-round. Due to the cold water, the river here is often shrouded in mist during the warmer months. It is a haven for trout fishermen, paddlers, and tubers. In 2012, the U.S. Dept. of the Interior named this stretch of river from Buford Dam to Atlanta its first National Water Trail.

Outfitters Two facilities provide tube and boat rentals on this section of the river:

Allsouth Tubing, 4349 Abbotts Bridge Rd., Duluth, Ga. 30097, 678-349-6880, www.gorivertubing.com

Chattahoochee Outfitters, 203 Azalea Dr., Roswell, Ga. 30075, 770-650-1008, www.shootthehooch.com

Points of Interest

MILE 86.5 (34.161072, -84.076282) Buford Dam & Goats. Atop the grassy knoll above the dam's powerhouse, you may see several goats. Since the 1980s, the U.S. Army Corps of Engineers has maintained a small herd to keep vegetation atop the dam trimmed.

MILE 87.3 (34.151755, -84.082201) Bowman's Island. This large island splits the river, and near this site archaeologists have found evidence of prehistoric Native American occupation. The preferred route is river right.

MILE 88.2 (34.140653, -84.087092) Fish Weir. Built by Native Americans, the W-shaped rock shoal here (visible only in extreme low water) was once used to capture fish. Traditionally, a line of people would walk in the shallow water upstream of the dam, spooking fish to the point of the dam where a basket awaited to collect the fish. The National Park Service has documented 11 historic fish traps in the 48 miles between Buford Dam and Peachtree Creek in Atlanta.

MILE 88.4 (34.137667, -84.089486) Buford Trout Hatchery. This hatchery operated by the Georgia Department of Natural Resources takes advantage of the clear, cold water from Buford Dam. Water is pumped from the river into the hatchery's raceways where rainbow and brown trout are bred. The fish are then released to the Chattahoochee and other streams in North Georgia. Considered the southernmost trout waters in the United States, the Chattahoochee tailwater fishery that stretches from the dam to Atlanta annually hosts an estimated 115,000 fishing trips that add up to $10.5 million for the local economy. Of course, the fishery is completely artificial. Before the creation of Lake Lanier and the cold-water releases from the dam, water temperatures in this section of the river could not support trout populations. The hatchery, not accessible from the river, is open daily. The property includes a nature trail, a fishing pond, and viewing areas of the hatchery raceways. Buford Trout Hatchery: 770-781-6888.

MILE 88.9 (34.1305279, -84.093966) Rescue Rock Rapid. So named because this site is used by local emergency personnel to practice swiftwater rescue, and, in fact, has been the site of many a real-life rescue. The best route through the borderline Class II rapid starts center and follows the main flow to river right. When Buford Dam is releasing, this rapid is transformed into a formidable Class II obstacle with large waves. During releases, the route on river left is less challenging.

MILE 89.5 (34.123924, -84.095634) Trout Sluice. The pipe on river right is used by the Georgia Department of Natural Resources to sluice trout into the river. The state annually stocks approximately 200,000 rainbow, brown, and on occasion, even brook trout between Buford Dam and the Paces Mill Unit of the Chattahoochee River National Recreation Area.

MILE 91.7 (34.098435, -84.109812) Settles Bridge Unit CRNRA. Built in 1896, this Pratt metal truss bridge was typical of that period and based on a design patented by Thomas and Caleb Pratt in 1844. It was abandoned as a thoroughfare between Gwinnett and Forsyth Counties in the 1950s. The land surrounding the bridge is protected as part of the Chattahoochee River National Recreation Area. Facilities include a parking area and canoe-kayak launch.

MILE 92.4 (34.088871, -84.112199) Fish Weir. Running the full width of the river, this fish weir is believed to have been built by Cherokee Indians in the early 1800s. In 1993, it was described as being constructed of stones and several 30-foot-long timbers.

MILE 93.2 (34.077150, -84.113197) Proposed Re-regulation Dam. In 1986, the U.S. Congress authorized the U.S. Army Corps of Engineers to construct a dam at this site for the purposes of assuring water supply to Metro Atlanta and meeting minimum flow targets downstream. However, studies predicted both high costs and environmental impacts, so in 1989, the Corps scuttled it in favor of reallocating more of the water from Lanier for Metro Atlanta's water supply. That decision touched off a water dispute between Georgia, Alabama, and Florida that remains unresolved.

MILE 95.3 (34.053617, -84.104336) Trout Sluice. The Georgia Department of Natural Resources uses the pipe at river right to stock trout.

MILE 95.7 (34.050647, -84.097651) Littles Ferry Bridge & Bank Robbery Getaway. Now spanned by the modern steel and concrete bridge on McGinnis Ferry Road, this is the site of a great bank robbery getaway in the early 20th century. Two thieves who'd just robbed a Gwinnett County bank made their escape across the bridge here.

Upon reaching the Fulton County side, they reportedly stopped, hopped out, and tossed the timber planks of the bridge into the river, rendering the bridge impassable and securing their escape from Gwinnett County authorities. A boat ramp and parking area provide access on river right upstream of the bridge.

SHOALS, GWINNETT COUNTY

MILE 96.1 (34.046895, -84.101889) State Record Brown Trout. Near this site on November 12, 2001, Charlie Ford of Rome caught the state-record brown trout. The fish weighed 18 pounds, 6 ounces . . . and really, it should never have been found in the Chattahoochee. Brown trout are not native to Georgia waters and were certainly never found on the river here prior to 1957, when Buford Dam was completed. But the cold water coming downriver from the bottom of Lake Lanier has created a haven for state-stocked brown and rainbow trout, and this section of the river has become one of the most popular spots in the state for anglers wanting to catch them. The stocking program began in 1962, and the Chatta-hoochee has proven to be highly hospitable, especially to brown trout. A Georgia Department of Natural Resources study begun in 2005 determined that a sustainable wild population of reproducing brown trout had been established in the river, and in 2011 it announced that it would cease stocking the fish between Buford Dam and the Ga. 400 bridge near Roswell.

MILE 97.5 (34.034165, -84.120709) Abandoned Gwinnett County Water Intake. The structure on river left is a former water intake for Gwinnett County. This site was abandoned when the county moved its primary water withdrawal upstream to Lake Lanier. Lake Lanier serves up about 75 million gallons a day to the county's 824,000 residents.

MILE 98.7 (34.030654, -84.138936) Sand Dredge. The hulking barge, machinery, and pipes on river left are used to suck sand from the river bottom.

MILE 98.8 (34.030082, -84.1411193) Rogers Bridge. Rogers Bridge is named for John Rogers, an early white settler of the area who married Sarah Cordery, the daughter of a Cherokee mother and European father, in 1802. Together, John and Sarah raised 12 children along the river here, maintaining a 325-acre farm and operating a ferry across the river. According to local historian Don Shadburn, Rogers and his family originally lived on the east side of the river, but around 1819 moved their home downriver on logs and reconstructed it on the west bank in Cherokee territory. The home still stands in the town of Johns Creek. Rogers Bridge was the last operating metal truss bridge between Buford Dam and Atlanta, carrying cars across the river into the late 1970s.

MILE 98.8 (34.030258, -84.149101) Cauley Creek WRF. Originally constructed in 2002 to much fanfare, this state-of-the-art facility treated the sewage of Fulton County residents for reuse as irrigation at the many nearby private golf courses. Surrounded by upscale homes, operators boasted of an odorless facility and even neatly disguised the plant inside a bucolic red barn. Because the facility provided water for reuse, it was hailed as a way to reduce water withdrawals from the stressed Chattahoochee, but in 2012 after the completion of the new county-operated Johns Creek wastewater facility downstream, Fulton County commissioners voted to end the county's contract with the privately owned Cauley Creek facility. The Environmental Protection Division of the Georgia Department of Natural Resources objected to the move, arguing that the Cauley Creek facility had saved billons of gallons of water from the Chattahoochee. Commissioners from South Fulton countered with the argument that water ratepayers should not be asked to subsidize private golf clubs in upscale North Fulton.

MILE 100.8 (34.024800, -84.172431) Abbotts Bridge Unit CRNRA. This park includes restrooms, picnic tables and shelters, and a boat ramp.

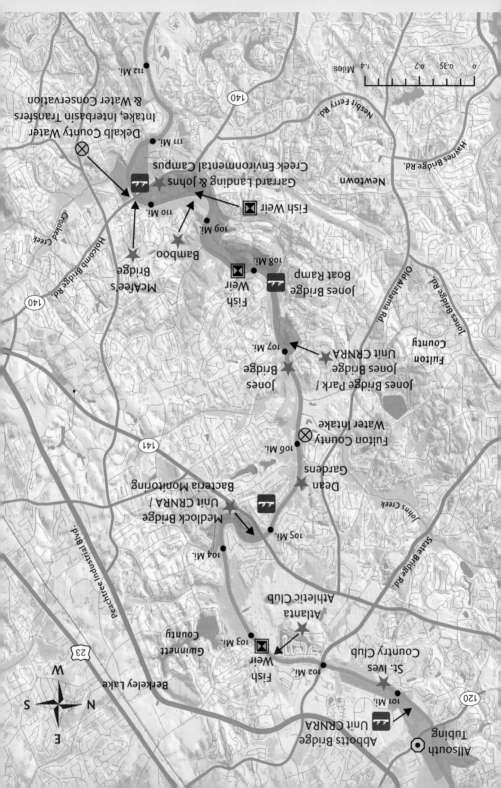

Jones Bridge

Length 10 miles (Abbotts Bridge to Holcomb Bridge)

Class 1

Time 4–6 hours

Minimum Level The river here can be run year-round, but releases from Buford Dam can create unsafe conditions. Boaters and anglers should use extreme caution when traveling this section. Hydropower releases from Buford Dam cause dramatic rises in water levels and flow velocity. Release schedules are issued by the U.S. Army Corps of Engineers daily and can be retrieved at http://water.sam.usace.army.mil/todaySched.htm or by calling 770-945-1466. The Chattahoochee River National Recreation Area (CRNRA) records on average two deaths each year on the river, and many such deaths are the result of river users being unaware and unprepared for the powerful releases from Buford Dam.

River Gauge The nearest river gauge is at McGinnis Ferry Road, http://waterdata.usgs.gov/ga/nwis/nwisman/?site_no=02334653.

Launch Site This site is part of the CRNRA. Amenities include parking area, boat ramp, restrooms, and picnic areas. User fees apply.

DIRECTIONS From the intersection of I-85 and Ga. 120 (exit 108), take Ga. 120 West for 3.9 miles into Duluth. Turn right onto Main Street and proceed 0.1 mile. Turn left onto Abbotts Bridge Road (Ga. 120) and proceed 3.1 miles. Turn left into the entrance of the Abbotts Bridge Unit of the CRNRA.

Take Out Site The take out is on river right just downstream of Holcomb Bridge Road. A city of Roswell park, Garrard Landing offers a boat ramp, restrooms, picnic facilities, and a recreational trail.

DIRECTIONS From the exit of the Abbotts Bridge Unit of the CRNRA, turn left and proceed 0.8 mile. Turn left onto Parsons Road and travel 0.7 mile. Turn left onto Medlock Bridge Road (Ga. 141) and proceed 2 miles. Turn right onto Old Alabama Road and travel 3.8 miles. Turn left onto Jones Bridge Road and proceed 0.7 mile. Bear right onto Barnwell Road and proceed 2.5 miles. Turn left onto Holcomb Bridge Road (Ga. 140) and proceed 0.6 mile to the Johns Creek Environmental Campus. Turn right into the campus and follow the signs to Garrard Landing.

Alternative Take Out Sites To create a 4-mile trip, paddlers and floaters can take out at the Medlock Bridge Unit of the CRNRA. This unit provides parking, a boat ramp, and walking trails. A 6-mile trip is also possible with a take out at the Jones

Bridge Unit of the CRNRA. This unit provides parking, a canoe-kayak launch, restrooms, picnic areas, and walking trails.

DIRECTIONS TO MEDLOCK BRIDGE UNIT CRNRA   From the exit of the Abbotts Bridge Unit of the CRNRA, turn left and proceed 0.8 mile. Turn left onto Parsons Road and travel 0.7 mile. Turn left onto Medlock Bridge Road (Ga. 141) and proceed 3.4 miles. Turn left into the entrance of the Medlock Bridge Unit.

DIRECTIONS TO JONES BRIDGE UNIT CRNRA   From the exit of the Abbotts Bridge Unit of the CRNRA, turn left and proceed 0.8 mile. Turn left onto Parsons Road and travel 0.7 mile. Turn left onto Medlock Bridge Road (Ga. 141) and proceed 2 miles. Turn right onto Old Alabama Road and travel 3.8 miles. Turn left onto Jones Bridge Road and proceed 0.7 mile. Bear right onto Barnwell Road and travel 0.9 mile. Turn left into the entrance of the Jones Bridge Unit and follow the road to the canoe-kayak launch.

Description   This section of the river flows through several units of the Chattahoochee River National Recreation Area, a national park that encompasses 10,000 acres along the river between Buford Dam and Atlanta. Due to Buford Dam, the water continues to run clear and cold as the river winds past upscale subdivisions, country clubs, and golf courses—including one of the largest residences in the state. Beneath the veneer of this 21st-century opulence is a region rich in history. Shoals at Jones Bridge interrupt what is mostly a gentle flatwater course.

Outfitters   Two facilities provide tube and boat rentals on this section of the river:

Allsouth Tubing, 4349 Abbotts Bridge Rd., Duluth, Ga. 30097, www.gorivertubing
.com, 678-349-6880

Chattahoochee Outfitters, 203 Azalea Dr., Roswell, Ga. 30075, 770-650-1008, www
.shootthehooch.com

Points of Interest

MILE 101.3 (34.017480, -84.176277) St. Ives Country Club. Located on river right, St. Ives is typical of North Fulton living. The 18-hole golf course winds through a gated community where home prices start at around $1 million. Golf balls can often be fished from the river bottom here.

MILE 102.7 (33.998287, -84.181320) Atlanta Athletic Club. For the next mile, the river parallels both of the Atlanta Athletic Club's 18-hole golf courses. The club dates to the late 1800s, and its history tells the story of the rise, fall, and rebirth of Atlanta's first suburbs and the metro area's unstoppable spread north along the Chattahoochee. Originally founded by Atlanta businessmen in 1898, the club built its first golf course in 1915 in the city's original "suburbs" at a site at the east end of the city's trolley line—5 miles from downtown. The course came to be known as East Lake Country Club. East Lake was the home course of the famed Bobby Jones and thrived into the middle 1900s, but by the 1960s most of East Lake's members had long since fled intown Atlanta for the burgeoning suburbs to the north. In 1963, the club sold parts of East Lake to fund a course and clubhouse at this new location overlooking the Chattahoochee. Since that move, the club has hosted three PGA championships. East Lake, on the other hand, languished; the land sold by the club became a housing project riddled with poverty, drugs, and violence, and the old course itself became mostly forgotten. Then in the early 1990s, restoration of the course and clubhouse began; since 2005, the East Lake Club has been the permanent host of the PGA Tour Playoff for the FedEx Cup. The surrounding neighborhood has risen with the tide and has become a model for urban renewal.

OAK AT ABBOTTS
BRIDGE UNIT OF
CHATTAHOOCHEE
RIVER NATIONAL
RECREATION AREA,
GWINNETT COUNTY

MILE 102.9 (33.996488, -84.183030) Fish Weir.

MILE 104.8 (33.996601, -84.201957) Medlock Bridge Unit CRNRA / Bacteria Monitoring. A boat ramp just upstream of Medlock Bridge Road marks the Chattahoochee River National Recreation Area. The park includes a parking area, a boat ramp, a picnic area, and walking trails. This is also the site of a water-quality monitoring program administered jointly by the U.S Geological Survey, the National Park Service, and Chattahoochee Riverkeeper. Bacteria levels are measured regularly and posted online at http://ga2.er.usgs.gov/bacteria.

MILE 105.6 (34.003903, -84.212278) Dean Gardens. On river right is what was once known as Dean Gardens, a 32,000-square-foot neoclassical mansion built between 1988 and 1992 by Larry Dean, a self-made man who made a mint developing data-processing software. In a river corridor flush with upscale homes, this one stands alone. It cost $25 million to build, as Dean spared no expense (he appointed one bathroom with a 24K gold sink costing $80,000). Shortly after its completion, Dean and his wife divorced, after which the megamansion went on the market—where it stayed for more than 15 years. Once listed at $40 million, the estate sold in 2010 for $7.6 million to actor-director-comedian Tyler Perry, who announced even before he took possession that he would raze the estate and build a new home on the site. Both men were attracted to the site largely because of its proximity to the river. In 2011, the *Atlanta Business Chronicle* reported: "one of the biggest selling points for Dean Gardens was not the house, but the land on which it sits. The property, with its 1,200 feet of Chattahoochee River frontage, could qualify for as much as $10 million in tax breaks by setting up a conservation easement that bars development of the acreage's green spaces."

MILE 106 (34.003665, -84.219343) Fulton County Water Intake. This pumping station on river right supplies water to Fulton County residents. Fulton (including the city of Atlanta) uses about 180 million gallons a day. Local water planners expect that demand to grow beyond 280 million by 2050.

MILE 106.8 (34.001607, -84.234229) Jones Bridge. This bridge dates to 1904, when it connected Gwinnett with the now-defunct Milton County. The bridge had a short life: it fell into disrepair in the 1920s and with the Great Depression gripping the country in the 1930s neither of the county governments could pay for repairs. In 1945 a crew arrived at the site (with a crane and other heavy equipment) and began dismantling the bridge. Questioned by local residents, the men claimed to be working for Gwinnett County. Gwinnett officials did not discover the ruse until half the bridge was gone. The thieves, cashing in on the high steel prices during World War II, were never apprehended.

MILE 107 (34.001060, -84.236192) Jones Bridge Park / Jones Bridge Unit CRNRA. The shoals just below the abandoned bridge mark the site of these two parks—the Gwinnett County park is on river left while the Chattahoochee River

National Recreation Area preserves the land on river right. The 30-acre county park features picnic facilities, a playground, soccer fields, and restrooms. It is possible to take out canoes and kayaks at the park, but there is no developed boat launch. The CRNRA on the opposite shore features parking, a canoe-kayak launch (below the shoals), restrooms, picnic areas, walking trails, and a boat ramp (0.6 mile downstream from the shoals). The shoals themselves are popular with sunbathers and anglers, not to mention Canada geese. The best route through the shoals is on river right.

MILE 107.7 (33.998641, -84.247711) Jones Bridge Boat Ramp.

MILE 108 (33.994516, -84.249755) Fish Weir.

MILE 109.3 (33.984919, -84.263431) Bamboo. An impressive stand of bamboo crowds the shore on river left. Bamboo is a nonnative, introduced species that the Georgia Exotic Pest Plant Control Council includes on its list of threats to Georgia's natural areas. The Asian giant can quickly take over the habitat of native species, crowding them out and significantly altering ecosystems. It should not be confused with native river cane, a smaller cousin of the invasive bamboo.

MILE 109.4 (33.985415, -84.263493) Fish Weir.

MILE 110.2 (33.973471, -84.263025) McAfee's Bridge. Just downstream of the modern-day Holcomb Bridge are the remains of this bridge, which dates to 1834. That year workers for landowner Robert McAfee built the pillars by stacking large flat stones atop one another. No mortar was used, but more than 160 years later the structure still stands. The 220-foot-long bridge that once sat on these pillars was set ablaze by Union troops during the Civil War. At that time, it was the only bridge spanning the Chattahoochee near Atlanta other than the Western & Atlantic railroad bridge. In 1906, the original Holcomb Bridge was set atop these same pillars. Prior to the construction of McAfee's Bridge, the river was crossed here via a ferry operated by early settler Charles Gates in the 1820s.

MILE 110.2 (33.972920, -84.263766) DeKalb County Water Intake, Interbasin Transfers & Water Conservation. The structure on river left serves as nearby DeKalb County's water intake and can pump as much as 140 million gallons a day (MGD) to meet the needs of the county's 700,000 residents. DeKalb, like many counties in the Metro Atlanta area, lies within two river basins (Chattahoochee and Ocmulgee). While it gets all of its drinking water from the Chattahoochee, much of the wastewater produced by residents is treated and discharged to the streams feeding the Ocmulgee. This shifting of water flows is known as an interbasin transfer. Each day, an average of about 37 million gallons is removed from the river here, never to be returned. This poses concerns for downstream water users and the river's health. In response, DeKalb was one of the first metro counties to enact a water conservation measure requiring owners of residences with old, water-wasting toilets to replace them prior to obtaining new water service after the sale of the property. The program is expected to save 6–18 MGD once fully implemented, thus reducing the water transferred from the Chattahoochee. Until 2013, when DeKalb County upgraded its water intake structure, a rock dam or jetty extended from the west bank of the river just below McAfee's Bridge. The rock dam deepened the river and forced the river to the intake, ensuring adequate water for withdrawals even during periods of low flow.

MILE 110.2 (33.973000, -84.264377) Garrard Landing & Johns Creek Environmental Campus. A city of Roswell park, Garrard Landing offers a boat ramp, restrooms, picnic areas, and a recreational trail. The city of Roswell chose the name Garrard Landing to honor the previous landowners at the site—not Union General Kenner Garrard, who was infamously responsible for burning the town's mills and then, under orders of General William T. Sherman, arresting the mill's owners and workers for treason. Sherman's order read thus: "I repeat my orders that you arrest all people, male and female, connected with those factories, no matter what the clamor, and let them foot it, under guard, to Marietta, whence I will send them by cars to the North . . . the poor women will make a howl. Let them take along their children and clothing, providing they have the means of hauling, or you can spare them." Garrard was also responsible for the burning of McAfee's Bridge. On the rise above the landing is the Fulton County Johns Creek Environmental Campus, a sewage treatment facility cleverly disguised to look like a textile mill from the late 1800s. Completed in 2009 at a cost of $138 million, the facility can treat up to 15 million gallons of sewage a day to reuse quality levels. Garrard Landing also serves as the launch site for the annual Chattahoochee Riverkeeper Back to the Chattahoochee River Race.

ANGLER NEAR JONES BRIDGE PARK, GWINNETT COUNTY

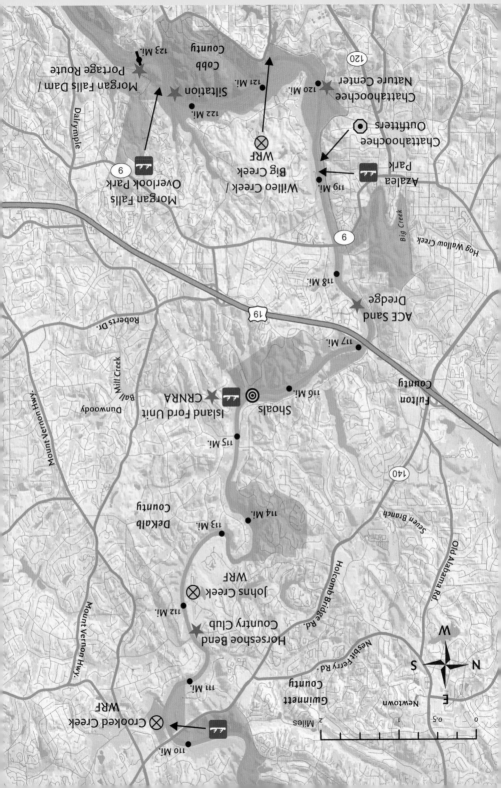

Morgan Falls

Length 13 miles (Holcomb Bridge to Morgan Falls Dam)

Class 1

Time 6–8 hours

Minimum Level The river here can be run year-round, but releases from Buford Dam can create unsafe conditions. Boaters and anglers should use extreme caution when traveling this section. Hydropower releases from Buford Dam cause dramatic rises in water levels and flow velocity. Release schedules are issued by the U.S. Army Corps of Engineers daily and can be retrieved at http://water.sam.usace.army.mil/todaySched.htm or by calling 770-945-1466. The Chattahoochee River National Recreation Area records, on average, two deaths each year on the river, and many such deaths are the result of river users being unaware and unprepared for the powerful releases from Buford Dam.

River Gauge The nearest river gauge is at Roswell: http://waterdata.usgs.gov/ga/nwis/nwisman/?site_no=02335450.

Launch Site A city of Roswell park, Garrard Landing offers parking, canoe-kayak launch, restrooms, picnic areas, and a recreational trail.

DIRECTIONS From the intersection of Ga. 400 and Holcomb Bridge Road (exit 7/Ga. 140), travel east on Holcomb Bridge Road for 4.8 miles. Turn right into the Johns Creek Environmental Center and follow the signs to Garrard Landing Park.

Take Out Site The take out site is Morgan Falls Overlook Park, which is on Bull Sluice Lake on river left 0.5 mile upstream of Morgan Falls Dam. This city of Sandy Springs park offers parking, a boat dock, restrooms, picnic pavilions, walking trails, and additional amenities. However, parking is 0.1 mile from the take out location. Those through-paddling and wishing to portage around Morgan Falls Dam may do so using the portage path on the east side of the dam. The carry is through a fenced area adjacent to the powerhouse. The put-in below the dam is at the edge of the fence down a steep riprap bank to the river.

DIRECTIONS From the entrance to the Johns Creek Environmental Campus, turn right onto Holcomb Bridge Road and proceed 0.7 mile. Turn right onto Spalding Drive and travel 2.6 miles. Turn left onto Jeff Ferry Road and proceed 0.6 mile. Turn right on Dunwoody Club Drive and travel 2.3 miles to reconnect with Spalding Drive. Turn left onto Spalding Drive and proceed 0.4 mile. Turn right onto Pitts Road and travel 0.7 mile. Turn left onto Roswell Road (Ga. 9) and proceed 0.6 mile. Turn right onto Morgan Falls Road and travel 1.2 miles to the park entrance on the right.

Alternative Take Out Sites To create a 5-mile trip, paddlers and floaters can take out at the Island Ford Unit of the Chattahoochee River National Recreation Area (CRNRA). This facility provides parking, a canoe-kayak launch, restrooms, picnic facilities, walking trails, and the park visitor center. A 9-mile trip can be created utilizing Azalea Park in Roswell. This city park provides parking, a boat ramp, rest-rooms, and picnic facilities.

DIRECTIONS TO ISLAND FORD UNIT CRNRA From the entrance to the Johns Creek Environmental Campus, turn left onto Holcomb Bridge Road and proceed 4.6 miles. Turn left onto Old Alabama Road and travel 1.1 miles. Turn right onto Riverside Road and proceed 1.3 miles. Turn left onto Ga. 9 and travel 0.2 mile. Turn left onto Roberts Drive and proceed 1.6 miles. Turn left into the entrance for CRNRA and follow Island Ford Parkway 1.2 miles to the park headquarters.

DIRECTIONS TO AZALEA PARK IN ROSWELL From the entrance to the Johns Creek Environmental Campus, turn left onto Holcomb Bridge Road and proceed 4.6 miles. Turn left onto Old Alabama Road and travel 1.1 miles. Turn right onto River-side Road and proceed 1.3 miles. Continue straight across Ga. 9 to Azalea Drive. Riverside park is 0.6 mile ahead on the left.

Description The Chattahoochee continues its meander through Metro Atlanta's northern suburbs where its corridor alternates between the preserved land of the Chattahoochee River National Recreation Area and intensely developed residential areas. Some homes are perched amazingly close to the water. Seven miles from the launch site, the current slackens as the river spreads into the backwaters of Bull Sluice Lake, which is formed by Morgan Falls Dam. Access points along the lake provide for out-and-back float trips.

Outfitters Chattahoochee Outfitters offers tube and boat rentals: 203 Azalea Dr., Roswell, Ga. 30075, 770-650-1008, www.shootthehooch.com.

Points of Interest

MILE 110.6 (33.972246, -84.267978) Crooked Creek WRF. This water reclama-tion facility (WRF), otherwise known as a sewage treatment plant, sits just upstream on Crooked Creek, a tributary entering on river left. Collecting and treating the sewage of Gwinnett County, one of Georgia's fastest growing coun-ties, its history tells the story of the area's dramatic growth. Originally built in 1972 to treat 1 million gallons a day (MGD), the plant has expanded continuously during the past four decades. In 2016, it is expected to treat up to 25 MGD. During that time the lexicon of sewage treatment has also evolved. In 1972, such facilities were referred to as "sewage plants," that evolved into "wastewater treatment plants" and finally the present and sanitized "water reclamation facilities." The standards for treatment have also evolved; the effluent now issuing forth from most "reclamation facilities" is considered cleaner than the water in the receiving streams.

MILE 111.7 (33.976045, -84.284961) **Horseshoe Bend Country Club.** Named for the bend in the river that it occupies, the site for this golf course was the original home of the Atlanta Steeplechase in 1966. The course hugs the right bank of the river for the next 1.5 miles. It is common to hear, and sometimes see, errant tee shots flying into the river here; golf balls litter the river bottom.

MILE 112.3 (33.975752, -84.290884) **Johns Creek WRF.** Sandwiched between the golf club's fairways is this now-defunct sewage treatment plant. Fast-paced growth in the area outstripped the facility's treatment capacity and in 2002, the Environmental Protection Division of the Georgia Department of Natural Resources issued a moratorium on new sewage hookups in the area because of frequent water-quality violations associated with the plant. The facility was replaced by the new Johns Creek Environmental Campus upstream; the land at the old WRF site is slated to become public greenspace.

BLUFFS ON BULL SLUICE LAKE, FULTON COUNTY

MILE 115.5 (33.987184, -84.323156) Island Ford Unit CRNRA. Located on river left, this unit of the national park holds the park's headquarters. Established in 1978 with a stroke of the pen by President Jimmy Carter, the Chattahoochee River National Recreation Area (CRNRA) was one of the federal government's first experiments with "urban national parks" designed to give city dwellers a respite in nature close to home. By all accounts, the CRNRA has been a huge success. It has led to the protection of 10,000 acres and hosts more than 3 million visitors each year. But, its creation was not without controversy. Conservative U.S. Congressman Larry McDonald, whose district included large portions of the proposed park, famously panned the multiunit recreation area as "bumps on a log that would provide refuge for hooligans, drug users and nudists." McDonald died tragically when the Soviet Union shot down Korean Air Lines Flight 007 in 1983, but were he alive today he'd see more mothers and baby strollers than nudists and drug users. The park headquarters overlooking the river was originally the summer home of Georgia Supreme Court Justice Sam Hewlett. Built in the 1930s, the structure features timbers from the Okefenokee Swamp and gneiss stones harvested from Stone Mountain. The unit provides parking, a canoe-kayak launch, restrooms, picnic areas, walking trails, and a gift shop.

MILE 115.6 (33.988714, -84.323800) Shoals. A series of shoals extends over the next 0.7 mile to the end of Island Ford.

MILE 117.6 (34.008380, -84.340172) ACE Sand Dredge. The odd-looking barge on river right here is a dredge used in harvesting sand from the river bottom. Sand and water are pumped on shore through the series of floating pipes. The sand is used primarily as an ingredient in concrete, but it is also employed as a conditioner for local lawns and golf courses. The Georgia Environmental Protection Division regulates these operations, the primary water-quality concerns being the turbidity of the water discharged back to the river and the protection of vegetation along the riverbank. According to Georgia's riparian laws, operators who do not own land on both sides of the river can mine only to the river's centerline.

MILE 119.1 (34.001487, -84.363346) Azalea Park. This city of Roswell facility provides parking, a boat ramp, restrooms, picnic areas, and recreational trails. Chattahoochee Outfitters has its headquarters here and provides boat rentals for out-and-back trips on Bull Sluice Lake.

MILE 120 (34.001096, -84.380083) Chattahoochee Nature Center. This 127-acre facility has been educating children and adults about local wildlife and the Chattahoochee River since the 1970s. The center hosts 100,000 visitors each year and handles more than 1,000 injured or ill animals each year for rehabilitation and reintroduction to the wild, if possible. The center can be accessed on river right via a dock and a walking path that crosses Willeo Road here. Entrance fee applies.

MILE 120.7 (33.992975, -84.383699) Willeo Creek / Big Creek WRF. Upstream on Willeo Creek sits Fulton County's largest water reclamation facility. In 1969 when it first opened, the facility processed less than 1 million gallons of sewage a day. Today it can handle 24 million, and the county expects to expand operations to treat up to 38 million.

MILE 122.3 (33.974248, -84.377219) Siltation. Throughout Bull Sluice Lake you will find mud flats and islands like these. They weren't always here. More than a century of farming and land development upstream have resulted in the slow siltation of the lake. Step into the river upstream, and your feet settle into sand, but here, where the finer particles settle once the river's flow ceases, you will set foot into thick mud. The siltation has become so severe that Georgia Power Co. has been forced to dredge in front of the dam to enable continued power generation.

MILE 122.4 (33.972095, -84.378924) Morgan Falls Overlook Park. This city of Sandy Springs park on river left offers parking, a boat dock, restrooms, picnic pavilions, walking trails, and additional amenities. However, parking is 0.1 mile from the take out location. Standing sentinel over the river in the middle of the park is a chimney that is original to the home built here by Joseph and Isabella Power in the 1820s. The Powers operated a ferry across the river here, as did Joseph's brother downstream at what has come to be known as Powers Ferry.

MILE 122.9 (33.968767, -84.382701) Morgan Falls Dam / Portage Route. At the time of its construction in 1904, this dam was the largest hydroelectric facility in the South. The majority of the power it produced was used to run the Atlanta streetcar system. In fact, before its construction, Bull Sluice Lake was touted in the *Atlanta Constitution* as "the greatest summer resort in the southern states," and plans called for a trolley line to extend from downtown to the lake. That line never materialized, but lines to Marietta and Stone Mountain did. Today, the facility still produces electricity, but only a fraction of the city's needs (enough to power about 4,000 homes). In fact, Georgia Power Co.'s 20 hydropower plants across the state supply just 3 percent of the total electricity it sells. In the 1940s, as a nation, 40 percent of the power we used came from hydropower plants like this one. A drought in 1925 caused a shortage of water to turn the dam's turbines, but the construction of Buford Dam, with its guaranteed flows, solved that problem. To portage around the dam take out just east of the dam and carry through a fenced area adjacent to the powerhouse. The put-in below the dam is at the edge of the fence down a steep riprap bank to the river.

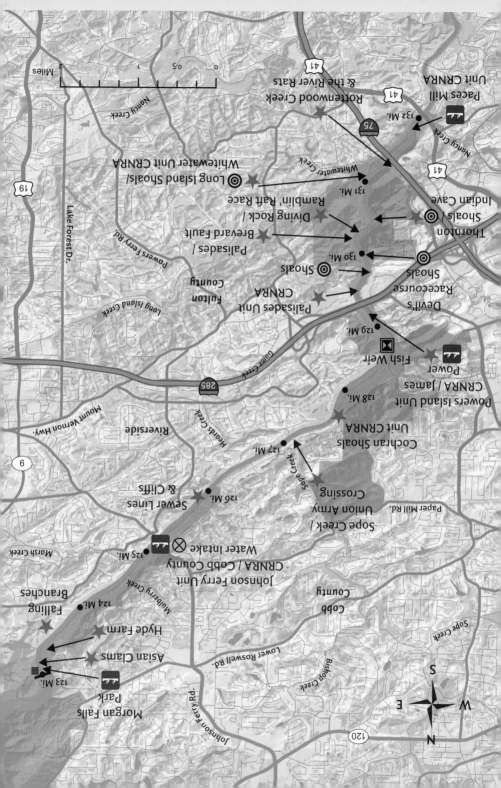

Palisades

Length 9 miles (Morgan Falls Dam to Paces Mill Unit of CRNRA)

Class 1

Time 4–7 hours

Minimum Level The river here can be navigated year-round.

River Gauge: The nearest river gauge is on the river below Morgan Falls Dam: http://waterdata.usgs.gov/nwis/uv?site_no=02335815.

Launch Site A Fulton County facility, Morgan Falls Park provides parking and a boat ramp.

DIRECTIONS From the intersection of Ga. 400 and Northridge Road (exit 6), travel west on Northridge Road 0.5 mile. Turn left onto Roswell Road (Ga. 9) and proceed 1.1 miles. Turn right onto Morgan Falls Road and travel 1.5 miles to the parking area at the boat ramp.

Take Out Site The take out site is in the Paces Mill Unit of the Chattahoochee River National Recreation Area (CRNRA) 0.5 mile downstream of the I-75 bridge. The national park facility provides parking, a boat ramp, restrooms, picnic areas, and recreational trails. User fees apply.

DIRECTIONS From the intersection of Morgan Falls Road and Roswell Road, turn right onto Roswell Road and travel 4.2 miles. Turn right onto the ramp for I-285 West and travel 5 miles. Take exit 20 to I-75 South and then take the first exit (Cumberland Blvd.). Turn right onto Cumberland Boulevard and proceed 0.3 mile. Turn left onto U.S. 41/Cobb Parkway and proceed 0.4 mile to the entrance to Paces Mill Unit on the right.

Alternative Take Out Sites To create a 2-mile trip, paddlers and floaters can take out at the Johnson Ferry Unit of the CRNRA. A 6-mile trip can be created utilizing the Powers Island Unit of the CRNRA. Both sites provide canoe-kayak launch, parking, restrooms, picnic areas, and recreational trails. User fees apply.

DIRECTIONS TO JOHNSON FERRY UNIT CRNRA From the intersection of Morgan Falls Road and Roswell Road, turn right onto Roswell Road and proceed 1 mile. Turn right onto Dalrymple Road, which soon becomes Riverside Drive. Proceed 2.7 miles. Turn right onto Johnson Ferry Road and proceed 0.2 mile to the park entrance on the right.

From the intersection of Morgan Falls Road and Roswell Road, turn right onto Roswell Road and proceed 4.2 miles. Take I-285 West for 2.8 miles to exit 22 (Powers Ferry Rd./Northside Dr.). Bear right at the exit onto Interstate North Parkway and proceed 0.9 mile. Turn right into the driveway for the Powers Island Unit of CRNRA and follow it to the parking area.

Description This 9-mile run is perhaps the most heavily traveled section of the entire river . . . and with good reason. It is arguably the most beautiful section of the river's 436 miles—all sandwiched between Georgia's busiest interstate highways and within 10 miles of downtown Atlanta. Rugged cliffs flank the river's banks in places, and shoals are frequent. On weekends during the summer, expect to see all manner of floats, tubes, canoes, and kayaks—not to mention a host of anglers. Much of the river corridor is protected as the Chattahoochee River National Recreation Area, making for many land-based respites along the way.

Outfitters Three outfitters provide tube, raft, canoe, and kayak rentals on this section of the river:

Chattahoochee Outfitters, 203 Azalea Dr., Roswell, Ga. 30075, 770-650-1008, www.shootthehooch.com

High Country Outfitters, 3906B Roswell Rd., Atlanta, Ga. 30342, 404-814-0999, www.highcountryoutfitters.com

Urban Currents, 2479 Peachtree Rd. NE, Suite 1615, Atlanta, Ga. 30305, 404-449-0612, www.urbancurrents.org

Points of Interest

MILE 123.3 (33.964828, -84.382515) Asian Clams. Littering the base of the rocky bluffs on river left are mounds of shells from Asian clams, an invasive mollusk. Asian clams first entered the United States in 1924 in the Pacific Northwest, and in just 50 years conquered the continent. They are now found in virtually every waterway in the country—an impressive feat for an immobile invertebrate. Highly tolerant of poor water quality and prolific reproducers, they survive in many habitats, but they are not thought to have displaced native mussels. Reservoirs, polluted water, and overharvesting did that. As evidenced by the mounds here, they have filled an important hole left by the disappearing native mussels— a food source for muskrats and otters as well many fish and crayfish.

MILE 123.7 (33.961435, -84.385319) Hyde Farm. Seeing suburban sprawl surround his property over the years, J. C. Hyde kept a promise he made to his father, Jesse Hyde, never to sell the family farm along the river. J. C. died in 2004 at the age of 94, having farmed the land until his dying year. Before his death he made arrangements to preserve the land permanently. The Trust for Public Land facilitated the deal, ultimately conveying 135 acres to the National Park Service. The farm, including a 180-year-old log cabin originally occupied by the pioneering Power family, and several historic farm structures, are now part of the Chatta-hoochee River National Recreation Area. A massive flood on the Chattahoochee actually made it possible for the sharecropping Hyde family to purchase the land in 1920. The flood left a thick deposit of sand across the bottomlands, which devalued the property and enabled Jesse Hyde and his wife, Lela, to purchase the farm and move in with their six children. The Hyde Farm is on river right.

MILE 123.8 (33.958659, -84.387980) Falling Branches. Passing by this spot you might hear the tinkle of water hitting stone. If so you'll know that Falling Branches is flowing. This tiny waterfall drops off an impressive cliff at river left. The fall is on private property. However, on river right, the land from Morgan Falls Dam to Johnson Ferry Road is part of the Chattahoochee River National Recreation Area.

MILE 125.2 (33.944578, -84.404611) Johnson Ferry Unit CRNRA / Cobb County Water Intake. Located just upstream of Johnson Ferry Bridge, this facility pumps water to the Cobb-Marietta Water Authority James E. Quarles treatment plant, which can produce up to 86 million gallons a day. The Chattahoochee is the work-horse for Metro Atlanta's water supply, providing 75 percent of the more than 500 million gallons used each day in the 15-county area. The Johnson Ferry Unit pro-vides parking, restrooms, picnic areas, and recreational trails. User fees apply.

MILE 125.8 (33.936207, -84.413060) Sewer Lines & Cliffs. On river left snaking down the high bluffs are long pipes. They are sewer lines, connecting some of the cliff-top homes with Fulton County's main trunk line at the base of the cliff, and they serve as a visual reminder of the workings of our modern sewage sys-tems. Because sewage is conveyed via gravity, sewer lines are often sited along our rivers and streams (the lowest land to be found), carrying the waste to river-side treatment facilities. Thus, it is not uncommon to get a whiff of sewage when traveling our rivers. During floods, and when sewer lines become clogged, spills can occur. Sewer lines parallel the Chattahoochee for most of its course through Metro Atlanta.

MILE 127.2 (33.925174, -84.429801) Sope Creek / Union Army Crossing. In the Civil War's Atlanta Campaign, the Chattahoochee was the last geographic defense preventing the Union Army from capturing Atlanta, and the Confeder-ates intended to make a stand at their heavily fortified "river line." Union Gen-eral William T. Sherman had other ideas. Rather than risk an assault of the Con-federates' impenetrable defenses, he ordered his troops to flank the defenders. The first Union soldiers crossed the Chattahoochee here on July 9, 1864, forcing a Confederate retreat. Atlanta would fall less than two months later. Prior to the Civil War, locals spelled the creek name as "Soap," but Union maps identified the tributary as "Sope" and that name has stuck.

FALLING BRANCHES, FULTON COUNTY

THE "INDIAN CAVE," PALISADES
UNIT OF CHATTAHOOCHEE
RIVER NATIONAL RECREATION
AREA, FULTON COUNTY

MILE 127.7 (33.920759, -84.437847) Cochran Shoals Unit CRNRA. For the next 2.5 miles the river parallels this part of the Chattahoochee River National Recreation Area and its popular recreational trail. There is no boat access in the unit.

MILE 128.8 (33.907925, -84.447289) Fish Weir.

MILE 129.3 (33.903416, -84.443759) Powers Island Unit CRNRA / James Power. An alternative take out for a 6-mile trip, this facility includes a parking area and restrooms. In the 1820s the Chattahoochee here was the border between Georgia and Cherokee territory. James Power, for whom the island is now named, ran a ferry and blacksmith shop at this site. An account documented in *The First Hundred Years: A Short History of Cobb County*, published in 1935, tells the story of one of Power's encounters with the native people: "On the northern bank of the river there was good deer hunting and it was not only Mr. Power's liking for this sport but the opportunity which it afforded for the replenishment of his larder which caused him to cross the river at intervals. . . . On one occasion, at least, Mr. Power's ardor for hunting was somewhat quenched. The Cherokees burst upon him from the woods. The necessity for a speedy escape was such that he loaded his and his friend's horses too quickly upon the bateau upon which they had crossed the river. The badly balanced boat capsized. Swimming the Chattahoochee was not enjoyable at any time; it was far from agreeable on a cold winter's day. The Indians stood upon the bank and shouted taunts as the men struck out across the river with their horses and finally climbed up the steep muddy bank on the other side." Upon removal of the Native population, Power crossed the river permanently and built the cabin, now preserved at Hyde Farm.

MILE 129.4 (33.899050, -84.441967) Palisades Unit CRNRA. On river left here, the East Palisades Unit extends downstream nearly 2 miles.

MILE 129.6 (33.895913, -84.444102) Shoals.

MILE 130 (33.892827, -84.442884) Devil's Racecourse Shoals. For 0.2 mile here the majority of the river's flow shoots through a narrow passage flanked by protruding shoals. During the 1800s these rugged shoals stretched shore to shore, but boatmen, tired of navigating the nettlesome obstacle, used dynamite to blast a more friendly course, creating the chute that smoothly moves paddlers today. Those same early river men lent the place its name, as the shoals were a "devil" to get through.

MILE 130.3 (33.890101, -84.440792) Palisades / Brevard Fault. Devil's Racecourse Shoals give way to a deep, canyon-like stretch of river that is the heart of the Palisades. The granite outcroppings that vault more than 50 feet above the river here are the handiwork of the Brevard Fault, a geological fault that stretches from the northeast corner of Georgia along a southwesterly route toward Alabama and forms a channel for the river for about 100 miles.

MILE 130.4 (33.888936, -84.442214) Diving Rock / Ramblin' Raft Race. Jutting out of the palisades about 20 feet above the water on river left is a popular spot for taking a plunge. During the 1970s the Diving Rock was a focal point of the annual Ramblin' Raft Race, a uniquely Atlanta cultural phenomenon that in its heyday attracted some 300,000 rafters and spectators. What started in 1969 as a Georgia Tech fraternity party soon became Atlanta's equivalent of Woodstock with equal parts beer, drugs, nudity, and the river. The event recurred through 1980. That year the National Park Service (NPS) spent $50,000 in an attempt to manage the crowds; meanwhile, Fulton County had an estimated 4,000 improperly parked cars towed. The following year, the NPS told race organizers they would have to foot the bill for security and cleanup. They declined, thus ending the race's amazing, albeit controversial, run. Opposite the Diving Rock, the NPS has constructed restroom facilities to help minimize the impact of visitors to this still-popular location.

MILE 130.6 (33.885610, -84.443871) Thornton Shoals / Indian Cave. The best route through this obstacle is far river right and then back to river left. At the top of the shoals on river left, trails lead to what is known as the Indian cave, an impressive overhanging rock believed to have sheltered Native Americans for thousands of years. This is one of 180 archaeological sites identified in the Chattahoochee River National Recreation Area.

MILE 131.1 (33.878600, -84.443292) Long Island Shoals / Whitewater Unit CRNRA. At the head of Long Island on river left is another National Park Service access point. This unit provides canoe-kayak access, parking, and access to walking trails through the East Palisades Unit. User fees apply.

MILE 131.4 (33.876635, -84.447782) Rottenwood Creek & the River Rats. Rottenwood Creek, entering on river right here, is considered the rallying point of the fight to save the Chattahoochee from development. It was here in 1970 that river lovers first noticed zoning notices posted along the creek and river. Cobb County had plans to lay a sewer line along the river, and Fulton County had similar plans for the east bank. The Fulton sewer line was designed to run through the palisades and required blasting a shelf out of the outcroppings (including the Diving Rock) bordering the river. The River Rats, who would later form the river protection group Friends of the River, were set into action. Three years later, the Georgia General Assembly passed the Metropolitan River Protection Act, and finally in 1978, the national recreation area was created. Taking up where the Friends left off, Chattahoochee Riverkeeper formed in 1994, and since that time, the river has had a full-time advocate working to protect and restore it.

MILE 131.9 (33.870412, -84.452074) Paces Mill Unit CRNRA. This is the final access point in the Chattahoochee River National Recreation Area, providing parking, boat launch, restrooms, picnic areas, and recreational trails. User fees apply.

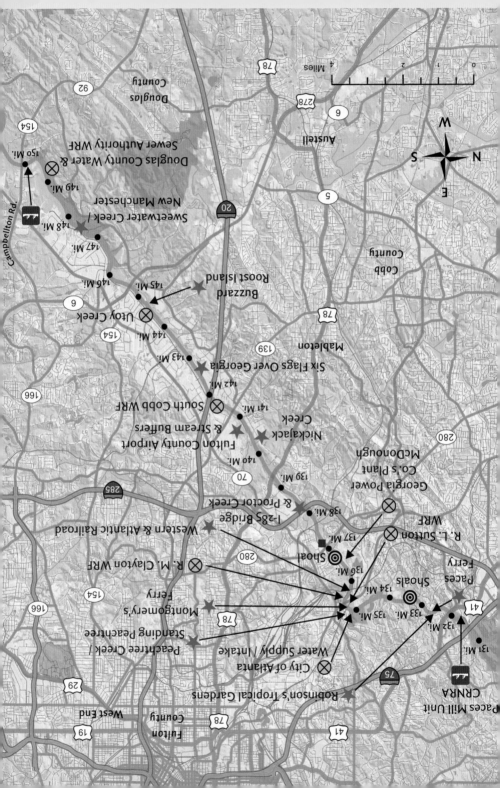

Buzzard Roost

Length 18 miles (Paces Mill Unit of CRNRA to Campbellton Road / Ga. 154)

Class 1

Time 8–10 hours

Minimum Level The river here can be run year-round.

River Gauge The nearest river gauge is at Paces Ferry Road, 1 mile downstream from the launch site: http://waterdata.usgs.gov/ga/nwis/uv?site_no=02336000.

Launch Site The launch site is in the Paces Mill Unit of the Chattahoochee River National Recreation Area (CRNRA). The national park facility provides parking, a boat ramp, restrooms, picnic areas, and recreational trails. User fees apply.

DIRECTIONS From the intersection of I-75 and Mt. Paran Road (exit 256), travel west on Mt. Paran Road 0.1 mile. Turn right onto U.S. 41 (Cobb Pkwy.) and proceed 1 mile to the Paces Mill Unit entrance on the left.

Take Out Site The take out site is a Georgia Department of Natural Resources boat ramp on river left just upstream of the Ga. 154 (Campbellton Rd.) bridge. A private recreational softball campus is adjacent to the ramp.

DIRECTIONS Return to U.S. 41, turn right (north), and proceed 0.5 mile. Turn right on Cumberland Boulevard and travel 0.5 mile. Take the entrance ramp to I-75 North and proceed 0.7 mile. Take the exit for I-285 West (exit 259B) and travel 9.3 miles to the interchange with I-20. Take the exit for I-20 West (exit 10B) and proceed 1.7 miles. Take the exit for Ga. 70/Fulton Industrial Boulevard (exit 49). Turn left onto Fulton Industrial Boulevard and travel 7.4 miles. Turn right onto Ga. 154 (Campbellton Rd.) and proceed 0.8 mile. Turn right into the entrance for the softball complex on the right and follow the drive for 0.1 mile to the parking area at the boat ramp.

Alternative Take Out Sites There are no developed public access points between Paces Mill and Ga. 154. However, it is possible to plan trips utilizing the rights-of-way of the numerous roadways that cross the river in this section. Those choosing these options should be prepared for strenuous carries to and from the river.

Description While the preceding 9 miles are perhaps the most heavily traveled of the entire river, this 18-mile section is likely the least traveled of any of the river's 436 miles. That's because just 3 miles below Paces Mill, the South's largest sewage treatment plant discharges to the river. Over the next 15 miles, six more facilities do the same. For some 50 years Atlanta's inadequate sewage treatment left this portion of the river with a well-deserved reputation as a cesspool. However, recent strides in collecting and treating the area's sewage have enabled the river to recover, and today a venture into the river's industrialized reaches along Atlanta's western flank is a surprisingly enjoyable journey. The homes that crowd the river upstream disappear and the industrial sites, by and large, are off river, leaving a wooded and wild corridor. Along the route are numerous significant historic sites, including Buzzard Roost Island, where archaeological evidence dates human occupation back to 10,000 BC.

Outfitters No outfitters service this section of the river.

Points of Interest

MILE 132.7 (33.859797, -84.4545117020607) Robinson's Tropical Gardens. On river right here sits Canoe Restaurant. Opened in 1995, it is considered one of Atlanta's finest restaurants. During the middle part of the 20th century, the site was home to Robinson's Tropical Gardens, a restaurant that ranks high in the pantheon of Atlanta's historic meeting places. Uniquely situated on the banks of the river, it was "the place to be" from the 1940s through the 1960s in the segregated city—a place where white college students could dance to live performances by the likes of Little Richard and Otis Redding. At one point in the restaurant's colorful history, the proprietors even operated an excursion boat on the river. A Robinson advertisement in a 1949 Georgia Tech student newspaper encouraged the students to "Dine and Dance Under the Stars."

MILE 132.8 (33.859016, -84.454522) Paces Ferry. This is the site of a ferry operated in the 1800s by Hardy Pace, one of the area's first white settlers. During the Civil War, the unpredictable currents of the river played into the hands of the Union Army. On July 5, 1864, after a Confederate cavalry and wagon train crossed the river here on a pontoon bridge, the defending army cut loose the pontoons, thinking the structure would drift downriver and come to rest in an area still controlled by the Confederates. Instead, the structure lodged on its side and fell into the hands of Union soldiers, who later employed it in their own crossing of the river. A day after the Confederates' pontoon disaster, Union General William T. Sherman would have his first view of the city of Atlanta from atop Vinings Mountain, just west of this river crossing. Hardy Pace is buried atop that same mountain. Today, the old iron bridge allows pedestrians to cross the river and is also the site of a water-quality monitoring program administered by the U.S Geological Survey, the National Park Service, and Chattahoochee Riverkeeper. Bacteria levels are measured regularly and posted online at http://ga2 .er.usgs.gov/bacteria. When bacteria levels exceed water quality standards, the National Park Service posts health advisories on this webpage.

MILE 133.4 (33.852471, -84.460353) Shoals.

MILE 135 (33.827662, -84.455048) City of Atlanta Water Supply / Intake. An island splits the river here, and paddlers can choose a route on far river right or navigate a rapid created by a rock weir below the city of Atlanta's water intake pipes on the left side of the river. Both the rock weir at the head of the island and the weir below the intake are efforts to insure that the river flows deep at the intake pipes even during low flow conditions. The weirs are symbolic of Atlanta's 170-year struggle with water supply. Unlike Georgia's other cities that grew up along waterways (Savannah, Augusta, Columbus) Atlanta was founded on a high ridge 6 miles from the diminutive Chattahoochee. In fact, the only other major U.S. metropolitan area at a higher elevation is Denver, Colorado. With no reliable groundwater sources and only small streams flowing through the city center, Mayor W. A. Hemphill in 1893 had pipes laid in the river and began pumping the river water to town. Periodic droughts rendered that solution tenuous and necessitated the construction of the weirs here. It wasn't until the construction of Buford Dam and Lake Lanier in 1956 that Atlanta was guaranteed flows even during drought. In the throes of a 1958 drought, the *Atlanta Journal* editors wrote: "Without the dam, Atlanta water users surely would have been on ration basis weeks ago. They should be thankful for the big impounding system and the water it doles out every day." However, Metro Atlanta's millions continue to

SHOALS NEAR PEACHTREE CREEK, FULTON COUNTY

strain the Chattahoochee, making finding new water supplies—through con-servation measures and new reservoirs—a priority of Atlanta leaders, just as it was in the late 1800s when Atlanta first entered into its partnership with the Chattahoochee. Paddlers choosing the river left route should navigate with care. At the right water levels, the chute created by the rock weir below Atlanta's water intake consists of a small ledge followed by several large waves. At higher levels, the rapid washes out, making navigation easier.

MILE 135.1 (33.826881, -84.455311) Peachtree Creek / Standing Peachtree. Atlanta traces its history (and the names of many of its streets) to this spot where, in 1814, U.S. soldiers constructed a fort to control the Creek Indians along what was then the western frontier of Georgia. The fort was built near an Indian trad-ing post known as Standing Peachtree. Wash Collier, one of the region's earli-est mail carriers in the mid-1800s, relayed this explanation of the site's unique name in an article published in the *Atlanta Constitution* in 1897: "There was a great huge mound of earth heaped up there . . . and right on top of it grew a big peach tree. It bore fruit and was a useful and beautiful tree. But, it was strange that it should grow on top of that big mound, wasn't it? So they called the post office out there Standing Peachtree and the creek they began to call Peachtree Creek. I've passed it many a time going on with my mails. There's nothing remaining of it now." Other accounts of the origins of the name trace it to a large pine tree at the location that oozed sap, or pitch—a "pitch tree." Either way, Atlanta's most recognized thoroughfare, Peachtree Street, fittingly runs along the ridge sepa-rating the Chattahoochee River basin from the adjacent Altamaha River basin.

MILE 135.1 (33.826528, -84.455976) R. L. Sutton WRF. On river right is the dis-charge from Cobb County's primary sewage plant. This water reclamation facil-ity treats up to 60 million gallons of sewage a day, and is on the receiving end of a giant 9.5-mile tunnel blasted 200 feet underground. Completed in 2005, this 18-foot-diameter tunnel collects sewage from the county's 500 miles of sewer lines and stores it to prevent it from bypassing full treatment at the plant dur-ing periods of peak flow. Protecting the river's not cheap, though . . . the tunnel project cost $113 million.

MILE 135.2 (33.825973, -84.456104) Montgomery's Ferry. The railroad bridge here marks the site of Montgomery's Ferry, an early river ford operated by James Montgomery, who was among the soldiers to establish Fort Peachtree in 1814. Montgomery operated the ferry as a private facility until 1837 when he received a state franchise. In the same era, the Chattahoochee was being employed to ship goods to points north and south. This historic account conveys the uncertainty of early river travel: "From the mouth of Peachtree Creek . . . he shipped in large canoes a cargo of goods. The canoes were worked by strong negroes and Indi-ans. . . . The dangerous voyage was safely made (to a point in Troup County near present-day LaGrange), but a great calamity came at the last moment. In turning the canoes in the bend of the river to land, the cargo capsized, and everything was lost."

MILE 135.4 (33.824997, -84.459489) R. M. Clayton WRF. On river left is the discharge from the South's largest sewage treatment plant. Operated by the city of Atlanta, this facility can treat up to 120 million gallons a day. During the 1960s, a much smaller plant each day received more than twice its capacity, and every day, up to 50 million gallons of untreated sewage was diverted directly to the river. Passage of the Clean Water Act in 1972 provided hope that the mess would be cleaned up, but progress was slow. Today, the pollution continues, but to a much lesser degree. In 1998, a lawsuit brought by Chattahoochee Riverkeeper resulted in the city agreeing to a schedule to upgrade its sewer infrastructure and the river from here downstream is slowly recovering from years of neglect and pollution.

MILE 135.7 (33.827240, -84.463357) Western & Atlantic Railroad. A railroad bridge has crossed the river here since 1842. At the time of the Civil War, this was the only bridge across the river in the Atlanta area, with the exception of McAfee's Bridge in Roswell.

MILE 136.5 (33.824338, -84.473281) Georgia Power Co.'s Plant McDonough. The same droughts of the 1920s that forced the city of Atlanta to build a rock weir upstream at its water intake also forced Georgia Power Co. to rethink its reliance on hydropower—a source that proved unreliable when Mother Nature failed to fill the river. Construction of this power plant in 1930 marked the beginning of the company's long marriage with coal-fired power plants that continues today . . . except at this plant that started it all. Because of air- and water-quality concerns, in 2000 Georgia Power began to overhaul the plant, installing a new water cooling system and replacing coal with cleaner-burning natural gas. Prior to these changes, the plant pumped 344 million gallons a day (MGD) from the river for its operations and discharged that same amount back to the river at elevated temperatures. The result was depleted oxygen levels in a stretch of river already burdened with wastewater discharges. Today, the facility uses only 20 MGD, and the river is better for the company's $96 million investment.

MILE 136.8 (33.821326, -84.476822) Shoal.

MILE 138.2 (33.807855, -84.496048) I-285 Bridge & Proctor Creek. Emptying into the river just below the I-285 bridge on river left is Proctor Creek, one of several streams that tell the story of Atlanta's sewer history. Because the city had no major water body close to the city center to receive and dilute its sewage, the city dumped its sewer lines into tiny creeks like this one. During a dry spell in 1908, up to 30 percent of this creek's flow consisted of raw sewage. Not surprisingly, at that time, typhoid death rates in the city were among the highest in the nation.

PADDLING OUT OF A STORM DRAIN, COBB COUNTY

This environmental and public health crisis pushed the city to the cutting edge of wastewater treatment in 1914, when it installed Imhoff tanks, the forerunner to today's septic tanks, at the ends of its sewer lines. The tanks were the first of their kind in the country.

MILE 140.3 (33.787866, -84.520531) Nickajack Creek. This creek marks the southernmost reaches of Johnston's River Line, built to stop the Union Army's siege of Atlanta during the Civil War. On July 9, 1864, the invading army successfully crossed the Chattahoochee far upstream and forced a Confederate retreat to the south side of the river. In the four days that followed, the two armies rested and put down their arms. Facing one another across the cool inviting waters and dirty from weeks of fighting, soldiers from both sides stripped and plunged into the river to bathe and swim; newspapers were exchanged, southern tobacco was traded for northern coffee. A week later, they would return to killing one another.

MILE 140.8 (33.783543, -84.528835) Fulton County Airport & Stream Buffers. On river left is the Fulton County Airport. In 2011, a plan to cut 17 acres of trees along the banks of the river and nearby Sandy Creek was stopped by a legal appeal filed by Chattahoochee Riverkeeper. The plan would have clear-cut vegetation in the state's 25-foot protected buffer along the river and creek, eliminating the important pollution control and habitat services the trees provide. The appeal led to revisions in the state's buffer laws to prevent large-scale cutting of trees along rivers without appropriate mitigation.

MILE 141.7 (33.773778, -84.536678) South Cobb WRF. This Cobb County water reclamation facility on river right treats up to 40 million gallons of sewage daily.

MILE 142.8 (33.763626, -84.550636) Six Flags Over Georgia. Since its opening in 1967, this 238-acre park on river right has been a mainstay of the local tourism economy. Cobb County officials wooed the park developers away from a planned site in Fulton County with cheaper land along the river and I-20. The park features 35 rides, including 11 rollercoasters.

MILE 144.5 (33.745822, -84.572952) Utoy Creek. Pipes on river left at the mouth of the creek carry wastewater from the city of Atlanta's Utoy Creek, South River, and Entrenchment Creek water reclamation facilities. As many as 78 million gallons a day are discharged here.

MILE 144.7 (33.743875, -84.575921) Buzzard Roost Island. For at least 12,000 years, people have used this spot to cross the river. Archaeological evidence dates human habitation around this spot to 10,000 BC. The Sandtown Trail, named for the Indian settlement just east of the river here, served as a trade route for Native Americans and was among the first routes whites took into Georgia's western frontier in the 1800s. Today, humans continue to cross the river here—on Camp Creek Parkway just downstream of the island. Camp Creek is the primary thoroughfare to Atlanta's Hartsfield-Jackson International Airport, the busiest in the country, serving 56 million passengers each year.

MILE 147.4 (33.717134, -84.605318) Sweetwater Creek / New Manchester. Upstream on this creek located on river right are the remains of New Manchester, a mill village situated along Sweetwater's rocky shoals. Taking advantage of the creek's precipitous fall to power their operations, Charles J. McDonald and James Rogers in 1849 built a textile mill at the site. By the advent of the Civil War in 1861, New Manchester was a thriving community, making cloth for use by the Confederate Army—an employ that did not sit well with the invading Union Army. When the town was captured in 1864, the mill was destroyed and the mill workers were marched and railed north to Ohio. Today, the brick ruins of the mill remain, and the land is protected as a state park. The city of East Point uses Sweetwater as its water source, with a pumping station 1 mile upstream from the mouth of the creek, and the creek is home to what is considered the largest blue heron rookery in Georgia not on the state's Atlantic coast, with some 150 birds during the peak breeding season. Finally, the creek also inspired the name of Atlanta's best-known craft beer—SweetWater—after one of the brewery's founders took a kayak trip through the rapids that once powered New Manchester.

NEAR PEACHTREE CREEK, FULTON COUNTY

MILE 149.3 (33.702680, -84.628071) Douglas County Water & Sewer Authority WRF. At river right is this 3-million-gallon-a-day sewage treatment plant.
With a population of 133,000, Douglas is typical of many of Metro Atlanta suburban counties, where many residences use septic systems rather than public-
sewer systems. In Douglas more than 50 percent of residents use septic tanks.
Improperly maintained septic systems can cause water pollution problems; and
as population growth demands more withdrawals from the Chattahoochee,
septic systems have come under increasing fire because by discharging into the
ground rather than directly into the river, they result in a reduction in river levels
for wildlife and for downstream water users. The preponderance of septic tanks
has prompted Douglas County to become a leader in managing septic tanks; the
county will no longer provide water service to new subdivisions that plan to rely
on septic systems.

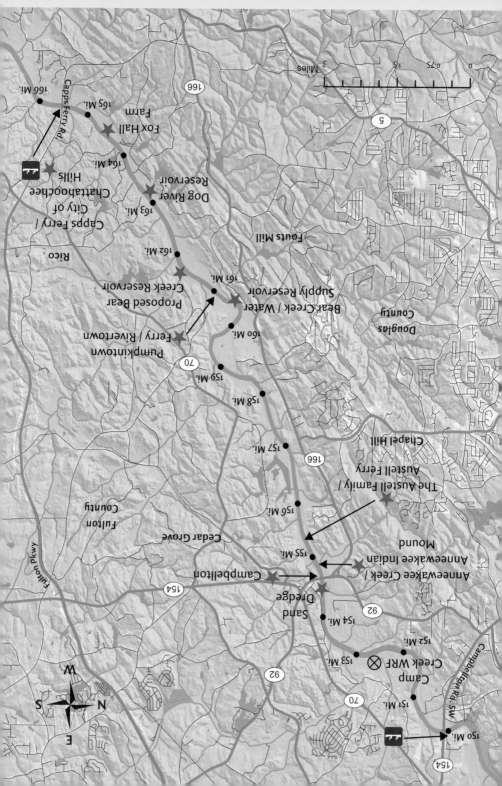

Chattahoochee Hill Country

Length 15 miles (Campbellton Road / Ga. 154 to Capps Ferry Road)

Class 1

Time 7–9 hours

Minimum Level The river here can be run year-round.

River Gauge The nearest river gauge is near Fairburn: http://waterdata.usgs.gov/ga/nwis/uv?site_no=02337170.

Launch Site The launch site is a Georgia Department of Natural Resources boat ramp on river left just upstream of the Ga. 154 (Campbellton Rd.) bridge. A private recreational softball campus is adjacent to the ramp.

DIRECTIONS From I-20 west of Atlanta, take exit 49 (Ga. 70/Fulton Industrial Blvd.). Travel on Fulton Industrial Boulevard south for 7.4 miles. Turn right onto Ga. 154 (Campbellton Rd.) and proceed 0.8 mile. Turn right into the entrance to the softball complex and follow the drive for 0.1 mile to the parking area at the boat ramp.

Take Out Site There is no developed take out site at this location, but it is possible to use the right-of-way along Capps Ferry Road to access the river.

DIRECTIONS From the entrance to the softball complex, turn left onto Campbellton Road and travel 0.8 mile. Turn right onto Fulton Industrial Boulevard and proceed 4.8 miles. Turn right onto Cochran Mill Road (Ga. 70) and travel 1.8 miles. Turn right onto Cedar Grove Road (Ga. 70) and proceed 8 miles. Turn right onto South Fulton Parkway (Capps Ferry Rd.) and travel 1.8 miles to the river. The access is on the east side of the river.

Description Leaving behind the city, the Chattahoochee rolls into Metro Atlanta's southwestern suburbs. Though more wastewater treatment plants discharge to the river, the scenery is decidedly rural, and those living in the area want to keep it that way. The final 10 miles of this run lie within the city of Chattahoochee Hills, incorporated in 2007 with a vision of preserving the rural landscape of the area. Flatwater dominates the full 15 miles.

Outfitters Georgia Trail Outfitters provides guide services and canoe and kayak rentals on this section: 18 Old Fish Camp Rd., Whitesburg, Ga. 30185, 404-852-3372, www.georgiatrailoutfitters.com.

Points of Interest

MILE 152.6 (33.670492, -84.651954) Camp Creek WRF. Upstream on this creek on river left sits another Fulton County sewage treatment facility. The Camp Creek facility handles the waste of nearby College Park, East Point, Fairburn, Hapeville, Palmetto, and Union City, treating up to 24 million gallons a day and discharging it to the creek.

MILE 154.6 (33.656678, -84.672145) Sand Dredge. Located on river left here is a sand dredge. Dredging the river for sand is not a new phenomenon. Historic photos from this area show a dredge operating here in 1954. Most commonly used as an ingredient in concrete, sand is also employed in making glass, filtering water, and manufacturing asphalt. It was even a key component of the tiles on the bottom of NASA's space shuttles, protecting the crafts on reentry to Earth's atmosphere.

MILE 154.7 (33.656500, -84.673926) Campbellton. Along the left bank of the river here between 1830 and 1835, the city of Campbellton sprang up as the seat of the newly formed Campbell County. The town and county were named in honor of Duncan Campbell, who negotiated the 1825 Treaty of Indian Springs with the Creek Indians to cede all their remaining land in Georgia to the U.S. government. Campbellton thrived with farms along the banks of the river and a ferry across it, but in the 1840s when the townspeople declined construction of the Western & Atlantic Railroad (reportedly because of the noise created by the iron horse), the populace shifted to nearby Fairburn, where the railroad was ultimately constructed. By 1870 that town would become the county seat. During the Great Depression, Campbell County went bankrupt and was folded into Fulton County. Despite the demise of the town, Campbellton Ferry (originally known as Francis Irwin's Ferry) continued operation until 1958, when a bridge was constructed here. It was the last operating ferry in the region.

MILE 154.9 (33.655231, -84.677703) Anneewakee Creek / Anneewakee Indian Mound. On river right here once stood what is locally known as the Princess Anneewakee Indian Mound. In the mid-1800s, a traveling preacher and amateur historian and archaeologist visited the site and described it thus: "[The tomb was] opposite the village of Campbellton, on the western bank of the Chattahoochee, in a tuft of trees, on one of those mounds so common in Georgia; rests the remains of Anawaqua, an Indian Princess, the former proprietor of the soil. It is situated in a meadow, in a bend of the Chattahoochee, and near the foot of a considerable hill. Ancient fortification are traced all around the plain, extending from the river to the hill." The mound was later destroyed by a landowner unaware of its significance. An excavation of the mound remains in 1972 turned up 1,400-year-old potsherds. Anneewakee Creek itself is the site of yet another sewage treatment plant, discharging up to 4 million gallons a day to the creek. Anneewakee is believed to be a Cherokee word meaning "cow people."

MILE 155.3 (33.651338, -84.685299) The Austell Family / Austell Ferry. A plantation and ferry near this location served as the home of one of Atlanta's most notable Reconstruction leaders—General Alfred Austell. An Atlanta banker and member of the Georgia militia, he was one of eight men who rode out to the Union Army under a white flag to surrender Atlanta. After the war, he established the First National Bank of Atlanta—what would become the longest continually operating bank in the city. In the 1870s he purchased a plantation and ferry near here, which his family operated until the 1930s. Since Austell was instrumental in financing the railroad that went through Douglas County, in 1885 the nearby community of Irvine was renamed in his honor. Austell died in 1881. In 1902, Alfred Jr., the Austells' youngest son, drove home from his Yale University graduation in a red, steam-powered automobile. The trip from Connecticut to the Chattahoochee reportedly took three months, and that vehicle is said to be the first to ever cross the river at Austell Ferry. The auto was quite the novelty in town as, apparently, was Alfred Jr., who became one of Douglas County's more colorful residents. He and his longtime companion, Miss Mamie Wier, were known for throwing all-night dances at their riverside home. After Alfred's death in 1923, Mamie continued to manage the property and ferry. Fannie Mae Davis, author of *Douglas County, Georgia: From Indian Trail to Interstate 20* (1987) described Mamie as the "guardian angel of the river bottom."

MILE 160.5 (33.630363, -84.752920) Bear Creek / Water Supply Reservoir. Just up Bear Creek on river right sits Douglas County's Bear Creek Dam, which was completed in 1980. The reservoir created by the dam supplies 4 million gallons a day to county residents. The county quickly outgrew its capacity, and in 1992 the county water authority built another dam on Dog River just to the west.

MILE 160.8 (33.625217, -84.754594) Pumpkintown Ferry / Rivertown. In the 1820s, Walter Colquitt, one of the area's first white landowners, established a plantation and ferry here and in 1829 lobbied the Georgia legislature to declare Pumpkintown as the county seat for Campbell County. His pleas went unheeded, and soon thereafter, he pulled up stakes and moved to Columbus. Rivertown, like Campbellton, has faded into history, but as late as 1886, according to the *Georgia State Gazetteer and Planter's Dictionary* there lived here on river left a population of 300 served by two churches, schools, and several gins and mills powered by steam and water.

MILE 161.7 (33.614853, -84.762505) Proposed Bear Creek Reservoir. If the cities of Fairburn, Palmetto, and Union City have their way, Bear Creek on river left in Fulton County will be inundated to create a water supply reservoir. The $100

NEAR BEAR CREEK, DOUGLAS COUNTY

million project would dam Bear Creek to fill a 440-acre reservoir by pumping up to 32 million gallons a day (MGD) from the river. Proponents say the project will provide 16 MGD to the South Fulton cities and help solve the region's water needs. Opponents claim the reservoir is expensive and unnecessary. A 2012 report by Chattahoochee Riverkeeper showed that Metro Atlanta could save as much as 34 MGD by replacing the region's water-wasting toilets. Likewise, expansion of the Dog River reservoir across the river in Douglas County could produce similar yields at half the cost of the new reservoir.

MILE 163.2 (33.603916, -84.783705) Dog River Reservoir. Completed in 1992, this dam and reservoir provides up to 23 million gallons a day (MGD) to Douglas County residents. Originally designed to provide 6 MGD, the county quickly outgrew its capacity and in 1998 the Douglas County Water & Sewer Authority initiated plans to add another 10 feet to the dam's height. The work was completed in 2009, and today the 256-acre reservoir holds 1.9 billion gallons of water. It is possible to paddle into the mouth of the Dog and up to the base of the dam, which is within sight of the Chattahoochee.

MILE 164.7 (33.589367, -84.802030) Fox Hall Farm. On river right sits this 1,100-acre, mixed-use residential-resort community begun in 2008. Plans for the community ultimately call for 830 single-family homes surrounded by all manner of recreational and sporting amenities, including shooting, equestrian, fishing, hiking, biking, and even bocce ball. Its location along the Chattahoochee—and a 20-minute ride to the Atlanta airport—are among its selling points.

MILE 165.5 (33.589367, -84.802030) Capps Ferry / City of Chattahoochee Hills. Capps Ferry sits near the center of the Chattahoochee Hill Country and the 33,000-acre city of Chattahoochee Hills, which was incorporated in 2007. The idea for the city began when major landowners in the area gathered to discuss ways to control the inevitable development headed to South Fulton and preserve the rural character of the area. The city's stated goal is to concentrate sustainable development in specific areas and preserve 60 percent of the land. The Chattahoochee Hill Country stretches from near Anneewakee Creek in Douglas County 20 miles downriver to Ga. 16. Development plans for the city call for 98 miles of trails though the property and along the river.

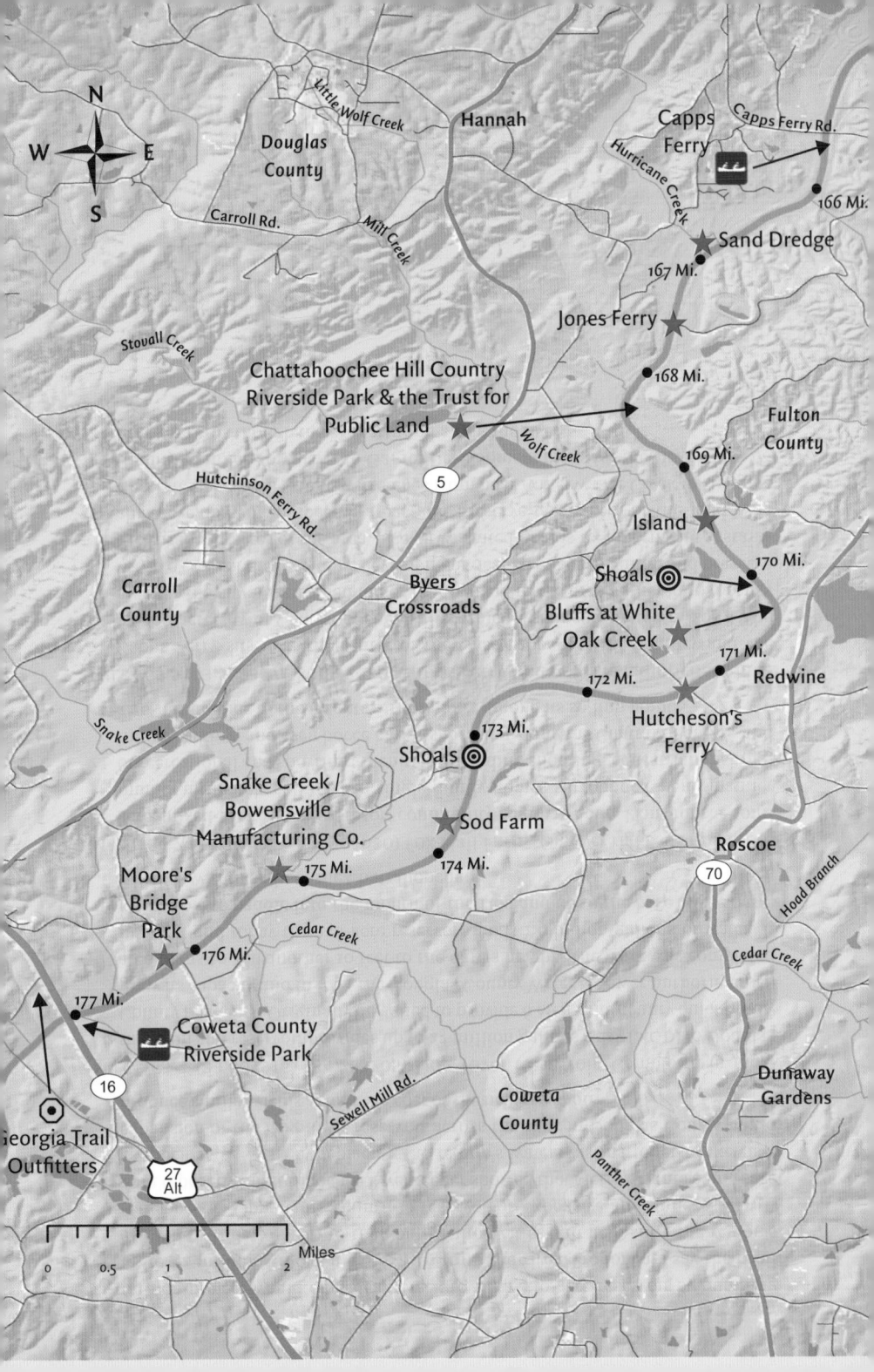

Whitesburg

Length 11 miles (Capps Ferry Road to Ga. 16)

Class 1

Time 4–6 hours

Minimum Level The river here can be run year-round.

River Gauge The nearest river gauge is at Whitesburg: http://waterdata.usgs.gov/ga/nwis/uv?site_no=02338000.

Launch Site There is no developed launch site at this location, but it is possible to use the right-of-way along Capps Ferry Road to access the river.

DIRECTIONS From I-20 west of Atlanta, take exit 34 (Bill Arp Rd.). Travel south on Bill Arp Road for 9.8 miles to the roundabout. Follow around the roundabout to Ga. 166 (Duncan Memorial Hwy.) and proceed 0.4 mile. Turn right onto Capps Ferry Road and travel 3.2 miles to the river.

Take Out Site The take out site is a Coweta County park with a boat ramp on river left just upstream of the Ga. 16 bridge at Whitesburg. The take out site provides parking, a boat ramp, and picnic tables.

DIRECTIONS From Capps Ferry Road at the river, return 3.2 miles. Turn left onto Ga. 166 (Duncan Memorial Hwy.) and proceed 0.4 mile to the roundabout. Follow around the roundabout to Ga. 5 (Bill Arp Rd.) South and travel 10.7 miles to the roundabout at Ga. 16 in Whitesburg. Follow around the roundabout to Ga. 16 and proceed 1.4 miles to the Coweta County park entrance on the left.

Description Just downstream from Capps Ferry, the Chattahoochee enters Carroll and Coweta Counties and the river continues its recovery from the urban landscape and the discharges from the sewage treatment facilities for Metro Atlanta. From Capps Ferry Road to Whitesburg, it takes on a decidedly rural feel, with forest and farmland dominating the terrain. Shoals become more frequent, and signs of bygone ferries and bridges punctuate this peaceful section of river.

Outfitters Georgia Trail Outfitters provides guide services and canoe-kayak rentals on this section: 18 Old Fish Camp Rd., Whitesburg, Ga. 30185, 404-852-3372, www.georgiatrailoutfitters.com.

Points of Interest

MILE 165.6 (33.578654, -84.808340) Capps Ferry. One of several ferries crossing the river in the 1800s and into the early 1900s, Capps Ferry ceased operation in 1932 as more bridges spanned the river.

MILE 167 (33.564253, -84.823843) Sand Dredge.

MILE 167.7 (33.556921, -84.827233) Jones Ferry. This is the site of a ferry that operated from the 1800s until the 1920s. The land on river left tells the story of more recent history—the economic collapse of 2007–8. The 1,000-acre tract known as Chabboquassett Farm was once a world-class thoroughbred farm. Sold in 2005 to a developer, the property later went into foreclosure. The land includes 2 miles of river frontage.

MILE 168.5 (33.5465590, -84.833231) Chattahoochee Hill Country Riverside Park & the Trust for Public Land. On river left here, the city of Chattahoochee Hills owns 234 acres that is slated for development as a city park. The land is part of more than 16,000 acres along the Chattahoochee that the Trust for Public Land (TPL), the Nature Conservancy, and other partners acquired between 1995 and 2011 to create a green corridor along the river from Helen to Columbus. The project has protected 75 miles of river frontage at a cost of more than $250 million.

MILE 169.4 (33.533610, -84.823038) Island.

MILE 170 (33.526992, -84.817395) Shoals.

MILE 170.5 (33.522842, -84.814756) Bluffs at White Oak Creek. The rocky outcroppings on river left are reminiscent of the bluffs at the Palisades farther upriver. The Brevard fault—a 160-mile geological fault that cuts across North Georgia from the northeast tip of the state to the Alabama line at West Point—is responsible for these outcroppings. The bluffs along the river formed by the Brevard fault often harbor trees and shrubs associated with North Georgia's mountains, including rhododendron and mountain laurel.

MILE 171.4 (33.514290, -84.825463) Hutcheson's Ferry. A ferry here was established in the 1800s and ran until after 1940. In 1878 it is believed that the ferry was used to carry the body of state senator Cheadle Cochran for burial in the Laseter Cemetery on a rise overlooking the river just west of this location. Cochran operated a mill (now Cochran Mill Park) on the east side of the river during the early days of Campbell County (later Fulton County).

MILE 173.1 (33.508530, -84.851384) Shoals.

NEAR GA. 16, COWETA COUNTY

MILE 173.7 (33.500156, -84.852886) Sod Farm. At river right here is North Georgia Turf, a sod farm that produces turfgrass for homes, athletic fields, golf courses, and other uses. Where corn and cotton were once the dominant crops of Georgia's river bottoms, turfgrass is now proving more profitable. Between 2005 and 2010 anywhere from 27,000 to 50,000 acres of sod was grown annually in the state, and in 2009, sod sales totaled $116 million, ranking in the top 20 of the state's farm commodities. Georgia's corn crop, though planted on 420,000 acres, accounted for just $203 million in sales. Sod is touted as a means to quickly cover bare soil at development sites, helping to prevent soil erosion, but the intensive nature of sod farming—requiring frequent fertilization and the removal of topsoil with each harvest, can lead to water pollution and soil erosion at production sites.

MILE 175.2 (33.492497, -84.875202) Snake Creek / Bowensville Manufacturing Co. Though the fall on the Chattahoochee here is minimal and shoals are infrequent, just upstream on Snake Creek, the geology was well suited for harnessing the creek's water power. In 1847, the Bowen brothers established Carroll County's first cotton mill, with Snake Creek's fall powering 500 spindles. A cotton mill then operated almost continuously here until 1970. Though remote, Bowensville—later called Banning—was among the first Georgia communities to enter the electric age thanks to its strategic location along the creek. It is said that Atlanta residents, who were still without the modern convenience—would

NEAR WHITE OAK CREEK, FULTON COUNTY

take excursions to the little mill village to witness the electric lights. Today, the creek still fuels the local economy—the old mill site is home to the Lodges at Historic Banning Mills, a retreat center that features the "world's largest zip line," which spans the deep gorge formed by the creek.

MILE 176.2 (33.48313, -84.887218) **Moore's Bridge Park.** The remains of a circa-1917 metal bridge connecting Coweta to Carroll County mark the original site of Moore's Bridge, a 480-foot-long covered bridge built in 1858 by noted Chatta-hoochee bridge builder and former slave Horace King. The bridge was the scene of an intriguing episode during the Civil War. Looking to encircle Atlanta and cut off rail transportation to the city from the south, the Union Army sent cavalry downstream along the river to seek potential crossings. They found Moore's Bridge. When the first Union soldiers arrived at the bridge (disguised in Confederate uniforms) they surprised a small contingent of Confederate soldiers skinny-dipping in the river. Those who escaped capture did so unclothed and barefoot on the Coweta County side of the river, riding on to nearby Newnan to warn that the "Yankees were coming." An artillery skirmish followed this initial contact, and the fight for the bridge ended with the Union Army setting fire to it. In 1867, King rebuilt the bridge, only to see it washed away by a flood in 1881. In 2009 the Trust for Public Land purchased the property on the west bank of the river; Carroll County is expected to develop the property as a passive recreation park complete with canoe-kayak launches along the 1.4 miles of river frontage.

MILE 177.1 (33.476766, -84.900425) **Coweta County Riverside Park.** This take out site on river left, maintained by Coweta County, provides picnic tables and benches as well as a boat ramp and parking.

NEAR WHITE OAK CREEK, FULTON COUNTY

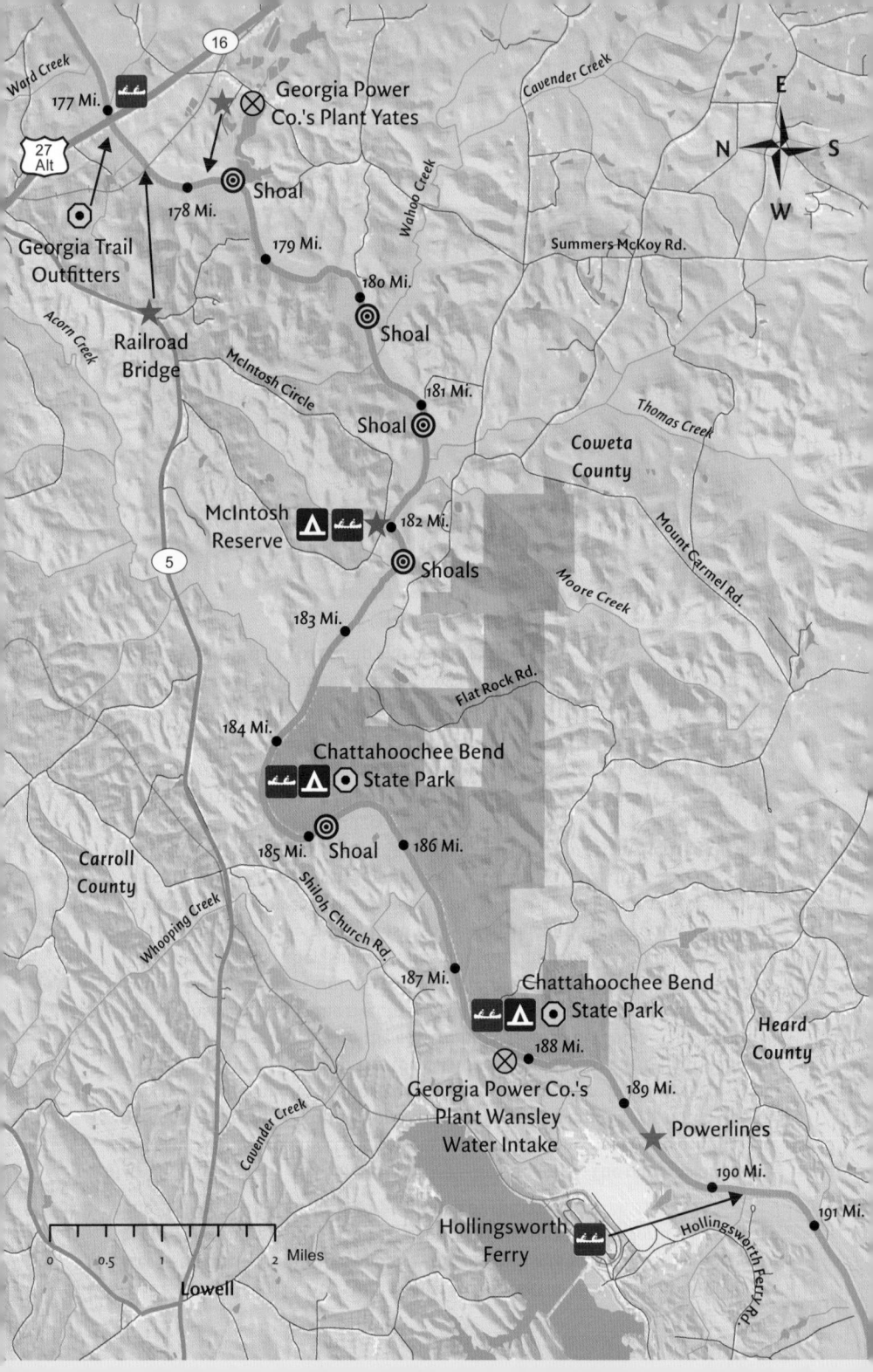

McIntosh

Length 13 miles (Ga. 16 to Hollingsworth Ferry Road)

Class 1

Time 6–8 hours

Minimum Level The river here can be run year-round.

River Gauge The nearest river gauge is at Whitesburg: http://waterdata.usgs.gov/ga/nwis/uv?site_no=02338000.

Launch Site The launch site is a Coweta County park with boat ramp just upstream of the Ga. 16 bridge at Whitesburg. Riverside Park provides parking, a boat ramp, and picnic tables.

DIRECTIONS From the intersection of Ga. 34 and I-85 in Newnan (exit 47), travel west on Ga. 34 (Bullsboro Dr.) 0.8 mile. Turn right onto Ga. 34 Bypass (Millard Farmer Industrial Blvd.) and proceed 4 miles. Turn right onto Ga. 16/U.S. 27 toward Whitesburg and travel 7.1 miles to the entrance to Coweta County Riverside Park on the right.

Take Out Site The take out site is a Georgia Department of Natural Resources boat ramp with a parking area on Hollingsworth Ferry Road near Georgia Power Co.'s Plant Wansley, a coal-fired power plant.

DIRECTIONS From the Coweta County Riverside Park, turn right onto Ga. 16 and proceed 1.3 miles to the roundabout in Whitesburg. Follow around the roundabout to Ga. 5 South. Proceed on Ga. 5 for 11.4 miles. Turn left onto Star Point Road and travel 3.5 miles. Turn left onto Glenloch Road and proceed 0.2 mile. Turn left onto Hollingsworth Ferry Road and travel 3.1 miles to a fork in the road. Bear to the right at the fork onto Hollingsworth Ferry Road and travel 0.4 mile to the boat ramp.

Alternative Take Out Sites To create 5- and 10-mile trips, boaters can utilize access points at McIntosh Reserve and Chattahoochee Bend State Park.

DIRECTIONS TO MCINTOSH RESERVE From the Coweta County Riverside Park, turn right onto Ga. 16 and proceed 1.3 miles to the roundabout in Whitesburg. Follow around the roundabout to Ga. 5 South. Proceed 2.3 miles on Ga. 5 South. Turn left onto West McIntosh Circle and continue 2 miles to the park.

DIRECTIONS TO CHATTAHOOCHEE BEND STATE PARK From the Coweta County Riverside Park, turn left onto Ga. 16 and proceed 2.3 miles. Turn right onto Wagers Mill Road and travel 3.3 miles. Turn right onto Boone Road and proceed 1.4 miles.

SHOALS NEAR MCINTOSH RESERVE, CARROLL COUNTY

Turn left onto Peyton Road and travel 0.4 mile. Turn left onto Mt. Carmel Road and proceed 3 miles. Turn right onto Bud Davis Road (Hewlett South Road) and proceed 1.9 miles. Turn right onto Flat Rock Road. At 1.3 miles, Flat Rock Road becomes Bobwhite Way. Continue on Bobwhite Way 0.8 mile to the park entrance.

Description A tour of 19th-century history and 20th-century industry, this 13-mile run makes the river's recent brush with urban Atlanta seem all but forgotten as it winds past beautiful bluffs and picturesque shoals. Two coal-fired power plants still operate in this section, which also contains Carroll County's historic McIntosh Reserve, the site of Creek Indian Chief William McIntosh's plantation, as well as one of Georgia's newest state parks—Chattahoochee Bend, which protects 5 miles of river frontage in Coweta County.

Outfitters Two facilities offer canoe and kayak rentals.

Georgia Trail Outfitters, 18 Old Fish Camp Rd., Whitesburg, Ga. 30185, 404-852-3372, www.georgiatrailoutfitters.com

Chattahoochee Bend State Park, 425 Bobwhite Way, Newnan, Ga. 30263, 770-254-7271, http://gastateparks.org/ChattahoocheeBend-Paddling

Points of Interest

MILE 177.5 (33.471871, -84.906729) Railroad Bridge. A railroad has spanned the river here since 1872, when the Savannah, Griffin & North Alabama Railroad was extended to Carrollton. In 1882, it took a train 5 hours to run the 60 miles from Griffin to Carrollton, with stops in Brooksville, Senoia, Turin, Sharpsburg, Newnan, Sargent, and Whitesburg.

MILE 178 (33.464425, -84.908681) Georgia Power Co.'s Plant Yates. Built in 1950, Yates is considered one of the state's oldest—and dirtiest—coal-fired power plants. Burning an average of 5,500 tons of coal per day (about 220 tractor-trailer loads), the plant emits into the air carbon dioxide, mercury, sulfur dioxide, nitrogen oxide, and particulates—pollutants associated with acid rain, smog, asthma, chronic bronchitis, brain damage, and heart problems—not to mention global warming. In 2013, Georgia Power announced that it would shutter five of the plant's units and convert the remaining two units to natural gas—dramatically reducing the plant's environmental impact. This announcement followed the 2007 installation of cooling towers to reduce impacts on the river. The towers eliminated 93 percent of the plant's daily withdrawals from the river as well as its hot-water discharge. In 1999 at the height of a summer drought, thousands of fish died when water temperatures topped 100 degrees downstream of the plant's discharge pipes. All water-intensive processes, coal-, nuclear-, and natural-gas-powered generation facilities in Georgia account for about half of all water withdrawals from Georgia's rivers, lakes, and streams.

BODY SURFING, CARROLL COUNTY

MILE 178.2 (33.461543, -84.908510) Shoal. The shoal here is created by a rock dam constructed to raise water levels at Plant Yates water intake pipes and ensure a steady flow of water to the plant during low-flow conditions.

MILE 180.0 (33.444356, -84.924699) Shoal.

MILE 181.1 (33.436567, -84.937059) Shoal.

MOON AT MCINTOSH RESERVE, CARROLL COUNTY

MILE 182 (33.440891, -84.950953) McIntosh Reserve. The bluff on river right marks the site of the plantation that Creek Indian Chief William McIntosh established around 1817, naming it Lockchau Talofau (Acorn Bluff). The plantation was worked by 72 slaves, and McIntosh's home served as a tavern and inn, owing to its location on the Federal Road and a strategic crossing of the river. As a leader of the Creek nation, McIntosh signed the Treaty of Indian Springs that relinquished all remaining Creek lands in Georgia to the U.S. government. This did not sit well with many of his fellow tribesmen. On April 30, 1825, 200 Creek warriors set fire to his plantation and killed him. His dramatic murder was witnessed by many because high waters on the Chattahoochee had kept travelers holed up at his inn, waiting for an easier river crossing. After his death, his wife, Peggy, relayed her plight to the *Cherokee Advocate*: "It was by Government my husband lost his life—Government say to my husband 'Go Arkansas, go to Arkansas, and you will be better off.' My husband wished to please the Government—my house is burned, myself and my children run—my children naked—

WILLIAM MCINTOSH GRAVE,
CARROLL COUNTY

no bread—one blanket, is all—like some stray dog, I suffer." General Alexander Ware, whose plantation was nearby on the east side of the river, provided aid for the McIntosh family and more than 100 other Creek refugees who feared for their lives following the murder of McIntosh. Georgia Governor George Troup, a cousin of McIntosh's, offered only meager assistance. A staunch advocate of the removal of the Creeks, Troup defied the federal government when President John Quincy Adams withdrew the questionably negotiated Treaty of Indian Springs. In a states'-rights showdown 35 years before the Civil War, Troup organized the state militia to fight federal troops should they intervene to prevent the removal of the Creeks. President Adams backed down, the treaty stood, and by 1927 many of the Creeks were forcibly removed from their homes. McIntosh Reserve is now a Carroll County park offering campsites along the river, restrooms with showers, pavilions, picnic tables, and walking trails. A take out–launch site is just downstream (and around the bend) from the bluff with vehicle access and parking. User fees apply. 770-830-5879.

MILE 182.4 (33.439772, -84.955051) Shoals. A series of shoals spans the river for the next 0.4 mile.

MILE 184.4 (33.45729834719391, -84.982560) Chattahoochee Bend State Park. A canoe-kayak launch on river left marks this state park, which opened in 2011—the state's first new park since 1993. At 2,900 acres, it ranks as the state's fifth-largest park and protects 5 miles of river frontage. Amenities include riverside canoe-in campsites, a boat launch, walking trails, restrooms, and observation towers overlooking the river. The take out here is for paddle-in camping only; no vehicle access is available. User fees apply.

MILE 185 (33.450924, -84.988783) Shoal.

MILE 187.5 (33.430297, -85.012730) Chattahoochee Bend State Park. A boat launch here provides access to park amenities, including a parking area, restrooms, camping areas, picnic tables, and a playground. User fees apply.

MILE 187.8 (33.425426, -85.015540) Georgia Power Co.'s Plant Wansley Water Intake. Operational since 1976, Plant Wansley, on river right, burns coal, oil, and natural gas to produce 2,852 megawatts of power daily. Though much larger than Plant Yates upstream, it emits about a fourth of the air pollution due to newer pollution controls and a greater reliance on natural gas. Water is pumped from the river here for use as cooling water in the power generation process.

MILE 189.4 (33.407283, -85.026755) Powerlines. These powerlines carry the electricity generated at Plant Wansley. The humming that is commonly heard below high-voltage lines is caused by the discharge of energy that occurs when the electrical field strength on the wires is greater than the breakdown strength (the field intensity necessary to start a flow of electric current) of the air surrounding

MORNING AT ACORN BLUFF, CARROLL COUNTY

the wires. They buzz and hum louder during rain or high-humidity conditions because moisture increases the conductivity of the air surrounding the lines.

MILE 190.3 (33.394537, -85.032664) Hollingsworth Ferry. This Department of Natural Resources boat ramp on river right was once the site of land owned by Levi Hollingsworth. In 1857, Hollingsworth obtained a permit from the Georgia General Assembly to build a dam across the river at this location to power a gristmill and sawmill. Whether the dam was constructed remains unclear, but Hollingsworth did operate a brick kiln, furniture factory, and woolen mill here. A family history claims that Hollingsworth also built a bridge across the river. The bridge was said to have been destroyed around the time of the Civil War. Hollingsworth would later operate a ferry at the site—one that would operate until 1978. During the early 1900s, the ferryman, who was often away working his nearby farm, was summoned by means of a dinner bell mounted on a tree.

Hilly Mill

Length 12 miles (Hollingsworth Ferry Road to Franklin)

Class 1

Time 5–7 hours

Minimum Level The river here can be run year-round.

River Gauge The nearest river gauge is at Franklin: http://waterdata.usgs.gov/ga/nwis/uv?site_no=02338500.

Launch Site The launch site is a Department of Natural Resources boat ramp with a parking area on Hollingsworth Ferry Road near Plant Wansley, a Georgia Power Co. coal-fired power plant.

DIRECTIONS From the intersection of U.S. 27 and I-20 near Carrollton (exit 11), travel south on U.S. 27 for 22.4 miles. Turn left onto West Ferry Road and proceed 5.2 miles to a fork in the road. At the fork, bear right and continue 0.3 mile to the boat ramp.

Take Out Site The take out site is a boat ramp just downstream of the Ga. 100/U.S. 27 Bus. bridge in Franklin, adjacent to a county park with softball-baseball fields. The take out site provides a boat ramp, parking, restrooms, and walking trails.

DIRECTIONS From Hollingsworth Ferry Road boat ramp, return 1.2 miles. Turn left onto Five Notch Road and proceed 7 miles. Continue across U.S. 27 and travel 0.2 mile. Turn left onto U.S. 27 Bus. (Franklin Parkway) and proceed 2.5 miles. Turn right onto Glover Road and continue into Heard County Park.

Description Picturesque islands, beautiful shoals, and breathtaking waterfalls on tributaries make this one of the most special stretches of the river between Atlanta and Lake West Point. Located along extensive island complexes, Bushhead Shoals and Daniel Shoals serve up whitewater, including the largest natural rapid on the river from Atlanta to West Point, while cascades on Hilly Mill and Red Bone Creeks provide worthy diversions from the main channel. Still, the impacts of Metro Atlanta are visible in sometimes-massive trash flotillas that collect at the heads of the islands in this 12-mile run. Nearing Franklin, the current slows noticeably as you reach the backwaters of Lake West Point.

Outfitters Georgia Trail Outfitters provides guide services and canoe and kayak rentals on this section: 18 Old Fish Camp Rd., Whitesburg, Ga. 30185, 404-852-3372, www.georgiatrailoutfitters.com.

Points of Interest

MILE 192.7 (33.373980, -85.058311) Shoal.

MILE 192.9 (33.372994, -85.055779) New Ferry. In the 1920s, a ferry was established here on Cemetery Road. The ferry operated only for about 15 years.

MILE 193.6 (33.370055, -85.047196) Shoals. The next half mile serves up a steady diet of shoals and swift-moving water.

MILE 194.3 (33.362887, -85.0475826) Hilly Mill Creek & Alan Jackson. On river left here is the mouth of Hilly Mill Creek. A short distance up the creek on private property is Hilly Mill Falls, a beautiful cascade of about 20 feet that spills into an equally beautiful swimming hole. The falls were the site of a gristmill in the 1800s operated by William S. Hilley. In the early days of Heard County and into the 20th century the falls were a popular community gathering spot; the pool at its base was also employed for baptisms by nearby Enon Grove Baptist Church. Hilly Mill inspired Newnan native and country music superstar Alan Jackson to pen "Chattahoochee," a song that was voted country music's top single in 1993. Like many generations of Coweta and Heard County residents, Jackson grew up swimming at the creek "way down yonder on the Chattahoochee."

MILE 195.9 (33.348764, -85.059620) Red Bone Creek. The falls on Red Bone Creek are visible from the river. Though only about 10 feet high, the cascade is worth exploring via a short walk up the mouth of the creek. The falls here and at Hilly Mill are more evidence of the Brevard fault that is also displayed upstream at the mouth of White Oak Creek, in the Palisades Unit of the Chattahoochee River National Recreation Area and other locations.

MILE 197 (33.338134, -85.064641) Shoal.

MILE 197.7 (33.33121, -85.067194) Bushhead Shoals Islands & Atlanta's Pollution. This set of three islands totaling 20 acres is perhaps the largest island complex on the length of the river. In high water numerous channels can be navigated, leading to Bushhead Shoals at the end of the islands. At the head of each island it is not uncommon to find mammoth flotillas of trash—today's very visible signs of Metro Atlanta's impact on the river. In the 1940s, timber on these islands was harvested by crews using axes and saws. A team of mules and horses dragged the timbers to the river, where they were then winched across the channel to a waiting diesel-powered sawmill. While the horses and mules stayed on the islands for the duration of the six-month operation, the work crew ferried themselves to work each day. The sawmill hands reported that there were the remains of many moonshine stills on the islands. Today, the land is fully forested and worthy of exploration. The Nature Conservancy was instrumental in

DANIEL SHOALS, HEARD COUNTY

purchasing the islands as well as adjacent and nearby land on both sides of the river for protection as state park lands.

MILE 199.7 (33.307366, -85.078331) Daniel Shoals. The largest natural shoal on the river between Atlanta and Lake West Point, Daniel Shoals is a long ledge that is best navigated from far river left. An island marks the beginning of the shoals, and the river becomes very shallow adjacent to the island. Paddlers should move to the left of the island and hug the bank on river left. Look for the large chute that flows to the center of the river. In high water, the shoal is navigable on both sides of the island.

MILE 201.1 (33.289629, -85.088631) U.S. 27 Bridge. In 2005 the U.S. 27 bypass of downtown Franklin opened, and along with it this bridge, which is one of the newest bridges spanning the Chattahoochee.

MILE 201.5 (33.289772, -85.094725) Centralhatchee Creek. Flowing in from river right, this tributary's moniker comes from the Creek language: "Sundal" meaning "perch," and "hatchee" meaning "creek." The stream was recorded on earlier maps as Sundalhatchee. You'd hardly guess by looking at it now, but in the 1800s this tributary was of economic significance. In 1834 the Georgia General Assembly adopted a law requiring that "Central Hatchie" creek remain open for the free passage of lumber boats from Tompkins Mill upstream to its confluence with the Chattahoochee. That same year, legislators adopted a law prohibiting the use of poisons in killing fish in the state's streams. Native Americans

and early white settlers alike had been releasing crushed buckeye seeds into the stream to kill the fish in order to harvest them. The toxins were also known to kill livestock. Violation of this law carried a $15 fine (nearly $400 today). Today, Centralhatchee remains important to the area, serving as one of Heard County's water sources.

MILE 202.7 (33.279350, -85.100668) City of Franklin / Chattahoochee Old Town. Overlooking the banks of the river here is the city of Franklin, the county seat of Heard County named to honor Benjamin Franklin. The city is believed to sit on the site of the Creek Indian town of Chattahoochee, from which some believe the river got its name. In 1799, Benjamin Hawkins, the U.S. Indian agent for the area wrote: "The name of the river derived from 'Chatto,' a stone, and 'hoche,' marked or flowered; there being rocks of this description in the river above Hoithletigua at an old town Chattahoochee."

HILLY MILL FALLS, HEARD COUNTY

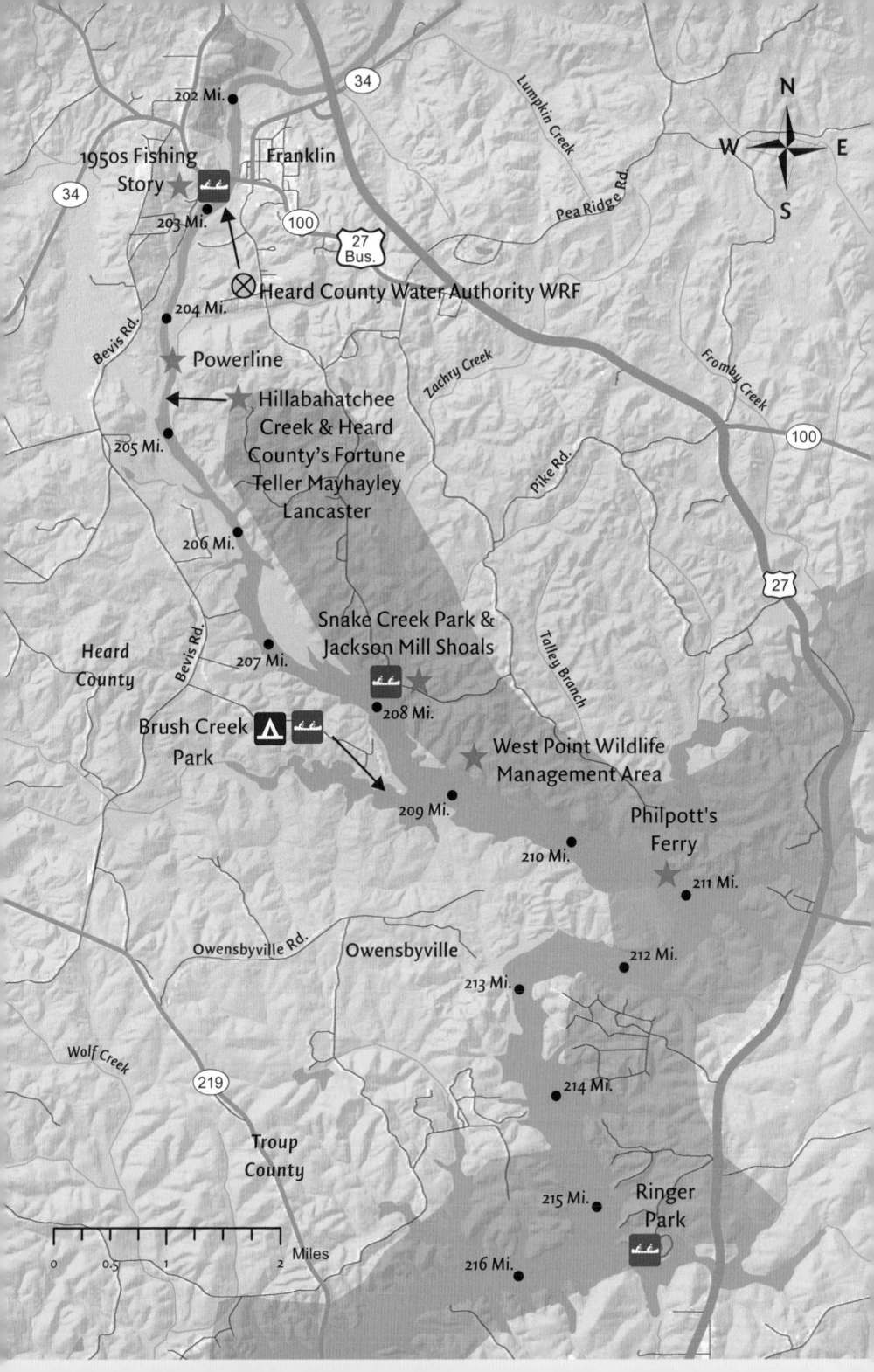

Lake West Point Backwaters

Length 12 miles (Franklin to Ringer Park)

Class 1

Time 5–9 hours

Minimum Level The lake is navigable year-round. Information on Lake West Point water levels is at http://water.sam.usace.army.mil/acfframe.htm. Lake levels can change dramatically with rainfall, but generally fluctuate 7 feet annually from 628 to 635 feet above mean sea level, with the highest levels occurring in the summer months and the lowest levels during the fall and winter.

River Gauge The nearest river gauge is at Franklin: http://waterdata.usgs.gov/ga/nwis/uv?site_no=02338500.

Launch Site The launch site is a boat ramp on river right just downstream of the Ga. 100/U.S. 27 Bus. bridge in Franklin, adjacent to a county park with softball-baseball fields. The launch site provides a boat ramp, parking, restrooms, and walking trails.

DIRECTIONS From the intersection of U.S. 29 and I-85 near Grantville (exit 35), travel west on U.S. 29 for 3.1 miles. Turn right onto Coweta-Heard Road and proceed 5.3 miles. Turn right onto Ga. 100 and travel 5.7 miles. Turn right onto U.S. 27 and proceed 2.4 miles. Turn left onto U.S. 27/Ga. 100 and travel 2.2 miles through Franklin and across the river. Turn left onto Glover Road. The entrance to the park is on the left.

Take Out Site The take out site is a U.S. Army Corps of Engineers boat ramp on river left. Ringer Park provides a boat ramp, a parking area, restrooms, and water.

DIRECTIONS From the boat ramp in Franklin, return to Ga. 100, turn right, and return 2.2 miles. Turn right onto U.S. 27 and proceed 9 miles. Turn right onto Ringer Access Road and travel 1.1 miles to the boat ramp.

Alternative Take Out Sites To create 6- and 7-mile trips, boaters can utilize the boat ramps at Snake Creek Access and Brush Creek Park.

DIRECTIONS TO SNAKE CREEK PARK From the boat ramp in Franklin, return to Ga. 100. Turn right onto Ga. 100 and proceed 0.4 mile. Turn right onto South River Road and travel 4.7 miles. Turn right into Snake Creek Park.

DIRECTIONS TO BRUSH CREEK PARK From the boat ramp in Franklin, return to Ga. 100. Turn left onto Ga. 100 and proceed 0.4 mile to the intersection with Ga. 34.

Turn left onto Ga. 34 and proceed 0.1 mile. Turn left onto Bevis Road and travel 5.6 miles on Bevis Road. Turn left into the entrance of Brush Creek Park and proceed 1.6 miles to the boat ramp.

Description Mostly a lake paddle, this 12-mile run takes in the backwaters of Lake West Point, offering off-river excursions up Snake and Potato Creeks as well as the New River. Where the current slows, the trash from up the river also falls out, often leaving coves and eddies littered with refuse. However, much of this section skirts 10,000 acres of the West Point Wildlife Management Area, lending the section a wilderness feel. Wildlife is abundant; don't be surprised to see a bald eagle or two.

Outfitters No outfitters service this section of the river.

NEAR HILLABAHATCHEE CREEK, HEARD COUNTY

RINGER PARK,
TROUP COUNTY

Points of Interest

MILE 202.7 (33.277781, -85.101033) 1950s Fishing Story. Throughout the mid-20th century, before Metro Atlanta's overwhelmed and inadequate sewer system turned the river into a cesspool for miles below the big city, the river in Heard County was a sportsman's paradise and many local residents earned a portion of their living fishing, hunting, and trapping wildlife along the river corridor. From the 1920s to the late 1950s, local trappers sold pelts to Sears & Roebuck, which offered credits to their catalog, while fish and other river game was sold to local restaurants. In the 1950s, Franklin's Jefferson Stallings netted a 78-pound alligator snapping turtle that he sold to Green's Restaurant in nearby Hogansville at 75 cents a pound. Today, alligator snapping turtles are considered threatened species in Georgia, making it illegal to capture, kill, or sell these reptiles.

MILE 202.8 (33.270982, -85.106387) Heard County Water Authority WRF. On river left here this small stream receives the treated wastewater from this plant that serves the city of Franklin. The plant treats about 90,000 gallons a day from the city's 1,000 residents and businesses. The vast majority of Heard County's 11,000 residents rely on septic tanks.

MILE 204.4 (33.255587, -85.108994) Powerline.

MILE 204.8 (33.248822, -85.110206) Hillabahatchee Creek & Heard County's Fortune Teller Mayhayley Lancaster. Mayhayley Lancaster became nationally famous as a soothsayer in 1948 when she directed Coweta County Sheriff Lamar Potts to the remains of a body that helped him solve a murder. That story was made famous in the book *Murder in Coweta County*, which later became a made-for-TV movie. The Heard County Historical Society, in *Chattahoochee River Stories*, recorded an account in which Lancaster's powers helped solve a tragedy near the mouth of Hillabahatchee Creek (at river right). In the 1940s, a young man ventured out on the river in high water to catch some fish. When he did not return that evening, a search party was deployed but was unsuccessful. Desperate, the family turned to Lancaster, who was known for her ability to locate lost objects. Lancaster told the family to go to Hillabahatchee Creek: "Travel south about a mile and you will find his boat and his body on the side of the river. His hair will be a swinging in the water. He is in the bushes." The body was found at that very location. Among Lancaster's other powers was a savvy business sense. She operated several businesses, managed rental properties and a farm, and even ran for state senator. She died in 1955.

MILE 207.9 (33.214945, -85.082719) Snake Creek Park & Jackson Mill Shoals. A slough on river left leads a short distance to this boat ramp. Facilities include a parking area, picnic tables, and restrooms. Hidden beneath the water of Lake

PADDLING LAKE WEST POINT

West Point (and several decades of sediment) here is a place known to the Creek Indians as Chaukeethlucco, or Big Shoals. In the 1800s a mill operated near here that was powered by a dam on the river erected at those shoals—thence, the shoals became known as Jackson Mill Shoals. In 1882, Jackson Mills were destroyed in a fire; a year later it is believed that a flood wiped out the dam that powered the mill.

MILE 208.7 (33.203226, -85.081686) **Brush Creek Park.** A slough on river right here leads to a boat ramp that provides access to this Heard County park that offers camping, restrooms with showers, water, and picnic areas. User fees apply. 706-645-377.

MILE 208.9 (33.202880, -85.076936) **West Point Wildlife Management Area.** This state-managed land extends on both sides of the river for the next 1.5 miles to the mouth of the New River on river left. Beyond the New River, the Wildlife Management Area (WMA) extends downriver along the west bank another 6 miles to the Ga. 219 bridge. The various units of this WMA protect 10,000 acres of land around the lake.

MILE 210.7 (33.192358, -85.0458445) **Philpott's Ferry.** At this site just downstream of the mouth of New River in the late 1700s, Robert Grayson established a trading post and ferry across the Chattahoochee. Like many men of Georgia's early frontier, Grayson took a Creek wife. Their daughter, Eliza, would become one of Chief William McIntosh's wives. David Philpott eventually acquired this land and operated the ferry. During the Civil War, Philpott's slaves and ferry played a critical role in helping hundreds of retreating and exhausted Union cavalry escape capture. Defeated at the Battle of Brown's Mill near Newnan, one Union force fled southwest to this spot on the river. On arrival they found no ferry and, fearing capture, they made desperate attempts at crossings. Some tied fence rails together to form rafts; others forced their horses into the water and hitched rides by holding onto their tails. While the riders in tow reached the other side, many of the exhausted horses could not pull themselves up the western bank and drowned. Eventually, one of Philpott's slaves directed the Union troops to the ferryboat that had been poled up New River and sunk using stones. The soldiers pulled the stones from the ferry, it rose to the surface, and within a short while, they began the tedious process of moving horses and men across the river on the 20-by-8-foot raft. Despite these efforts, hundreds of Union soldiers were captured here—trapped on the east side of the river.

MILE 215.5 (33.145681, -85.049189) **Ringer Park.** This U.S. Army Corps of Engineers recreation area provides a boat ramp, a parking area, restrooms, water, and picnic areas.

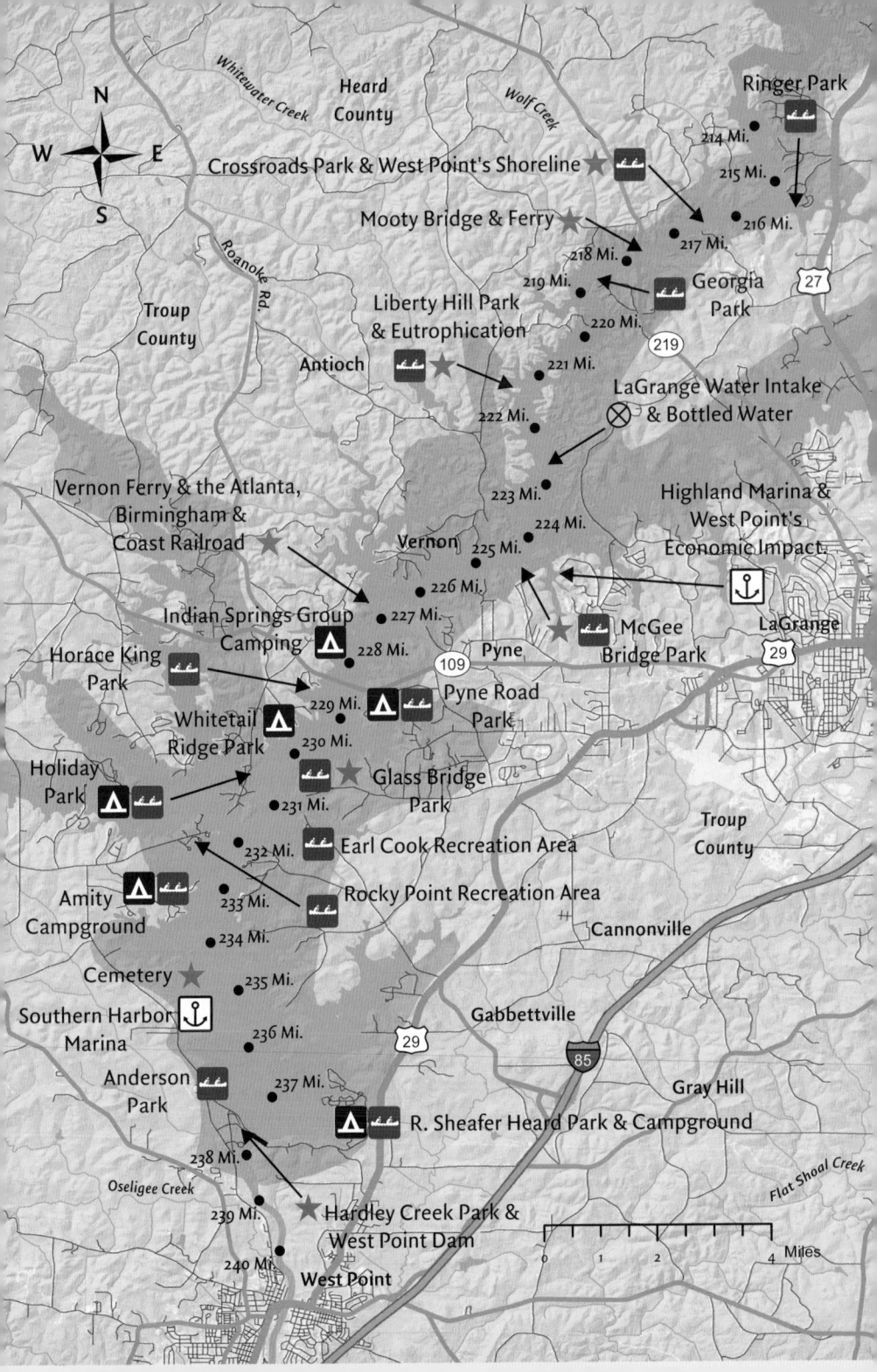

Lake West Point

Length 20 miles (Ringer Park to West Point Dam)

Class 1

Time 10+ hours

Minimum Level The lake is navigable year-round. Information on Lake West Point water levels is at http://water.sam.usace.army.mil/acfframe.htm. Lake levels can change dramatically with rainfall, but generally fluctuate 7 feet annually from 628 to 635 feet above mean sea level, with the highest levels occurring in the summer months and the lowest levels during the fall and winter.

River Gauge The nearest river gauge is upstream at Franklin: http://waterdata .usgs.gov/ga/nwis/uv?site_no=02338500.

Launch Site The launch site is a U.S. Army Corps of Engineers boat ramp on the east side of the river north of LaGrange. Ringer Park provides a boat ramp, a parking area, restrooms, and water.

DIRECTIONS From the intersection of Ga. 109 and I-85 (exit 18), travel west on Ga. 109 for 3.5 miles. In LaGrange, turn right onto U.S. 27 (Morgan St.) and proceed 8.5 miles. Turn left onto Ringer Park Road and travel 1.1 miles to the boat ramp.

Take Out Site There are multiple access points on Lake West Point. Lake users can create many trips utilizing U.S. Army Corps of Engineers campgrounds and boat ramps as well as local parks. On the mainstem of the river, you'll find at least 15 boat landings in the 20 miles from Ringer Park to West Point Dam. Most facilities charge a nominal parking or user fee; campgrounds also charge fees.

Description With almost 26,000 acres of water and an estimated 500 miles of shoreline, Lake West Point offers many exploration opportunities. Completed in 1974, West Point Dam was the last dam built on the mainstem of the Chattahoochee and the first to be authorized by the U.S. Congress with recreation as one of the project's primary purposes. Thus, there are six campgrounds operated by the U.S. Army Corps of Engineers on the lake, along with 26 day-use facilities. Unlike Lake Lanier upstream, where lake homes crowd the shoreline, West Point's shore has a decidedly wild appeal thanks to the Corps' strictly enforced shoreline management plan that greatly reduces private docks and other structures. Publicity stemming from Atlanta's continued pollution of the river and warnings of algae blooms and fish kills on the lake dramatically impacted use of the lake in the late 1980s and into the 1990s. Bans on phosphorus detergents, more stringent limits for Metro Atlanta wastewater treatment plants, and a $2 billion investment in sewer infrastructure in the city of Atlanta have aided the lake's recovery.

Outfitters Two private marinas operate on the lake:

Highland Marina Resort, located midlake just west of LaGrange, offers a boat ramp, docks, marine service, jet ski and boat rentals, fishing guides, RV campsites (no tent camping), cabin rentals, and a gift shop/bait-and-tackle store: 1000 Seminole Rd., LaGrange, Ga. 30240, 706-882-3437, www .highlandmarina.com.

Southern Harbor Resort & Marina, near West Point Dam on the west shore of the lake about 5 miles north of West Point, offers a boat ramp, docks, boat and cabin rentals, and camping: 1133 County Rd. 294, Lanett, Ala. 36863, 334-644-3881, www.southernharbor.com.

Points of Interest

MILE 216.5 (33.140949, -85.073162) Crossroads Park & West Point's Shoreline. This access point on river left offers a boat ramp and a parking area. West Point's relatively undisturbed shoreline provides a stark contrast to Lake Lanier upstream and the several Georgia Power–managed lakes just downstream, where private docks and homes clutter the landscape. On West Point, the U.S. Army Corps of Engineers shoreline management plan permits private docks on just 25 percent of the lake's shoreline; 46 percent of the shoreline is designated for public recreation. A 100-foot setback on all construction further protects the view from the lake as well as water quality.

MILE 217.7 (33.132983, -85.088041) Mooty Bridge & Ferry. Just upstream of the Ga. 219 bridge, the remains of Mooty Bridge lie at the bottom of the lake. A ferry crossing was here prior to the construction of the original bridge.

MILE 218.8 (33.128659, -85.096058) Georgia Park. A boat ramp is in a cove on river left. Facilities include a parking area and restrooms.

MILE 221.4 (33.102033, -85.121163) Liberty Hill Park & Eutrophication. A boat ramp is in a cove on river right here. Facilities include a parking area and restrooms. Eutrophication is the accumulation of phosphates and nitrates in lakes. In the proper amounts, these nutrients support healthy ecosystems and thriving fisheries, but an excess of these same nutrients can accelerate growth of algae, ultimately leading to fish kills when the algae dies, decomposes, and robs oxygen from the water. On most lakes the eutrophication process takes decades, but on West Point it was occurring within a decade of the closing of the gates at the dam. The culprit was upstream discharges from Metro Atlanta sewage treatment plants. In 1984, the phosphorus load in the Chattahoochee below Atlanta peaked at 1,800 tons; 11 years later after a phosphorus detergent ban was implemented and improvements to upstream wastewater treatment plants were completed, the phosphorus load entering West Point from the Chattahoochee dropped to 400 tons. Phosphorus entering the lake continues to be a point of controversy as lake stakeholders debate exactly how much is good for the lake and its fishery.

MILE 222.8 (33.078633, -85.112518) LaGrange Water Intake & Bottled Water. On river left, you'll see the raw-water intake for this city of 29,000—the first community downstream of Atlanta to use the Chattahoochee for its water supply. You will also likely see a surprising number of plastic bottles. Not only do plastic water bottles become a source of litter, but bottled water can cost 10,000 times more per gallon than tap water. If you received your recommended daily supply of water from bottled water, you would spend up to $1,400 annually. The same amount of tap water would cost about 49 cents—and wouldn't be delivered in plastic.

MILE 224 (33.056139, -85.109887) Highland Marina & West Point's Economic Impact. The cove on river left leads to Highland Marina, which offers a boat ramp, docks, marine service, jet ski and boat rentals, fishing guides, RV campsites (no tent camping), cabin rentals, and a gift shop/bait-and-tackle store. Highland is one of two private marinas on the lake that helps drive the economy of surrounding communities. More than 2 million people visit the lake each year, and the economic impact of it has been estimated at between $150 and $700 million. Tourism rises and falls with lake levels, and local leaders, advocating for optimal pool levels during the recreation season, often butt heads with the U.S. Army Corps of Engineers over management of the lake.

MILE 224.4 (33.057992, -85.120841) McGee Bridge Park. A boat ramp and fishing pier on river left mark this U.S. Army Corps of Engineers park that also offers picnic tables and restrooms. The park is named for the bridge that once spanned the river here—the remains of which lie on the lake floor. Also covered by the lake is one of the extensive orchards that once occupied river bottomland in the region.

MILE 226.8 (33.047331, -85.156236) Vernon Ferry & the Atlanta, Birmingham & Coast Railroad. Vernon Ferry operated just upstream of this railroad bridge during the 1800s and early 1900s. Prior to the impoundment of the lake, the A, B & C Railroad crossed the river just downstream from the present causeway and bridge. Completed in 1908, the A, B & C came to be known as the "Bee Line" because it was the most direct route from Birmingham to Brunswick on the Georgia coast.

MILE 227.8 (33.039135, -85.166547) Indian Springs Group Camping. At river right here this campground's covered picnic shelter is visible. The campground provides primitive camping only, but drinking water is available. 706-645-2937.

MILE 228.5 (33.027927, -85.173414) Horace King Park. Just downstream from Ga. 109 is the U.S. Army Corps of Engineers Horace King Park on river right, with a boat ramp, parking, picnic areas, restrooms, and water.

MILE 228.5 (33.026182, -85.160282) Pyne Road Park. Directly opposite Horace King Park on river left is Troup County Pyne Road Park, with a boat ramp, parking, picnic areas, camping, restrooms, drinking water, and ball fields. 706-884-1414.

MILE 229.7 (33.018680, -85.177121) Whitetail Ridge Park. This park maintained by the U.S. Army Corps of Engineers on river right has no boat ramp, but Whitetail Ridge offers camping, restrooms with showers, and water. 706-884-8972.

MILE 230.1 (33.009359, -85.175501) Glass Bridge Park. A boat ramp on river left marks the former site of Glass Bridge, built in 1896 and named after a local family. The covered bridge was built by the sons of Horace King, the freed slave who designed and built more than 100 bridges in Georgia, Alabama, and Mississippi. This was the last major wooden bridge built across the Chattahoochee in the area and the last to remain in operation. It met its demise in 1956 when the Georgia Department of Transportation replaced it. When DOT attempted to dismantle the old bridge for safety reasons, they found it so well built that they resorted to burning it. This was an ironic end to this span, as its construction had resulted in such controversy (residents in

HIGHLAND MARINA, TROUP COUNTY

other parts of the county wanted the Chattahoochee bridge built near their communities) that opponents set fire to it. In fact, the history of this site is riddled with fire. In 1793, early white Georgians waded to the west bank of the river here under cover of darkness and set fire to a Native American village in retaliation for attacks on settlers. The site came to be known as Burnt Village.

MILE 230.5 (33.007092, -85.188418) Holiday Park. A boat ramp on river right provides access to this U.S. Army Corps of Engineers park with parking, restrooms with showers, water, picnic areas, camping, and walking trails. 706-884-6818.

MILE 231.6 (32.990284, -85.174149) Earl Cook Recreation Area. A sandy beach on river left marks this U.S. Army Corps of Engineers recreation area that offers a boat ramp, parking, restrooms with showers, and water.

MILE 232 (32.989978, -85.203138) Rocky Point Recreation Area. A sandy beach on river right marks this U.S. Army Corps of Engineers recreation area that offers a boat ramp, restrooms, drinking water, picnic areas, and a fishing pier.

MILE 233 (32.981995, -85.212022) Amity Campground. This U.S. Army Corps of Engineers campground offers campsites, restrooms with showers, and water. The boat ramp is in a cove off the main channel on river right. 334-499-2404.

MILE 234.6 (32.957239, -85.202112) Cemetery. About 25 feet below the water surface here is the site of a former cemetery. During the construction of the dam and impoundment of the lake, the U.S. Army Corps of Engineers removed and reinterned 258 graves that would have been inundated.

MILE 235 (32.950734, -85.201969) Southern Harbor Marina. On river right here is the entrance to Southern Harbor Marina. The private facility offers a boat ramp, docks, boat and cabin rentals, and camping.

MILE 236.4 (32.933716, -85.199260) Anderson Park. On river right, this U.S. Army Corps of Engineers facility offers a boat ramp, parking, a picnic area, and restrooms.

MILE 237.5 (32.92122, -85.164305) R. Sheafer Heard Park & Campground. Located on the east shore of the lake at the dam, this is the only U.S. Army Corps of Engineers campground on the lake with electricity and water that stays open year-round. The campground and day-use area (closer to the dam) offers a boat ramp, parking, campsites, restrooms with showers, water, and picnic areas. 706-645-2404.

MILE 237.9 (32.920790, -85.190053) Hardley Creek Park & West Point Dam. Hardley Creek Park hugs the west bank of the dam and is home to the U.S. Army Corps of Engineers Visitors Center, which provides interesting exhibits about the construction and operation of the dam. The dam rises 97 feet above the riverbed and stretches the length of 24 football fields. Interpretive displays at the visitors center boast that enough concrete was used in building the powerhouse to construct a sidewalk from Atlanta to San Diego. Completed in 1974, the project cost $132 million. It is possible to portage around the dam by carrying up the riprap on the west side of the dam and descending the grassy bank on the back side of the dam. There is no developed launch below the dam, but a parking area leads to a riprap bank where it is possible to launch small vessels.

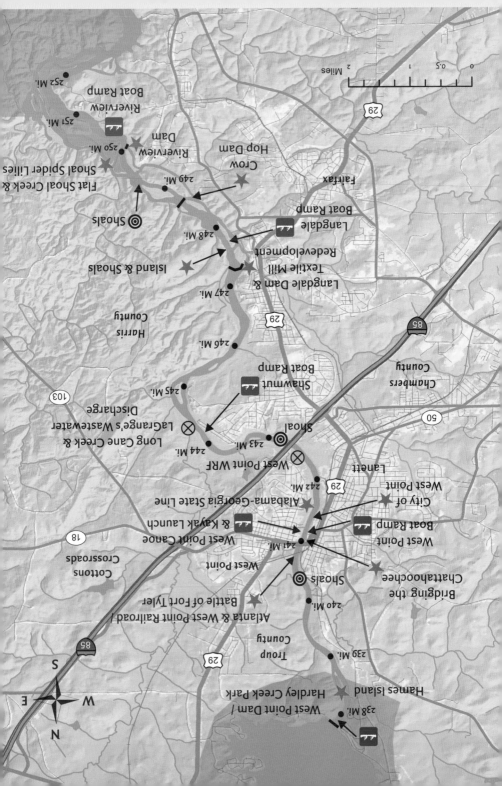

Langdale / Riverview

Length 12 miles (West Point Dam to Riverview)

Class 1

Time 5–9 hours

Minimum Level The river here is navigable year-round, but releases from West Point Dam can create unsafe conditions, with the river rising rapidly as much as 7 feet. Boaters and other river users should use extreme caution when traveling this section. Lowhead dams downstream at Langdale and Riverview add to the danger. These open spillways create strong hydraulics on the backside of the dams that can trap and drown boaters. Release schedules are issued by the U.S. Army Corps of Engineers daily and can be retrieved at http://water.sam.usace.army.mil/todaySched.htm or by calling 706-645-2929.

River Gauge The nearest river gauge is at West Point: http://waterdata.usgs.gov/ga/nwis/uv?site_no=02339500.

Launch Site Although there is no boat ramp, it is possible to launch small vessels on the west bank of the river near the base of West Point Dam in Hardley Creek Park. The park provides parking, restrooms, picnic and fishing areas, walking trails, and access to the U.S. Army Corps of Engineers West Point Visitors Center.

DIRECTIONS From the intersection of Ga. 18 and I-85 (exit 2), travel west on Ga. 18 (E. 10th St.) for 1.9 miles to the bridge over the Chattahoochee. After crossing the bridge, turn right onto West 9th Street and proceed 0.1 mile. Turn right onto 3rd Avenue and travel 3 miles. Turn right onto Stateline Road and proceed 0.3 mile to the parking area.

Take Out Site The take out site is a grassy bank on river right just below the end of the island separating Riverview Dam from the river's main channel. There is a small parking area here.

DIRECTIONS From West Point Dam return to 3rd Avenue (Co. Rd. 212). Turn left onto 3rd Avenue and proceed 3.2 miles back to West Point. Continue on 3rd Avenue (U.S. 29) for 2.3 miles to I-85. Continue straight on U.S. 29 for 2.8 miles through Langdale to the intersection with 63rd Street. Turn left onto 63rd Street and proceed a half block. Turn right onto 20th Avenue and travel 1.7 miles. At the fork, bear left onto School Street and continue straight for 0.7 mile. Turn left onto Library Street and proceed 0.1 mile. Turn left onto Lower Street and travel 0.1 mile to the industrial building. Bear to the right and follow the drive 0.3 mile along the river to the landing.

Alternative Take Out Sites To create a 3-mile trip, boaters can utilize a canoe-kayak launch on river left at the East 10th Street (U.S. 29) bridge or a boat ramp on river right 0.1 mile downstream in downtown West Point. A 6-mile or 9-mile trip can be created using the boat ramp at Shawmut Airport or Langdale, respectively.

DIRECTIONS TO WEST POINT CANOE AND KAYAK LAUNCH Return to and turn left onto 3rd Avenue (Co. Rd. 212), traveling 3 miles back to West Point. Turn left onto West 9th Street and proceed 0.1 mile. Turn left onto East 10th Street and proceed 0.2 mile. Turn right onto Avenue B and go one block. Turn right onto East 9th Street and follow the road to the parking area at the boat launch.

DIRECTIONS TO THE WEST POINT BOAT RAMP Return to and turn left onto 3rd Avenue (Co. Rd. 212). Proceed 3 miles back to West Point. At West 9th Street, continue straight on 3rd Avenue for two blocks. Turn left onto West 7th Street and proceed one block. At 2nd Avenue, continue straight on 7th Street one more block to 1st Avenue. The boat ramp is at the end of 7th Street.

DIRECTIONS TO SHAWMUT BOAT RAMP Return to and turn left onto 3rd Avenue (Co. Rd. 212), traveling 3 miles back to West Point. At West 9th Street, continue straight on 3rd Avenue (U.S. 29) for 2.7 miles. Turn left onto East 30th Street in Shawmut and proceed 0.6 mile. Turn left onto 12th Avenue and travel 1 mile to the boat ramp in the nonoperational Shawmut Airport.

DOWNSTREAM OF WEST POINT DAM, TROUP COUNTY

Return to and turn left onto 3rd Avenue (Co. Rd. 212), traveling 3 miles back to West Point. At West 9th Street, continue straight on 3rd Avenue (U.S. 29) for 5 miles. Turn left onto 63rd Street in Langdale and proceed 0.2 mile. After 63rd Street becomes Cemetery Road, continue 0.1 mile to the boat ramp.

Description From West Point Dam to Columbus the river drops 300 feet in 38 miles as it makes its way across the fall line from the piedmont to the Coastal Plain. Early industrialists recognized this geography and as a result the river here is clogged with seven dams. On this section to Riverview there are three. In their seminal book, *A Canoeing and Kayaking Guide to Georgia*, authors Bob Sehlinger and Don Otey disparaged this portion of the river as a "paddle trip suitable only for bad dreams." Though portages are a harsh reality, a trip here opens a window to the Chattahoochee's past as well as a pathway to some beautiful scenery. Lively shoals, especially below Langdale and Crow Hop Dams, punctuate a mostly flatwater journey as the river begins its descent through the fall line. The Trust for Public Land, the National Park Service, local governments, and the citizen group Middle Chattahoochee River Stewards are working to create a canoe-kayak trail from West Point Dam to Lake Harding. Improved river access and portage routes around the dams are planned.

Outfitters No outfitters operate on this section of the river.

PORTAGING AROUND CROW HOP DAM, HARRIS COUNTY

SHOALS BELOW CROW HOP DAM, HARRIS COUNTY

Points of Interest

MILE 238.4 (32.910779, -85.191134) Hames Island. This island marks the site of a Native American crossing of the river prior to the advent of ferries and bridges.

MILE 240.5 (32.885015, -85.180341) Shoals.

MILE 240.8 (32.879862, -85.179354) Atlanta & West Point Railroad / Battle of Fort Tyler. A strategic target during the Civil War, the railroad bridge here was the cause of one of the last (and perhaps most pointless) battles to be fought in the war. On Easter Sunday, April 16, 1865, more than 3,000 Union soldiers descended on West Point from Alabama with orders to destroy this bridge and a wagon bridge farther downstream. They were met by 120 Confederate soldiers from a hilltop fort just to the west with a commanding view of the bridge. The daylong battle left more than two dozen dead and dozens more wounded. After the outnumbered defenders surrendered, the two bridges were destroyed. Unbeknownst to both sides, the war was already over: seven days earlier, Confederate General Robert E. Lee had surrendered in Virginia.

MILE 241 (32.877555, -85.180255) Bridging the Chattahoochee. The first bridge over the river here was completed in 1838 by John Goodwin and Horace King. The timbers and other material used to construct it were reportedly floated downriver from Heard County. The 652-foot-long covered bridge cost $22,000 to build and proved profitable for its investors. In 1850, it cost 60 cents to cross the bridge in a wagon pulled by a team of mules. The bridge was destroyed during the Civil War.

MILE 241.1 (32.876213, -85.180386) West Point Canoe & Kayak Launch. The launch and parking area is on river left.

MILE 241.2 (32.875172, -85.181947) West Point Boat Ramp. Just downstream of the canoe-kayak launch, this access on river right is suitable for trailered boats.

MILE 241.2 (32.874996, -85.181457) City of West Point. Straddling the river here is West Point. The founders gave up the town's original name of Franklin when they learned that Heard County's seat upstream had already claimed the name. West Point's history is intrinsically linked to the river. In fact, Sidney Lanier's famous poem "Song of the Chattahoochee" (1877) celebrates the river's "duty" to man and the turning of the textile mills in West Point. Reportedly, Lanier wrote the poem at the bequest of relatives in West Point. A West Point newspaper boasted during the era that there was enough power to be harnessed from the Chattahoochee within several miles of West Point to "turn half the spindles in the world." For all that the river has done for the community, it has also proven extremely uncooperative. In the 1880s, the West Point–based Chattahoochee

Navigation Company drew up plans to build a lock and dam between the town and Franklin, to facilitate upstream steamboat travel, but their efforts proved fruitless because of the shallow, shoal-filled river. More problematic than the river's shoals, however, were the floods. West Point was hit by major floods in 1886, 1901, 1912, 1916, 1919, 1929, and 1961. The 1961 flood saw teenagers water-skiing down Main Street and prompted Congress to act on the construction of West Point Dam. Since the dam was completed in 1974, water has crept into town only once.

MILE 241.6 (32.870347, -85.183495) Alabama-Georgia State Line. At this slight elbow in the river, the western bank of the Chattahoochee becomes the state line. In most instances where a river forms a boundary, states share "ownership" of the river with property rights extending to the center of the river. But when Georgia's commissioners negotiated the cessation of lands west of the Chatta-hoochee to the federal government in 1802, they did so with the carefully worded provision that Georgia's western border ran "thence up the said River Chatta-hoochee and along the western bank thereof." Georgia's claim to the entire river prevented Alabama landowners from harnessing the river and handicapped that state economically for decades. In the mid-1800s, Alabamans challenged the border in court but failed and today, the "Welcome to Georgia" signs sit on the west bank of the river.

HAMES ISLAND, TROUP COUNTY

MILE 242.5 (32.856006, -85.179496) West Point WRF. On river left is the city's wastewater treatment plant.

MILE 242.8 (32.854240, -85.176191) Shoal.

MILE 244.2 (32.851432, -85.157115) Shawmut Boat Ramp. This access point on river right is suitable for trailered boats with parking and picnic areas.

MILE 244.4 (32.850112, -85.155442) Long Cane Creek & LaGrange's Wastewater Discharge. Though the Long Cane Creek Water Reclamation Plant for LaGrange is 11 miles northeast of here, its effluent is piped to this location and discharged beneath the river surface here. The plant can treat up to 12 million gallons of sewage daily. Long Cane Creek enters from river left.

MILE 247.3 (32.815497, -85.164738) Langdale Dam & Textile Mill Redevelopment. Built in 1908 to power the West Point Manufacturing Company's textile mills in Langdale, this 15-foot-high, 1,362-foot-long lowhead dam creates a picturesque but dangerous obstacle. Boaters should use caution when approaching the dam and should never attempt to run the falls. Hydraulics below the dam have trapped and drowned unsuspecting boaters. A buoy line upstream of the dam warns of its approach. The property around the dam is owned by Georgia Power Co., which is working with local governments and the Middle Chattahoochee River Stewards to designate and develop an official portage route around the dam. The best portage route around the dam is on river left at the eastern end of the dam. In 2000, after more than a century of a textile mill operating along the river here, the Langdale and Riverview mills closed. The city of Valley, hoping to turn this bowl of lemons into lemonade, purchased both properties and plans to develop the riverfront into a mixed-use retail-office-residential complex with improved access for boaters and the development of a 22-mile water trail from West Point to Lake Harding. Langdale, and its sister mill village of Riverview, dates back to 1866. Both villages are listed on the National Register of Historic Places, memorializing an era when mill employees lived in company houses and the company store and Chattahoochee River were central to their lives.

MILE 247.7 (32.809916, -85.166570) Langdale Boat Ramp. This access point on river right is suitable for trailered boats.

MILE 247.7 (32.810331, -85.163856) Island & Shoals. Below Langdale Dam, the river becomes braided and winds through a maze of islands leading up to Crow Hop and Riverview Dams, a pair of lowhead dams that should always be portaged. Georgia Power Co., which owns the property around the dams, is working with local governments and the Middle Chattahoochee River Stewards to designate and develop an official portage route around these dams. The best route around the dams is on river right, hugging the west bank of the river for the next mile until you reach the head of Hills Island (identifiable because of

NEAR RIVERVIEW, CHAMBERS COUNTY, ALA.

RIVERVIEW DAM, HARRIS COUNTY

the water treatment facility on river right). At the head of Hills Island, go left of the island and look for the portage route around Crow Hop Dam on Hills Island around the western end of the dam. This route avoids Riverview Dam, which lies at the downstream end of Hills Island between the island and the west bank of the river. There is no easy portage route around Riverview Dam.

MILE 248.5 (32.799221, -85.155627) Crow Hop Dam. This dam spans 944 feet across the river from Hills Island to the eastern bank of the river. It redirects water to the turbines at Riverview Dam on the west side of Hills Island. Crow Hop is a 15-foot-high stone masonry lowhead dam and should be approached with caution; a buoy line upstream of the dam warns of its approach.

MILE 249.3 (32.795406, -85.142978) Shoals. This series of shoals marks the downstream end of Hills Island.

MILE 249.7 (32.793675, -85.141207) Riverview Dam. Located on the western channel formed by Hills Island, this dam was built in 1918 to power the textile mills in Riverview. The city of Valley is attempting to restore and redevelop the old mill buildings and create a linear park along the river.

MILE 250 (32.787919, -85.138990) Flat Shoal Creek & Shoal Spider Lilies. Just opposite the end of Hills Island and concealed by Johnson Island is the mouth of Flat Shoal Creek on river left—which is home (several miles upstream) to a stand of shoal spider lilies (Hymenocallis coronaria). A state threatened plant, the lilies bloom each May in only a handful of places in Georgia. The geology that made this part of the state ideal for building dams and harnessing the river's power also provided the ideal habitat for the lilies that survive only in rocky shoals with swift-moving water. Though they once existed in the mainstem of the Chatta-hoochee, the river's fall-line dams have eliminated virtually all of their habitat. The property surrounding Flat Shoal Creek's lilies has been deeded to the Nature Conservancy by Steve Johnson, a West Point native whose family has lived in Harris County since the 1800s and also lent their name to the large island here.

MILE 250 (32.787027, -85.139716) Riverview Boat Ramp. A small parking area and Georgia Power Co. day-use park mark the take out for this section.

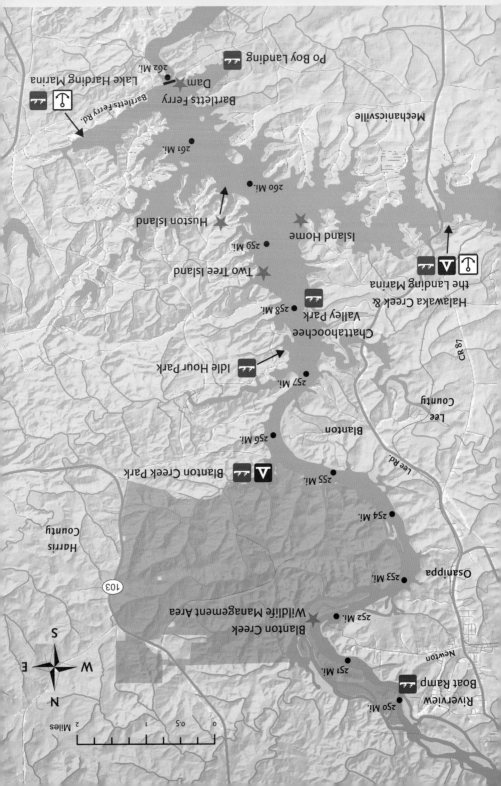

Bartletts Ferry

Length 11 miles (Riverview to Bartletts Ferry Dam)

Class 1

Time 5–8 hours

Minimum Level The river here is navigable year-round, but releases from West Point Dam can create unsafe conditions immediately below Riverview Dam. Release schedules are issued by the U.S. Army Corps of Engineers daily and can be retrieved at http://water.sam.usace.army.mil/todaySched.htm or by calling 706-645-2929. Lake Harding levels vary less than 1 foot daily and fluctuate between 518 and 521 feet above mean sea level throughout the year—except in the event of a maintenance drawdown.

River Gauge The nearest river gauge is at West Point: http://waterdata.usgs.gov/ga/nwis/uv?site_no=02339500.

Launch Site The launch site is in the Georgia Power Co. park adjacent to Riverview Dam. The park provides a boat launch and parking.

DIRECTIONS From the intersection of U.S. 29 and I-85 (exit 79), travel south on U.S. 29 for 2.8 miles through Langdale. Turn left onto 63rd Street and proceed a half block. Turn right onto 20th Avenue and travel 1.7 miles. At the fork in the road, bear left and continue straight on School Street for 0.7 mile. Turn left onto Library Street and proceed 0.1 mile. Turn left onto Lower Street and proceed 0.1 mile to the industrial building. Bear to the right and follow the drive 0.3 mile along the river to the landing.

Take Out Site Po Boy Landing is a boat ramp at Bartletts Ferry Dam in a cove on the west side of the river. The take out includes a dock, a parking area, and restrooms. From this take out, it is a 1-mile portage along roads to the boat launch below the dam.

DIRECTIONS From the Riverview launch site, return through Riverview on Lower Street for 0.2 mile until it merges with California Street. Bear left at the merge and continue on California Street for 0.6 mile. Turn right onto Newton Street and proceed 0.2 mile. Turn left onto Columbus Road and travel 2.1 mile. Merging with Co. Rd. 379 on the right, continue south on Co. Rd. 379 (McColloh Rd.) another 1.6 miles. At the crossroads with Co. Rd. 270, bear to the left and continue on Co. Rd. 379 for 7.1 miles. Turn left onto Lee Road and proceed 3 miles to the boat ramp and parking area on the left.

Description Part river, part lake, this 11-mile section tours the backwaters and main body of Lake Harding—one of Georgia's oldest manmade reservoirs and resorts. Completed in 1926, the lake was a popular getaway for Columbus's well-to-do. In contrast to the circa-1970s Lake West Point upstream, no shoreline construction guidelines impeded development here. The result is a jumble of homes and docks crowding the banks; some tiny islands host homes (and even churches). The 5,850-acre lake boasts of 156 miles of shoreline. On arrival at Bartletts Ferry Dam, adventurers wanting to continue downstream face a 1-mile portage to a launch below the dam. Shorter trips can be created using four public boat launches located on the lake.

Outfitters No outfitters operate on this section of the river.

Points of Interest

MILE 251.8 (32.772409, -85.122130) Blanton Creek Wildlife Management Area. This state-managed property hugs the east bank of the river for the next 4 miles, protecting 4,500 acres of land.

MILE 255.7 (32.741749, -85.111181) Blanton Creek Park. This Georgia Power Co. campground can be accessed via a boat ramp in a cove on river left. The facility provides a campground, restrooms with showers, a picnic area, and parking. 706-643-7737.

MILE 257.4 (32.716699, -85.115199) Idle Hour Park. This Georgia Power Co. boat ramp on river left provides parking and restrooms.

MILE 258.1 (32.706516, -85.120564) Chattahoochee Valley Park. The Georgia Power Co. maintains a parking area and a boat ramp on river right.

MILE 258.7 (32.701498, -85.112539) Two Tree Island. "Jet Ski, Boat or Swim. . . . Get there anyway you can! Join us this summer in the middle of Lake Harding for the most exciting worship service anywhere around." Thus reads the online advertisements for this nondenominational church that holds Sunday services at 11 a.m. from June through August. The tiny island is in the middle of the main channel.

MILE 259.4 (32.689709, -85.116417) Island Home. On river right here is a rare sight on the Chattahoochee's lakes: a dwelling place on an island. On Lake Harding there are a handful—holdovers from the era before Georgia Power restricted development in and around the lake.

MILE 259.9 (32.691387, -85.149396) Halawaka Creek & the Landing Marina. On river right here Halawaka Creek meets the Chattahoochee. Halawaka is derived from the Creek Indian word meaning "bad." About 1.5 miles up the creek, you'll find the Landing Marina, with restrooms, campsites, cabins, a store, a dock, gas, and a boat ramp.

MILE 260.2 (32.683569, -85.102534) Huston Island. Of all the island homes on Lake Harding, none is more famous than Tom Huston's "Halawaka." This sprawling log structure was built in the 1920s, and its history parallels the saga of its owner. Huston, a Columbus inventor who held patents on a peanut roasting process, a peanut-shelling machine, and even a cellophane peanut bag, began

selling peanuts in the river city during the early 1920s for . . . peanuts (5 cents a bag). By 1930 he was profiled by *Time* magazine as the "Farmer Boy Who Became Peanut King." When Bartletts Ferry Dam was completed in 1926, he ventured out onto the lake and fell in love with this island. Halawaka, named for the creek entering the river here on the Alabama side of the lake, endured misfortune, as did its owner. Huston's investments in developing a frozen

ANGLER ON LAKE HARDING, HARRIS COUNTY

peach business coincided with the stock market crash, and by 1932 he lost control of his Tom Huston Peanut Co. Halawaka would also meet its demise in the Great Depression, destroyed in a fire. Huston moved to Florida, where, like a phoenix, he rose from the business ashes to make a fortune growing peaches and developing pet products. Tom's Snacks, sold many times over since 1932, today remains one of the leading purchasers of Georgia-grown peanuts. A lone chimney is all that remains of Tom's summer getaway, and kudzu covers much of the island; thus locally it is often referred to as Chimney or Kudzu Island.

MILE 261.8 (32.674326, -85.072595) Lake Harding Marina. On river left in front of the dam a cove leads 1.3 miles to Lake Harding Marina, with restrooms, a store, gas, and a boat dock. 706-505-1395.

MILE 262 (32.663591, -85.090870) Bartletts Ferry Dam. This dam spans 1,900 feet across the Chattahoochee and is 120 feet tall. The dam's name comes from a family of Baptist ministers who once owned the land here and would likely be impressed with the baptismal "pool" the dam created. In addition to preaching the gospel, the *Bartley* family also operated a ferry at this site. Unfortunately for the family, the spelling of their name was corrupted. Lake Harding was named to honor Reynold Monroe Harding, who served as vice president of the Columbus Power & Electric Co., which was responsible for the construction of the dam. Also unfortunately, the company's dam projects—first Goat Rock and then Bartletts Ferry—diminished Columbus as a manufacturing center by sending electricity to rival towns like LaGrange, West Point, and even Atlanta.

MILE 262 (32.657165, -85.103215) Po Boy Landing. This landing 0.8 mile west of the dam provides a boat ramp, a parking area, a dock, and restrooms. From this take out, it is a 1-mile portage along roads to the boat launch below the dam.

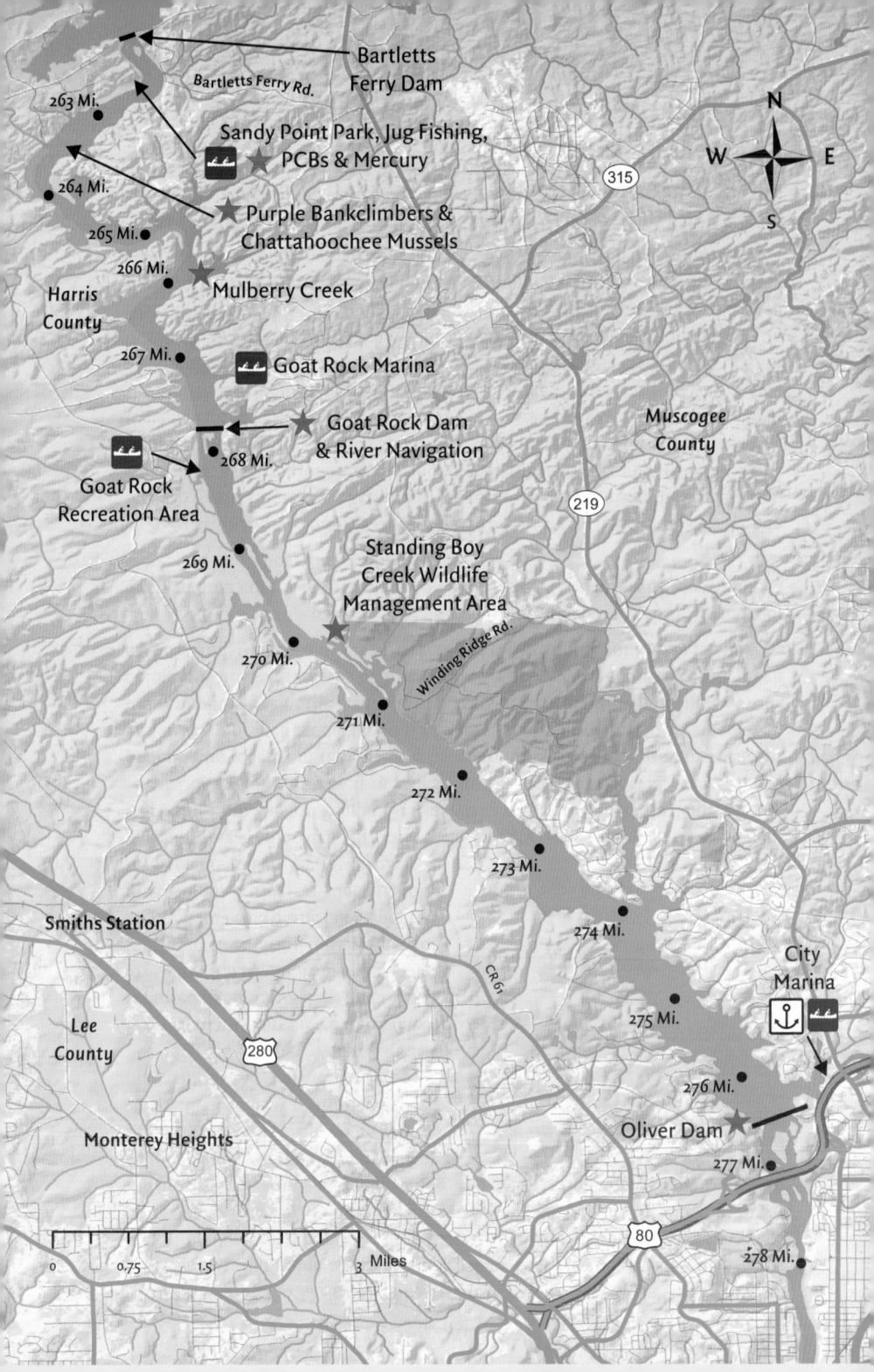

Bartletts
Ferry Dam

Bartletts Ferry Rd.

263 Mi.

Sandy Point Park, Jug Fishing,
PCBs & Mercury

264 Mi.

Purple Bankclimbers &
Chattahoochee Mussels

265 Mi.

266 Mi.

Mulberry Creek

Harris
County

267 Mi.

Goat Rock Marina

Muscogee
County

315

Goat Rock Dam
& River Navigation

268 Mi.

Goat Rock
Recreation Area

269 Mi.

219

Standing Boy
Creek Wildlife
Management Area

270 Mi.

Winding Ridge Rd.

271 Mi.

272 Mi.

273 Mi.

274 Mi.

Smiths Station

CR 61

City
Marina

Lee
County

280

275 Mi.

276 Mi.

Monterey Heights

Oliver Dam

277 Mi.

80

278 Mi.

N
W   E
S

0   0.75   1.5   3   Miles

Goat Rock

Length 13 miles (Bartletts Ferry Dam to Oliver Dam)

Class 1

Time 6–10 hours

Minimum Level The river here is navigable year-round. Water levels on Goat Rock Lake and Lake Oliver vary according to releases from West Point Dam. Release schedules for Georgia Power Co.'s Middle Chattahoochee dams can be obtained by calling 706-317-6000.

River Gauge The nearest river gauge is at West Point: http://waterdata.usgs.gov/ga/nwis/uv?site_no=02339500.

Launch Sites Sandy Point Park is on the west bank of the river below Bartletts Ferry Dam and provides parking, a boat ramp, picnic areas, and access to Goat Rock Lake. Goat Rock Recreation Area is on the west bank of the river below Goat Rock Dam and provides parking, a boat ramp, and access to Lake Oliver. There is no reasonable portage route around Goat Rock Dam. However, in 2013, plans were underway to create a water trail extending from West Point to Oliver Dam with the development of portage paths around Bartletts Ferry and Goat Rock Dams.

DIRECTIONS TO SANDY POINT PARK From the intersection of Fob James Drive and I-85 (exit 77), travel south on Fob James for 1 mile. Turn right onto the Fairfax Bypass and proceed 6 miles, at which point Fairfax Bypass becomes Lee Road. Continue on Lee Road another 6 miles. Turn left onto Old West Dirt Road and proceed 0.9 mile. Turn right upon arriving at the Bartletts Ferry Dam area and proceed 0.6 mile to the boat ramp downstream of the dam.

DIRECTIONS TO GOAT ROCK RECREATION AREA From the intersection of U.S. 280/U.S. 431 and I-85 (exit 62) in Opelika, proceed on U.S. 280 East for 12.2 miles. Turn left onto Co. Rd. 250 and proceed 3.2 miles. Turn right onto Lee Road and travel 0.5 mile. Turn left onto Co. Rd. 330 and proceed 1.8 miles. Turn right onto Co. Rd. 249 and proceed 0.5 mile. Turn left into the entrance to the Goat Rock Dam area and proceed 0.2 mile to the fork in the road. Bear right at the fork and travel 0.3 mile to the boat ramp.

Take Out Sites Due to the difficulty of portages around Goat Rock and Oliver Dams, boaters should consider out-and-back trips on these lakes. Take out sites are near both dams. Goat Rock Marina, 0.2 mile up a cove on the east side of the river 0.4 mile upstream of Goat Rock Dam, provides a boat ramp, a dock, restrooms, and parking. City Marina on Lake Oliver, on the east side of the river at Oliver Dam, provides a boat ramp, a dock, parking, restrooms, a store, and picnic areas.

DIRECTIONS TO GOAT ROCK MARINA From the intersection of River Road and U.S. 80 in Columbus, travel north on River Road for 8.1 miles. Turn left onto Goat Rock Road and proceed 1.6 miles. Turn right onto Adcock Road and travel 0.3 mile. Turn right onto Rocky Ridge Road and proceed 0.1 mile. Turn left into Peggy Lane and travel 0.5 mile to the boat ramp.

DIRECTIONS TO OLIVER MARINA Oliver Marina is at the intersection of River Road and U.S. 80 in Columbus. From the exit ramp of U.S. 80 West, proceed across River Road. From the exit ramp of U.S. 80 East, turn left onto River Road, pass underneath U.S. 80, and turn left. From either direction, the marina is on the right.

Description This 14-mile run, interrupted by Goat Rock Dam, is all lake. Goat Rock provides 1,050 acres of open water and 25 miles of shoreline—virtually all of it wild and undisturbed. The lake also provides access to Mulberry Falls, one of the most scenic spots in Harris County. Lake Oliver provides 2,150 acres and 40 miles of shoreline. Standing Boy Creek Wildlife Management Area protects about 2 miles of riverfront on the upper end of Oliver, but as the river nears Columbus, extensive riverfront development crowds both the Alabama and Georgia shores.

Outfitters No outfitters operate on this section of the river.

Points of Interest

MILE 262.5 (32.656905, -85.087644) Sandy Point Park, Jug Fishing, PCBs & Mercury. Goat Rock is a popular fishing lake, and this recreation area on river right is a common launch point. One of the techniques seen here is jug fishing— baited lines are tied to plastic soda or oil bottles and released to slowly float downstream. Jug fishing is legal in Georgia, but the buoys must be marked with the angler's name and address and must be attended regularly and removed at the completion of the trip. Fish in Goat Rock Lake, as well as Harding and Oliver (and other Chattahoochee lakes), have been found to contain unhealthy levels of mercury and polychlorinated biphenyls (PCBs). Therefore, the Georgia Department of Natural Resources has placed fish consumption advisories on some species. PCBs were used in electric transformers, televisions, refrigerators, and other appliances. PCBs were banned from use in the United States in 1979, but because they persist in the environment and bioaccumulate in fish they remain an ongoing health risk. Mercury continues to make its way into Georgia rivers as airborne mercury primarily from coal-fired power plants that falls into rivers and streams. Access Georgia fish consumption guidelines at http://www.gaepd .org/Documents/fish_guide.

MILE 263.6 (32.646878, -85.100733) Purple Bankclimbers & Chattahoochee Mussels. Near here in 2000, Carson Stringfellow, an environmental consultant and instructor at nearby Columbus State University, found a federally threatened purple bankclimber mussel—a species that had not been documented in the Chattahoochee since the 1800s. The Apalachicola-Chattahoochee-Flint River basin is home to 29 native mussel species, including four endangered species (fat threeridge, shinyrayed pocketbook, Gulf moccasinshell, and oval pigtoe) and two threatened species (chipola slabshell and purple bankclimber). Four species historically found in the basin are now extirpated or extinct. The river's dams have played a major role in the demise of mussels because most species cannot tolerate slack water like that found in a lake. The dams have also blocked the movement of fish, many of which are critical to the reproductive cycle of mussels. Female mussels release their fertilized young into the water column where host fish suck the "glochidia" into their gills. There the young mussels attach to the fish and grow. When they reach the right size, the young mussels fall from the fish to the river bottom to grow into adult mussels. In this manner, mussels are dispersed throughout the river. Mussels also play an important role in keeping the river clean by filtering nutrients from the water. Purple bankclimbers were once abundant on the Chattahoochee. Shell middens at archaeological sites show that they were a staple in the diet of Native Americans.

LAUNCHING BELOW BARTLETTS FERRY DAM, LEE COUNTY, ALA.

MILE 265.8 (32.631076, -85.082526) Mulberry Creek. A mile-long paddle up this creek on river left leads you to a 0.3-mile stretch of shoals that culminates in Mulberry Falls, a breathtaking example of fall line geology. The creek spills over several drops, including a 15-footer. Popular with whitewater paddlers, the rapids here are Class III–V, depending on flows.

MILE 267.4 (32.617439, -85.074532) Goat Rock Marina. A cove on river left leads to this take out that provides a boat ramp, a dock, restrooms, and parking.

MILE 267.8 (32.610265, -85.079769) Goat Rock Dam & River Navigation. In operation since 1912, Goat Rock Dam was the first of the big 20th-century dams along the Chattahoochee's fall line. Stretching 68 feet above the riverbed and spanning 1,320 feet, it was also the first dam that pitted hydropower proponents against proponents of river navigation—a conflict that continued for nearly a century. When the dam was built, it stored water from 6 p.m. until 6 a.m. daily, then released it to produce electricity and feed already-existing hydropower plants at Columbus. These daily

GOAT ROCK DAM, LEE COUNTY, ALA.

fluctuations rendered steamboat navigation below Columbus even more precarious. Columbus steamboat interests cried foul, but those protests were tempered by the realization that the hydroplant meant more electricity and business prospects in the city. Conflicts between navigation interests and hydropower producers persisted for a century. In 2012, the U.S. Army Corps of Engineers greatly curtailed operating hours for the Lower Chattahoochee's navigational locks because they receive so little use. This move, for all practical purposes, closed the book on 180 years of commercial navigation on the Lower Chattahoochee. Goat Rock received its name from a herd of goats that were once a common site atop a large boulder near the Alabama side prior to construction of the dam. During dedication ceremonies, Columbus Mayor L. H. Chappell anointed a goat, said to have descended from the original herd, with a splash of river water.

MILE 268.2 (32.603848, -85.078374) Goat Rock Recreation Area. Located 0.4 mile downstream from the dam on river right, this access point provides parking, a boat ramp, and a boat dock.

MULBERRY FALLS, HARRIS COUNTY

MILE 270.2 (32.580021, -85.064770) Standing Boy Creek Wildlife Management Area. With assistance from the Trust for Public Land, in 2001 Georgia purchased for $7.7 million this 1,578-acre property that stretches along the east bank of the river for the next 2 miles. Plans originally called for it to be developed into a state park providing hiking trails, campsites, and canoe-kayak launches. In 2013 it remained as a wildlife management area. The property is home to the federally endangered relict trillium, a wildflower found only in Alabama, Georgia, and South Carolina, with just 14 known populations in Georgia.

MILE 276.4 (32.521169, -84.992571) City Marina. A cove on the Georgia side of the dam leads to City Marina, which provides a boat ramp, a dock, parking, restrooms, a store, and picnic areas. This is the closest take out to the dam; there is no reasonable portage route around the dam.

MILE 276.6 (32.517655, -84.999109) Oliver Dam. Completed in 1959, Georgia Power Co.'s Oliver Dam is 70 feet high and 2,120 feet long. Nearly 120 years earlier the region's first white settlers harnessed the power of the river here. A Captain Johnson (the history books don't record his first name) felled a tree across the river gorge, nailed planks to it, and successfully diverted enough water to power a textile mill that supplied local residents with thread, cloth, meal, flour, and tanned leather. The mill provided supplies for the Confederate Army during the Civil War but was destroyed by the Union Army late in the war. The factory was rebuilt in 1866 and operated until the 1880s. The three-story wooden structure burned in 1910.

Columbus

Length 4 miles (Oliver Dam to Columbus)

Class I–IV

Time 2–4 hours

Minimum Level The river here is navigable year-round. Water levels vary according to releases from Oliver Dam. Release schedules for Georgia Power Co.'s Middle Chattahoochee dams can be obtained by calling 706-317-6000.

River Gauge The nearest river gauge is below Oliver Dam: http://waterdata.usgs .gov/ga/nwis/uv?site_no=02341505.

Launch Site The gateway to the longest urban whitewater run in the United States is on the east bank of the river below North Highlands Dam and provides parking, a boat ramp, picnic areas, restrooms, and walking trails.

DIRECTIONS From U.S. 80 (exit 1) in Columbus, take 2nd Avenue South for 0.9 mile. Turn right onto 38th Street and proceed one block. Turn left onto 1st Avenue and travel 0.2 mile. Turn right into the entrance to the Chattahoochee Riverwalk and proceed 0.3 mile to the parking area at the launch site adjacent to the North Highlands Dam.

Take Out Site The take out for this section is behind the Columbus Convention & Trade Center downstream from the Dillingham Street Bridge. The take out provides a boat ramp, parking, and restrooms.

DIRECTIONS From the launch site, return to 1st Avenue. Turn right onto 1st Avenue and proceed 0.1 mile. Turn left onto 32nd Street and proceed one block. Turn right onto 2nd Avenue and travel 2.1 miles. Turn right onto 9th Street and proceed 0.2 mile. Turn left onto Front Avenue and then immediately right into the Columbus Convention & Trade Center facility. Follow the drive to the boat landing behind the center.

Alternative Access Points Additional access points along the urban riverfront provide access to Bibb City Pond, which is formed by North Highlands Dam, Heaven's Gate Rapid on the Columbus side of the river, and Cut Bait Rapid on the Phenix City side of the river. These locations do not have developed boat launches.

DIRECTIONS TO BIBB CITY POND ACCESS From U.S. 80 (exit 1) in Columbus, take 2nd Avenue South for 0.7 mile. Turn right onto 41st Street and proceed one block. Turn right onto Hemlock Drive and take the left fork onto Poplar Street. Proceed on

Poplar Street 0.1 mile and then bear right onto Linden Point. Travel one block and bear to the left where the road forks. Continue to the trail leading to the river. There is roadside parking only; there is no developed launch site here.

DIRECTIONS TO HEAVEN'S GATE RAPID ACCESS From U.S. 80 (exit 1) in Columbus, take 2nd Avenue South for 3 miles. Turn right onto 12th Street and proceed 0.3 mile to Front Avenue. Continue across Front Avenue. Street parking is available on Front Avenue and in the parking deck at the corner of Front and 12th Streets.

DIRECTIONS TO CUT BAIT RAPID ACCESS From the U.S. 80/U.S. 431 and U.S. 280 interchange in Phenix City, travel south on U.S. 431 for 0.9 mile. Turn left onto Crawford Road and proceed 1.2 miles to the fork in the road. Bear left at the fork onto 13th Street. Proceed 0.6 mile to the entrance to the parking area on the right near the trail along the west bank of the river.

Description No other section of river has played a larger role in the cultural history of an area than has this 4-mile run from Oliver Dam to Columbus. Located at the fall line separating the piedmont from the Coastal Plain, the river drops at a rate of more than 25 feet per mile from the base of Oliver Dam to the Dillingham Street Bridge in downtown. This strategic spot at "Coweta Falls" prompted Native Americans to settle here in order to take advantage of the fish spawning runs that ended at the base of the falls. Those same falls attracted early white settlers, who quickly harnessed the river to turn grist and textile mills, damming it at three locations within 4 miles. More recently, those same historic dams have been removed to harness the river again—this time to restore some of the river's natural flow and to create a 2.5-mile whitewater course that has been billed as the longest urban whitewater run in the world. Rapids range from Class II–IV, depending on water levels. Access to portions of the river outside the whitewater run is very limited, but excursions between the Oliver and North Highlands Dams, as well as the whitewater run that begins below North Highlands Dam, can best be classified as "time travel," revealing this area's long relationship with the river.

Outfitters Whitewater Express offers guided raft trips and rentals on this section of the river: 1303 3rd Ave., Phenix City, Ala. 36867, 334-298-9521, www.whitewaterexpress.com.

Points of Interest

MILE 276.7 (32.512363, -84.994528) Magnolia Island & Clapps Factory Cemetery. During the time that Clapp's Factory was in operation (1830s–80s), this island, located directly below Oliver Dam, was a place of social gatherings. Prior to the Civil War, two footbridges extended from the Georgia and Alabama shores to the island, bringing picnickers. Reportedly, as many as 500 people visited the island in a single day. The scene from this spot must have been dramatic in those days, as the falls here splashed down about 15 feet. The Clapps Factory Cemetery is on river left. More than 500 people are believed to have been buried there, but a few headstones are all that remain.

MILE 277.3 (32.504578, -84.994068) Chattahoochee Riverwalk. On river left here is a bridge over a tributary—part of Columbus's 22-mile riverwalk that stretches from Lake Oliver through the city southward to Fort Benning. The walk is the result of mandates to upgrade the city's sewer system—trunk lines of which ran along the riverbank to the city's wastewater treatment plant. While repairing and replacing sewer lines, the city also built the walk. Today it is considered one of the city's top tourist attractions. This site is the best location to launch boats on Bibb City Pond and explore the river between Oliver and North Highlands Dams.

MILE 277.6 (32.499521, -84.996805) Lovers' Leap & North Highlands Dam. The location of this dam is said to be the Chattahoochee's legendary Lovers' Leap, a rocky bluff overlooking the Chattahoochee on river left from which two star-crossed Native American lovers from rival tribes leaped into the raging current of the Chattahoochee, choosing death together rather than life apart (a legend, or version thereof, that appears in many different locations). The rugged terrain here made construction of a mill difficult, and thus this otherwise-ideal spot to harness the river was not developed until technology allowed the transmission of electricity over long distances. North Highlands Dam went in service in 1900 and was billed as the "first large-scale dam" in the South. Lovers' Leap soon came to be known as Bibb City Pond. Buoys about 0.1 mile upstream warn of the lowhead dam's approach. A rugged portage route can be found on river right, but below the dam is almost a half mile of dry riverbed, as the bulk of the river flows river left and through this Georgia Power Co. facility's powerhouse.

MILE 278.1 (32.495244, -84.994814) Launch Site. This launch site on river left provides access to the Chattahoochee's 2.5-mile whitewater run.

MILE 278.2 (32.495425, -84.995197) Ambush Rapid & Columbus Whitewater Course. This manmade rapid—created using some 600 cubic yards of rock (about 34 dump truck loads)—was constructed to add another whitewater element to the course constructed in 2012–13, when two historic dams were blasted and dismantled. The idea for removing these dams has its origins in the 1990s, when local outdoorsman Neal Wickham suggested creating a whitewater course when Atlanta was to host the 1996 Olympic games. John Turner, an executive with the W. C. Bradley Co. in Columbus, ultimately led the effort to make Wickham's vision come to life. The city of Columbus chipped in $5 million for the project, with another $20 million coming from private donors and federal grants. By using the river's existing rapids and engineering others, the project

HEAVEN'S GATE RAPID, MUSCOGEE COUNTY

has yielded a 2.5-mile series of Class II–IV rapids. The course opened in May 2013 and during the first two months of operation, Whitewater Express, the only licensed commercial outfitter for the course, guided 7,500 people down the river.

MILE 279.2 (32.480259, -84.994268) City Mills Dam. The power of water has been harnessed here since 1828, when Seaborn Jones erected a wooden dam to power a gristmill. In 1906–7 the original wooden structure was replaced with a stone dam. In 2012 when the stone dam was breached to restore the river's natural flow and its rapids for a whitewater course, the skeleton of the original wooden dam was revealed. In 1895, power from this dam ran the Columbus trolley line. Remnants of the dam remain along both banks of the river.

MILE 279.2 (32.479754, -84.994638) Gooder 'n Grits Rapid. An ode to the product once produced at City Mills, Gooder 'n Grits is a Class II rapid through the center of the river, with a 6-foot drop followed by a series of waves.

CITY MILLS, MUSCOGEE COUNTY

MILE 279.4 (32.478175, -84.995054) Turner's Tumbler Rapid. This series of shoals creates a Class II obstacle beneath the railroad trestle here.

MILE 279.6 (32.474926, -84.994603) Lawsuits That Determined a State Boundary. In this vicinity in 1841, Girard resident Stephen Ingersoll installed a waterwheel along the Alabama shore to turn his mill. Four years later, Columbusite John Howard constructed a 4-foot-high dam across the river for the purposes of turning his mill; the backwaters from the dam quickly inundated Ingersoll's wheel, rendering it inoperable and setting off a comical tale of dueling lawsuits. Ingersoll sued in Alabama court and was awarded $4,000 in damages. Howard countersued in Georgia, claiming that Ingersoll trespassed on his property— and that he had caught fish in the commission of this trespass. A Georgia jury awarded him $600. These two lawsuits ultimately wound their way to the U.S. Supreme Court, which ruled that Georgia's boundary did, in fact, extend to the western bank of the river and that riparian landowners in Alabama did not enjoy the same rights as those on the Georgia side. And, that is why today you'll find no historic textile buildings on the western shore.

MILE 279.7 (32.472193, -84.996105) Muscogee Mills. Here on river left in 1882, a waterwheel that powered the Muscogee Mills produced the first electric light in Columbus. That year, hundreds of residents gathered on nearby Broad Street to watch the lighting of the first electric bulb in town. By 1887, the river powered lights throughout Columbus's downtown.

MILE 279.7 (32.472092, -84.996601) Wilson's Run Rapid. A Class III rapid with an 8-foot drop and large waves. The rapid is named for Union General James Wilson, a 27-year-old commander who led more than 13,000 cavalry troops into Alabama and Georgia near the close of the Civil War. Columbus was his final prize, as he learned of the war's end shortly after capturing and destroying much of the city's industrial complex on April 16, 1865—a week after General Robert E. Lee's surrender at Appomattox Courthouse in Virginia.

MILE 279.9 (32.469658, -84.997178) Eagle & Phenix Dam. Originally constructed in the 1840s and rebuilt in 1869, this dam powered what was, in the 1870s, the South's largest textile mill. Originally called Eagle Mills, the "Phenix" was added when the mill rebuilt and "rose from the ashes" after being torched by the Union Army late in the Civil War. In 2012, in a scene reminiscent of the lighting of Columbus's first electric light in 1882, hundreds of people came to watch the dam be blasted to restore the river's whitewater run. To commemorate

WHITEWATER RAFTING AT COLUMBUS, MUSCOGEE COUNTY

BIBB CITY POND, MUSCOGEE COUNTY

the historic occasion, a local deli baked a 6-foot-long, 500-pound "dam cake." The replica of the historic dam and powerhouse required 100 pounds of icing. While the dam was destroyed with explosives, the replica was devoured by those in attendance. Remnants of the old dam can still be seen on each of the river's banks.

MILE 280 (32.469493, -84.997706) Cut Bait Rapid. This Class IV rapid is to the right of the large island that splits the river's flow. During the early days of the opening of Columbus's whitewater course, a video of a series of rafts flipping in this rapid went viral on YouTube. Within a week of its posting, more than 100,000 had viewed it. The video made Cut Bait, which existed before the breaching of Eagle & Phenix Dam, instantly famous and fueled excitement for the whitewater course. Paddlers can choose to run this rapid, or they can ferry to the river's east bank to run Heaven's Gate.

MILE 280 (32.468939, -84.996870) Heaven's Gate Rapid. This rapid on the Georgia bank of the river was created using a "wave shaper," a massive metal structure that controls the height and intensity of water flow. In constructing the wave shaper and other features of this rapid, scuba divers anchored fabric bags on the river bottom and filled them with a special concrete mix. The rapid that resulted ranks as a Class IV obstacle with several large waves. A bridge from the Columbus riverbank to an island on river left gives spectators a clear view of boaters navigating this rapid.

HEAVEN'S GATE RAPID, MUSCOGEE COUNTY

HEAVEN'S GATE RAPID,
MUSCOGEE COUNTY

MILE 280.3 (32.465214, -84.997403) Woodruff Riverfront Park. The crown jewel
of the Columbus Riverwalk. The park provides great views of paddlers on the
river's whitewater run.

MILE 280.3 (32.464888, -84.998685) Hanging Tree Flats. The sandy area on river
right before the Phenix City Amphitheater is the site of the hanging of six Native
Americans in 1836. The Creek and Yuchi Indians were hanged for their role in
the attack on the frontier town of Roanoke 43 miles downstream on the Chattahoochee during the Second Creek War. The Creek attack on Roanoke was pro-
voked by the failure of the Alabama legislature to uphold an 1832 treaty guaran-
teeing Creek Indians land in the Chattahoochee Valley if they chose to remain in
their homeland rather than moving west.

MILE 280.4 (32.464127, -84.997875) Phenix City Amphitheater & "Sin City." The amphitheater on river right here signifies Phenix City's renaissance. Long handicapped by Georgia's claim to riparian rights to the western bank, Phenix City's history is tortured, albeit colorful. The town went bankrupt during the Great Depression and shortly thereafter resorted to generating revenue through a system of fines and licensing for gambling and liquor sales. Crime bosses and corruption soon took hold, managing extensive gambling, drug, and prostitution rings; meanwhile the young soldiers in training at nearby Fort Benning flocked across the river to partake of the town's offerings. In the city's most infamous incident, Phenix City lawyer Albert Patterson was gunned down outside his office after winning the state's Democratic primary in 1954 for attorney general on a campaign promise to "clean up" his town. This incident led Governor Gordon Persons to declare marshal law in the town. Troops were sent in, slot machines were confiscated and burned, pouring licenses were revoked, and soldiers from Fort Benning were turned back at the river bridges. From 1954 to 1968 the town was a "dry" municipality. Like Columbus, Phenix City has invested in revitalization of its riverfront, and when plans were drawn up for the river's whitewater restoration, local leaders agreed to locate one of the commercial rafting outfitters in Phenix City. In 2007 *BusinessWeek* magazine named Phenix City the nation's Best Affordable Suburb for raising a family.

MILE 280.5 (32.463476, -84.997511) Dillingham Street Bridge, John Godwin & Horace King. The site of the first bridge across the river built in 1832 by John Godwin and his slave Horace King. The covered bridge was washed away just nine years later, but Godwin and King rebuilt it. Then, 24 years later, the master bridge builders' work was destroyed again: with the Union cavalry charging from the west, Confederates defending Columbus set fire to the span to prevent the enemy from crossing it. In 1865, King rebuilt the bridge for a second time. That bridge lasted until the early 1900s, and in 1911 it was replaced with the current concrete and steel structure. King, who was granted his freedom by Godwin in 1846, became one of the South's most respected bridge builders and general contractors. He served in Alabama's reconstruction legislature, and ultimately settled in LaGrange, where a city street was named in his honor—unheard of for a black man in that era. On his death in 1885, newspapers heaped praise on him. Still, the *Atlanta Constitution* in its account of his death referred to him as "Uncle Horace King."

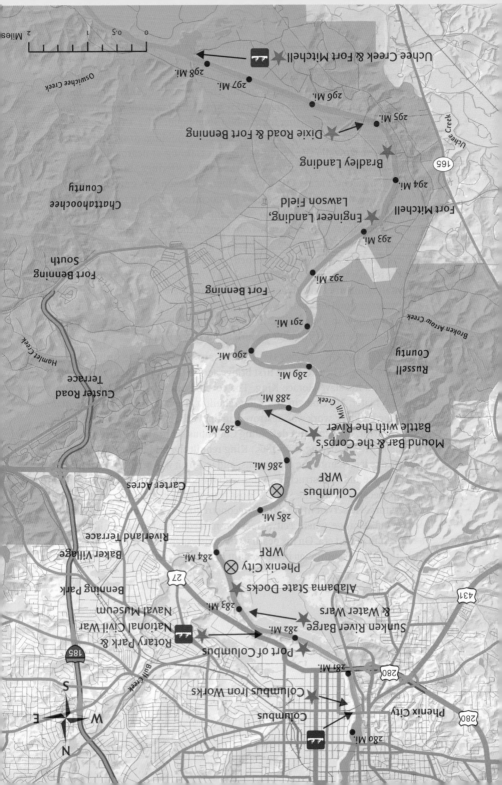

Fort Benning

Length 17 miles (Columbus to Uchee Creek)

Class 1

Time 8–10 hours

Minimum Level The river here is navigable year-round.

River Gauge The nearest river gauge is below Oliver Dam: http://waterdata.usgs.gov/ga/nwis/uv?site_no=02341505.

Launch Site The launch site is behind the Columbus Convention & Trade Center in downtown Columbus. The launch features a boat ramp and landing, parking, and restrooms. As an alternative, boaters can launch from Rotary Park, 1.8 miles downstream.

DIRECTIONS TO COLUMBUS CONVENTION & TRADE CENTER From the intersection of Wynnton Road and I-185 in Columbus (exit 6), travel west 2.7 miles. Turn left onto 10th Avenue and proceed 0.2 mile. Turn right onto 9th Street and travel 0.8 mile. Turn left onto Front Avenue and then immediately right at the Convention & Trade Center. Follow the drive to the parking area at the river.

DIRECTIONS TO ROTARY PARK From the intersection of Victory Drive and I-185 in Columbus (exit 1), travel west on Victory Drive 4.5 miles to the entrance of Rotary Park on the left.

Take Out Site The take out site is 0.1 mile up a slough at Uchee Creek on river right. A campground and recreation area managed by the U.S. Army within Fort Benning for use by soldiers and their families, the facility offers a boat ramp, docks, a parking area, restrooms, and a camp store with supplies. While civilians have access to the facilities (a small parking fee is required), the campground and associated amenities are available only to the military.

DIRECTIONS From the parking area at the Convention & Trade Center, return to Front Avenue and turn left. Proceed 0.1 mile. Turn left onto Dillingham Street and travel across the river 0.3 mile to Phenix City. Turn left onto Colin Powell Parkway (Broad St.) and proceed 0.1 mile and then bear to the right onto U.S. 431 (Martin Luther King Jr. Pkwy.). Travel on U.S. 431 South 3.7 miles. Turn left onto Ala. 165 and proceed 7 miles. Turn left onto 101st Airborne Division Road and travel 3.4 miles. Turn left onto Uchee Creek Road and proceed 1.5 miles to the parking area at the recreation area headquarters.

Description   Leaving behind the fall line and its whitewater, the Chattahoochee begins its slow winding way through the Coastal Plain. A historic corridor of commercial navigation, the remnants of that now-dead commerce remain in U.S. Army Corps of Engineers navigational buoys and mile markers. Still popular among recreational boaters, this section's most dominant feature is Fort Benning, a 182,000-acre army base occupying 16 miles of riverfront along both the Georgia and Alabama shores. The mostly wild riverfront landscape is often interrupted by the sights and sounds of training exercises—paratroopers spilling from transport planes overhead and the pop of rifle fire.

Outfitters   No outfitters operate on this section of the river.

Points of Interest

MILE 280.5 (32.461382, -84.997165) Columbus Iron Works. What is now the Columbus Convention & Trade Center was for more than a century the Columbus Iron Works. When established in 1853, it cast kettles, pots, and ovens; 10 years later as the Civil War raged, it was transformed into an armory for the Confederate Army and Navy, making cannons, mortars, and even an ironclad gunboat. The facility was destroyed when the Union Army captured Columbus, but investors quickly rebuilt it and were back in business by 1866. Its strategic location on the Chattahoochee and the steamboat landing connected the foundry with agricultural markets to the south, and after the war the ironworks turned "swords into plowshares" producing all manner of products for farmers in the Chattahoochee Valley. However, the ironworks may best be known as the manufacturer of the nation's best-selling ice machine in the late 1800s. The foundry was destroyed by fire again in 1902 but was rebuilt. In 1977, the city invested $8 million to restore the buildings into the Columbus Convention & Trade Center.

MILE 281.8 (32.446218, -84.983882) Port of Columbus. The facility on river left here is the port of Columbus, built to accommodate what was expected to be a thriving commercial shipping business on the Chattahoochee. In the 1950s and 1960s—some 20 years after any significant goods were shipped via steamboat on the river—the federal government spent more than $100 million building locks and dams in an effort to make Columbus (and some believed, even Atlanta) an inland port. But, the barges never came. In the mid-1970s, the U.S. Army Corps of Engineers predicted that 1.8 million tons of goods annually would be shipped on the river by 1990, but the most that was ever shipped was 1.2 million tons in 1985. The last commercial vessel to use the port of Columbus visited in 2000. In 2012, the Corps announced plans to greatly reduce the operating hours at the Lower Chattahoochee's locks due to lack of use.

MILE 282.3 (32.444317, -84.977263) Rotary Park & National Civil War Naval Museum. The public boat ramp and dock on river left provide access to Columbus's Rotary Park with restrooms, picnic tables, a bait shop, and the National Civil War Naval Museum. The museum houses the remains of the Confederate Navy's ironclad gunboat, the *Jackson*, which never fired a shot on the enemy due, in part, to the river's unpredictability. The Confederates hoped that an impenetrable ironclad built at Columbus's ironworks could steam downriver to Apalachicola and break the Union blockade. Instead, the 225-foot-long, 2,000-ton *Jackson*, which repeatedly failed to launch because of inadequate water levels, was set ablaze by Union troops on its capture in 1865. It drifted downriver for two weeks before finally sinking about 30 miles downstream. It was raised from the riverbed in 1961 and is now considered the "largest surviving Confederate warship."

MILE 282.9 (32.439733, -84.969197) Sunken River Barge & Water Wars. A relic of 20th-century commercial navigation, this partially sunken barge on river left is symbolic of the river's uncooperative nature and a long-standing water war between Georgia, Alabama, and Florida. Among the issues fought over is how the river's dams—particularly Buford Dam above Atlanta—are operated to provide a deep enough channel on the Lower Chattahoochee and Apalachicola Rivers to float commercial barges. In the early 1990s, the state of Alabama took legal action to prevent Metro Atlanta from taking more water from the river, partly because of concerns about the impact on the river's shipping channel. But, after 20 years of declining commercial use of the river, water supply trumped the river barges.

MILE 283.5 (32.433852, -84.966873) Alabama State Docks. Like Georgia, Alabama pinned its economic hopes on river navigation when the state built this terminal on river right. The silos rising above the riverbank date to the 1970s and can hold 426,160 bushels of grain. Of course, the barges no longer come to carry that grain.

MILE 283.7 (32.430881, -84.966090) Phenix City WRF. On river right here is the discharge from Phenix City's sewage treatment facility. The plant is allowed to discharge up to 7.7 million gallons of treated sewage to the river daily.

MILE 285.5 (32.409945, -84.979819) Columbus WRF. On river left here is the discharge from the city of Columbus water reclamation facility. In operation since 1964, this plant, after numerous upgrades, now treats up to 70 million gallons of sewage daily from Columbus and Fort Benning. In 2002 the facility embarked on a project to convert sewage into "green energy." Methane produced during the anaerobic digestion of sewage is captured and used to meet some of the facility's energy needs. An energy-intensive process, sewage treatment accounts for 4 percent of energy used in the United States, according to the U.S. Environmental Protection Agency. The Columbus facility has saved as much as $490,000 in energy costs annually as a result of the project, with the added benefit of reducing greenhouse gases emitted from the plant.

MILE 287.7 (32.390129, -84.973521) Mound Bar & the Corps's Battle with the River. Near here in 1828, commercial navigation of the Chattahoochee had an inauspicious start. After triumphantly arriving in Columbus, the steamer *Steubenville* (the second to reach Columbus) offered to provide free rides to Columbus residents on an excursion to see an Indian Mound located downriver on what was then the plantation of John Woolfolk. The trip to "Woolfolk's Mound" went off without a hitch, but the steamer, with its load of passengers, was unable to make progress upriver on its return to town.

UCHEE CREEK RECREATION AREA, RUSSELL COUNTY, ALA.

Many passengers gave up the ship and walked home. Some 70 years later, the U.S. Army Corps of Engineers battled the river in a similar fashion here—attempting to deepen the channel at a troublesome sandbar. From the Corps's 1892 report to Congress: "At Mound Bar there were removed 126 old piles and 805 cubic yards of gravel, and there were built 1,700 linear feet of dams and 400 square yards of bank protection mats. This work involved the driving of 1037 piles (wooden posts driven into the riverbed), cutting and placing 622 cords of brush, hauling and placing 592 cubic yards of ballast . . . 4,000 feet of lumber . . . and 600 pounds of nails and spikes." The report concluded (in pleading fashion): "Unless sufficiently large appropriation is made to renew these works, it is probable that boats will not be able to reach Columbus at all by another low-water season." In this manner, the Corps continued to receive federal funds to "improve" the river, climaxing in the 1950s with appropriations to build the Lower Chattahoochee's three locks and dams. No visible signs of the improvements here remain.

MILE 293.4 (32.346162, -85.002520) Engineer Landing, Lawson Field. The sandy landing on river left here leads to Fort Benning's Lawson Field. This airfield was originally constructed in 1920 as a hot-air-balloon landing field. The U.S. Army had been using manned reconnaissance balloons since the Civil War and during World War I, hundreds of missions were flown, often ending with soldiers parachuting out of the gondolas when they came under attack. Reconnaissance balloons are still used by the military, but today this airfield supports helicopters and planes. It is named in honor of Captain Walter Lawson, a decorated World War I veteran who died in a 1923 plane crash. The landing along the river is used for training in constructing pontoon bridges.

MILE 294.5 (32.330226, -85.006503) Bradley Landing. Like Engineer Landing, this location is sometimes used by Fort Benning to conduct "floating bridge training," in which a temporary bridge is laid across a series of pontoons to enable troops and equipment to cross.

MILE 295.2 (32.322014, -84.999678) Dixie Road & Fort Benning. The only bridge in the 40 miles between Columbus and Omaha, this span connects Fort Benning and Alabama. Fort Benning has been part of the Chattahoochee landscape since 1918; its mission is to train infantry soldiers. At the request of the Columbus Rotary Club, the fort was named after Confederate General Henry Benning. During his command of troops in the Civil War, Benning came to be known as "the Rock" because of his coolness under fire . . . but it wasn't always that way for Benning, a Columbus lawyer before the war. During one of his first battles, the greenhorn colonel came under attack and lost his cool, scampering to General James Longstreet in a tizzy: "General, I am ruined! My brigade was suddenly attacked and every man was killed. No one is to be found. Please, give orders where I can do some fighting." Longstreet coolly assessed that Benning was befuddled and responded with icy sarcasm: "Nonsense, Colonel. You are not so badly hurt. Look about you. I know you will find at least one man [to command]." Benning went on to redeem himself and move up the ranks, ending the war as a brigadier general. The training facility named in his honor has produced such notables as Omar Bradley, George Marshall, Dwight D. Eisenhower, George Patton, and Colin Powell.

MILE 298.2 (32.322014, -84.999678) Uchee Creek & Fort Mitchell. On river right, between the south bank of Uchee Creek and the Chattahoochee once stood the formidable Creek Indian village of Yuchi. In 1778 William Bartram described it in glowing terms: "it is the largest, most compact, and best situated Indian town I ever saw." Within 50 years of Bartram's visit the Yuchi were gone, forcibly removed from their town. In July 1836, U.S. soldiers and state militia gathered 1,600 Creek Indians from the surrounding area at Fort Mitchell—about 5 miles upstream on Uchee Creek—and marched them west to Montgomery, where they boarded steamboats bound down the Alabama River and up the Mississippi to points west. Today, Uchee Creek is home to a Fort Benning recreation area and campground catering to soldiers and their families.

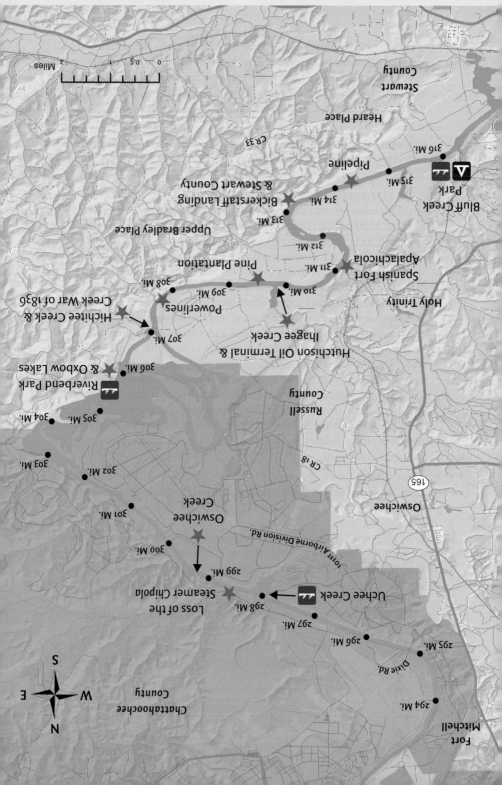

Riverbend

Length 17 miles (Uchee Creek to Bluff Creek)

Class 1

Time 8–10 hours

Minimum Level The river here is navigable year-round.

River Gauge The nearest river gauge is downstream at Ga. 39 near Omaha: http://waterdata.usgs.gov/ga/nwis/uv?site_no=02342881.

Launch Site The launch site is 0.1 mile off the mainstem of the river on Uchee Creek. A campground and recreation area managed by the U.S. Army within Fort Benning for use by soldiers and their families, the facility offers a boat ramp, docks, a parking area, restrooms, and a camp store with supplies. While civilians have access to the facilities (a small parking fee is required), the campground and associated amenities are available only to the military.

DIRECTIONS From Phenix City and Columbus, travel south on U.S. 431 from Phenix City for 3.7 miles. Turn left onto Ala. 165 and proceed 7 miles. Turn left onto 101st Airborne Division Road and travel 3.4 miles. Turn left onto Uchee Creek Road and proceed 1.5 miles to the parking area at the recreation area headquarters.

Take Out Site The take out site is 0.3 mile up Bluff Creek on river right. The U.S. Army Corps of Engineers campground provides a boat ramp, a dock, parking, restrooms with showers, water, and campsites. User fees apply.

DIRECTIONS From the Uchee Creek Recreation Area, return to 101st Airborne Division Road. Turn right and proceed 3.4 mile. Turn left onto Ala. 165 and travel 9.9 miles. Turn left onto Bluff Creek Road and proceed 1.5 miles to the parking area at the boat ramp.

Alternative Take Out Site To create a 7-mile trip, boaters can take out at Riverbend Park.

DIRECTIONS TO RIVERBEND PARK From the Uchee Creek Recreation Area, return to 101st Airborne Division Road. Turn right and proceed 3.4 mile. Turn left onto Ala. 165 and travel 13.9 miles. Turn left onto Ala. 208 (Ga. 39) and proceed 14.7 miles. Turn left onto U.S. 27 and travel 2.6 miles. Turn left onto Co. Rd. 43 and proceed 4.7 mile. Turn left onto Riverbend Road and travel 3.5 miles to Riverbend Park.

Description Flowing deeper into the Chattahoochee Valley, the timeless river rolls through a landscape rich in history, where the names of creeks (Oswichee, Hichitee, and Ihagee) echo the past when Native Americans plied the river in dugout canoes. This 17-mile run includes historic 19th-century steamboat landings, the sites of steamboat wrecks, and the relics of more recent attempts to transform this shallow, shifting, and uncooperative river into an avenue of commerce. The highlight of the trip is Riverbend, an extensive series of oxbow lakes that provide acres of off-the-main-channel exploration.

Outfitters No outfitters operate on this section of the river.

Points of Interest

MILE 298.5 (32.304356, -84.946923) Loss of the Steamer *Chipola*. Near this location, on September 19, 1867, the sternwheeler *Chipola* was steaming upstream en route to Columbus when her boilers exploded. Six crew members died in the blast that flung scalding water, wood, and metal. In the mayhem that followed, John Shaw, a black steward, swam to the rescue of Captain Van Marcus, who had been wounded and thrown from the vessel. Like many Chattahoochee steamers, the *Chipola*'s time on the river was short. She lasted just a year. Between 1829 and 1930, more than 200 steamboats operated on the Chattahoochee, Flint, and Apalachicola Rivers.

MILE 299.2 (32.300946, -84.937782) Oswichee Creek. Upstream on this tributary was the Creek Indian town of Oswichee, which existed until 1827. Oswichee is believed to be a Muskogee Indian word meaning "switchers."

MILE 305.9 (32.245248, -84.913277) Riverbend Park & Oxbow Lakes. Managed by Chattahoochee County since 2002, this park on river left offers a boat ramp, parking, and picnic areas and looks out over a vast network of oxbow lakes formed by the meandering river . . . and the backwater of Lake Walter F. George. At one time, the river flowed northwest from this landing and formed a massive loop back to the southeast—a journey of nearly 4 miles—but over time the river "cut through" the land, separating this bend. Today, the river's course from the top of the former bend to the bottom is but a mile. The river stays in its historic channel for another 20 miles before Walter F. George Dam causes it to spread over former bottomlands, but here—55 miles upstream of the dam—its effects are felt.

MILE 307.1 (32.231019, -84.922804) Hichitee Creek & Creek War of 1836. Another of the lyrical place names of Creek Indian origin in the Chattahoochee Valley, the Hichitee, or Hichiti, were a group of Creek Indians who in 1836 took up arms against white settlers to stop their forced removal from their ancestral lands. Near this spot on June 3, 1836, the Georgia militia opened fire on a group of Creek Indians as they launched their canoe from the western bank of the river.

The hour-long skirmish left at least six Creeks and one Georgia militiaman dead. Hichitee Creek enters on river left.

MILE 307.7 (32.222306, -84.924564) Powerlines.

MILE 309.7 (32.217731, -84.954669) Pine Plantation. On river left here for the next 3 miles, the river winds around a large pine plantation. In 2010 Georgia's forestry industry generated $14.5 billion in revenue—the vast majority of that income started on "farms" like this one, and an environmental price is paid. Erosion and sedimentation from harvesting practices can impact the health of nearby rivers and streams, and the conversion of diverse forests to monoculture farms reduces biodiversity and increases the need for herbicides and pesticides. Forestry management practices, such as leaving vegetation near waterways undisturbed, can help mitigate these impacts.

MILE 309.9 (32.217779, -84.959516) Hutchison Oil Terminal & Ihagee Creek. Another relic of 20th-century aspirations of inland ports, the Hutchison Oil Terminal on river right now sits silent. Ihagee Creek, which joins the river here, derives its name from a Creek Indian town once located nearby. The Creek word Ihagi is believed to mean "the groaners."

MILE 311.2 (32.212338, -84.978268) Spanish Fort Apalachicola. On river right here in 1689, a force of 24 Spanish soldiers, and 100 Apalachee Indians accompanying the Spanish upriver from Florida, constructed a square blockhouse

fort overlooking the river. The purpose of the fort was to thwart English efforts to gain control of the area by establishing a Spanish presence along the Chattahoochee. The effort proved unsuccessful, and a short time later the Spanish abandoned the fort, retreating downriver to Florida. The archaeological site was discovered by a Catholic monk at nearby Holy Trinity monastery in 1956. The moat that protected the fort is still visible.

MILE 313.2 (32.195370, -84.964210) Bickerstaff Landing & Stewart County. In the 1800s, during the heyday of steamboats on the river, Bickerstaff Landing on river left near this location was one of 240 steamboat landings between Columbus and Apalachicola. Such landings were the engines that drove the local economy. In 1850 with 16,000 residents, Stewart was Georgia's tenth most populous county and among the state's top three cotton-producing counties. At Bickerstaff Landing, cotton was loaded onto boats bound for Apalachicola, which at the time was the Gulf Coast's third largest port. But once the soil was expended and commerce shifted from steamboats to railroads (which bypassed Stewart), the county's fortunes turned. By 1950, the population was half what it was in 1850. In 2010, it was among Georgia's least populated of 159 counties.

MILE 314.4 (32.189105, -84.982148) Pipeline.

MILE 316 (32.185949, -85.011154) Bluff Creek Park. The take out is 0.3 mile up the slough on river right. The U.S. Army Corps of Engineers campground provides a boat ramp, a dock, parking, restrooms with showers, water, and campsites. User fees apply. 334-855-2746.

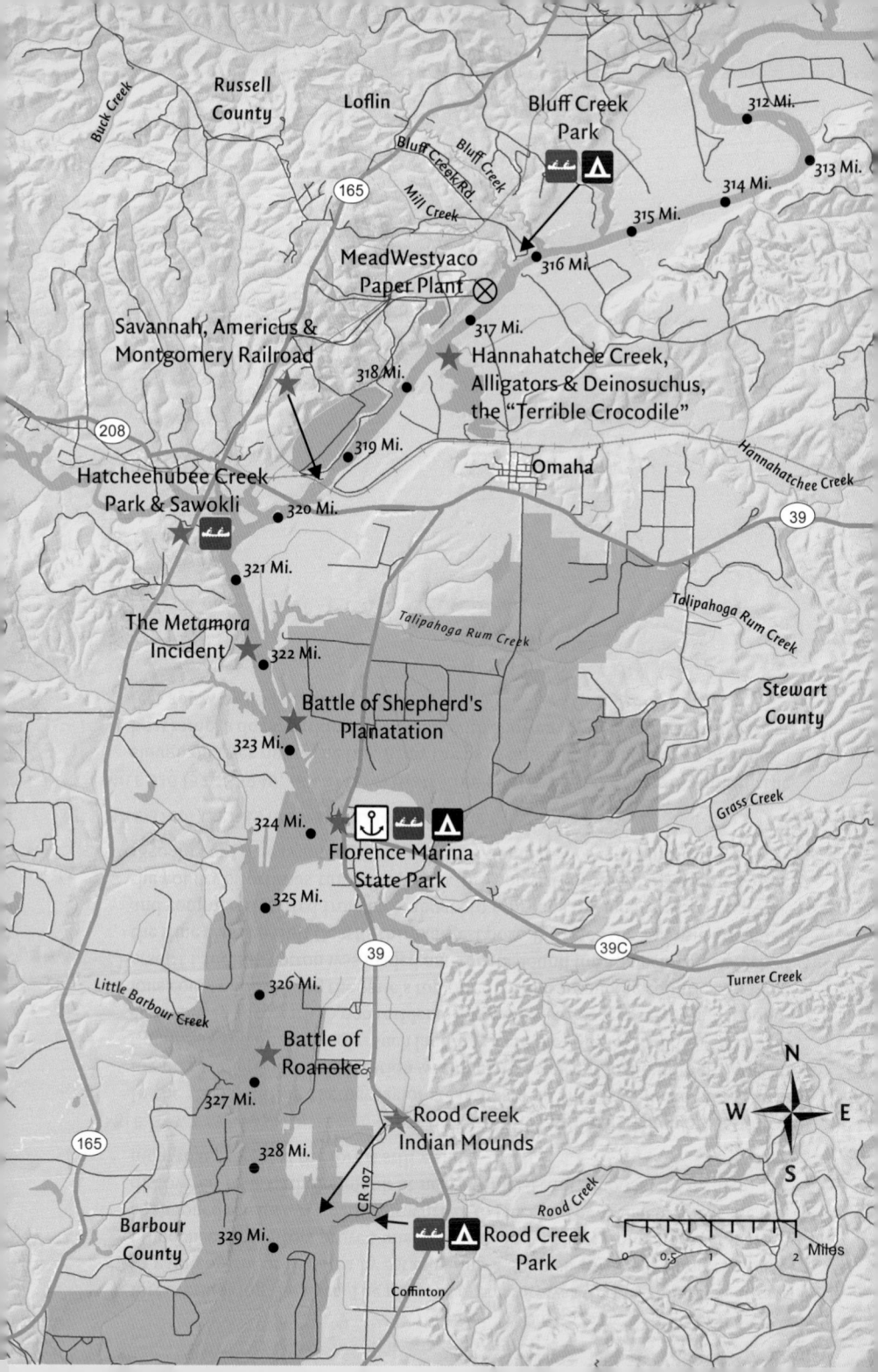

Rood Creek

Length 13 miles (Bluff Creek to Rood Creek)

Class 1

Time 6–9 hours

Minimum Level The river here is navigable year-round.

River Gauge The nearest river gauge is downstream at Ga. 39 near Omaha: http://waterdata.usgs.gov/ga/nwis/uv?site_no=02342881.

Launch Site The launch site is 0.3 mile off the mainstem of the river on Bluff Creek. The U.S. Army Corps of Engineers Bluff Creek Campground provides a boat ramp, a dock, parking, restrooms with showers, water, and campsites. User fees apply. 334-855-2746.

DIRECTIONS From Phenix City and Columbus, travel south on U.S. 431 from Phenix City 3.7 miles. Turn left onto Ala. 165 and proceed 16.9 miles. Turn left onto Bluff Creek Road and proceed 1.5 miles to the parking area at the boat ramp.

Take Out Site The take out site is 0.6 mile up Rood Creek on river left. This U.S. Army Corps of Engineers park provides a boat ramp, a dock, restrooms, water, primitive camping, and picnic areas. User fees apply.

DIRECTIONS From Bluff Creek Park, return to Ala. 165. Turn left and proceed 4 miles. Turn left onto Co. Rd. 208 and proceed 2.4 miles (crossing river). Turn right onto Ga. 39 South and travel 6.9 miles. Turn right onto Rood Creek Landing Road and proceed 1.4 miles to the parking area at the boat ramp.

Alternative Take Out Sites To create a 4-mile trip, boaters can utilize Hatcheehubee Creek Park or, for an 8-mile trip, Florence Marina State Park.

DIRECTIONS TO HATCHEEHUBEE CREEK PARK From Bluff Creek Park, return to Ala. 165. Turn left onto Ala. 165 and proceed 4.8 miles. Turn left onto Chub Creek Road and travel 0.3 mile to the boat ramp.

DIRECTIONS TO FLORENCE MARINA STATE PARK From Bluff Creek Park, return to Ala. 165. Turn left onto Ala. 165 and proceed 4 miles. Turn left onto Ala. 208 (Ga. 39) and travel 2.4 miles. Turn right onto Ga. 39 South and proceed 4 miles to Florence Marina State Park on the right.

Description The effects of Walter F. George Dam become noticeable and real between Bluff and Rood Creeks as the river slows and spreads. Sloughs at the mouths of tributaries grow. While the banks remain wooded and wild, this 13-mile run includes a passage by a massive paperboard plant as well as a stop at Georgia's Florence Marina State Park. In the 1830s, these 13 miles were at the center of fighting in the Second Creek War.

Outfitters No outfitters operate on this section of the river.

Points of Interest

MILE 316.7 (32.174684, -85.015430) MeadWestvaco Paper Plant. If you have ever bought a soft-drink 12-pack, there's a good chance the cardboard packaging for those drinks was made at this facility on river right. The MeadWestvaco Paper Plant produces coated paperboard, using water drawn from the river here. At the other end of the process, the plant discharges up to 30 million gallons of treated wastewater to the river daily. The Alabama Department of Environmental Management issues permits regulating the contents of that discharge and is charged with ensuring that the plant's effluent does not negatively impact the river. The 1,400-acre plant operates around the clock and produces 1 million tons of paperboard annually.

MILE 317.6 (32.165575, -85.025988) Hannahatchee Creek, Alligators & Deinosuchus, the "Terrible Crocodile." American alligators, once nearly extinct in Georgia and Alabama, have made a comeback after years of protection and

NEAR OMAHA, STEWART COUNTY

the backwaters of Lake Walter F. George—such as those spreading across the mouth of Hannahatchee Creek on river left—are often their haunts. Gators grow to 13 feet in length or greater, but 79 million years ago when this part of Georgia and Alabama was a coastal estuary, you might have encountered a much larger predator—Deinosuchus, the "terrible crocodile." Paleontologists have discovered fossilized remains of the giant crocodile along Hannahatchee Creek and in the Chattahoochee nearby. Based on those findings, they believe the creature attained lengths of 29 feet and was one of the apex predators of the Cretaceous period.

MILE 319.5 (32.143957, -85.045257) Savannah, Americus & Montgomery Railroad. The vertical-lift drawbridge here was constructed in 1969, but a railroad first crossed the river here in 1890 when the SA&M first connected nearby Louvale with points west toward Montgomery. The rail line is now abandoned.

MILE 320.5 (32.135326, -85.059714) Hatcheehubee Creek Park & Sawokli. This U.S. Army Corps of Engineers park on river right at the mouth of the creek provides a boat ramp, a dock, parking, restrooms, water, and picnic areas. User fees apply. On the north bank of the creek was the Native American town called Sawokli, which has been mentioned in accounts of French, English, and Spanish explorers and traders since the 1600s. Sawokli is believed to mean "Raccoon town."

SAVANNAH, AMERICUS & MONTGOMERY RAILROAD BRIDGE, STEWART COUNTY

MILE 321.8 (32.117352, -85.056036) The *Metamora* Incident. Near this location in June 1836 in the midst of the Second Creek War, the steamer *Metamora*, carrying 150 members of the Georgia and Alabama militia, came under fire from Creek warriors along the Alabama shore. After the militia returned fire, the ship made landfall so that troops could pursue the attackers, but steep and rugged terrain hampered their pursuit. The soldiers returned to the ship and continued north to Columbus.

MILE 322.7 (32.1056615, -85.052941) Battle of Shepherd's Plantation. On June 9, 1836, just to the east of the river here, 250 Creek Indians attacked Georgia militiamen. The Creeks initially overwhelmed the militia, but reinforcements from nearby Fort Jones to the south fended off the offensive. This was one in a series of skirmishes that represented the Creeks' last effort to push white settlers from their ancestral lands. Within two years, they would be defeated and forcibly removed from the Chattahoochee Valley.

MILE 323.8 (32.088992, -85.044809) Florence Marina State Park. The slough on river left leads to this state park that provides a boat ramp, a dock, boat gas, restrooms with showers, a campground, a store, cabins, and many other amenities. User fees apply. 218 Florence Rd., Omaha, Ga. 31821, 229-838-6870, www.gastateparks.org/FlorenceMarina. The park takes its name from the once-thriving river landing and frontier town of Florence, which was incorporated in December 1837 after Creek Indians burned the nearby town of Roanoke in 1836. In the 1840s, the community boasted of a covered bridge across the river, a news-paper, bank, and hotel, but in 1846 a flood washed away the bridge, diminishing the town's importance. When railroads later bypassed the community, Florence vanished into history. Its name, however, lived on in at least one resident of the Chattahoochee Valley: In 1897, the steamer *Naiad* ran aground in the river near here with an expectant mother on board. She gave birth on the ship and named the infant Florence Naiad, honoring both the steamboat and the nearest landing.

MILE 326.8 (32.050280, -85.056246) Battle of Roanoke. An incident along the east bank of the river here in the frontier town of Roanoke marked the "official" beginning of the Second Creek War. Though the 1832 Treaty of Cusseta guaranteed individual Creek Indians be provided 320 acres if they chose to stay in the Chattahoochee Valley of Alabama, neither white settlers nor the Alabama legislature honored the treaty. The result was a long-simmering conflict that exploded on May 15, 1836, when 200 Creeks attacked Roanoke. After crossing the river, the Creeks launched their offensive, killing more than a dozen people, capturing slaves, and driving off the remainder of the town residents. They then set fire to the town—among those killed were individuals trapped in the town hotel when it was set ablaze. The site of the town now lies beneath the water of the lake. The steamer *Georgian* was docked at the town's landing on the morning

VIEW FROM BLUFF CREEK PARK, RUSSELL COUNTY, ALA.

of the attack and narrowly escaped by stoking its furnaces with bacon and lard and then steaming away. For the next year, the Chattahoochee's steamers would be used by state militia and federal troops in the conflict with the Creeks, often coming under fire from Creeks stationed along the riverbanks.

MILE 328.9 (32.021903, -85.048178) Rood Creek Indian Mounds. The site of a Mississippian period Native American settlement (700–1600 AD), the Rood Mounds, on river left at the mouth of Rood Creek, are considered the largest native site in the Chattahoochee Valley. The 35 acres are dotted with eight mounds, and archaeologists believe that it was home to the dominant people of that era. Access to the site is restricted, but Florence Marina State Park runs regular tours of the mounds. Native Americans congregated their towns along the river because of the transportation routes these locations provided. They plied the water in dugout canoes, some of which would hold 30 men, and traded all the way to the Gulf Coast. There are more than 1,000 known Native American archaeological sites between Columbus and Apalachicola, Florida.

MILE 328.9 (32.024217, -85.036922) Rood Creek Park. A slough on river left here leads 0.6 mile up the creek to this U.S. Army Corps of Engineers park that provides a boat ramp, pit toilets, parking, camping, and water. User fees apply.

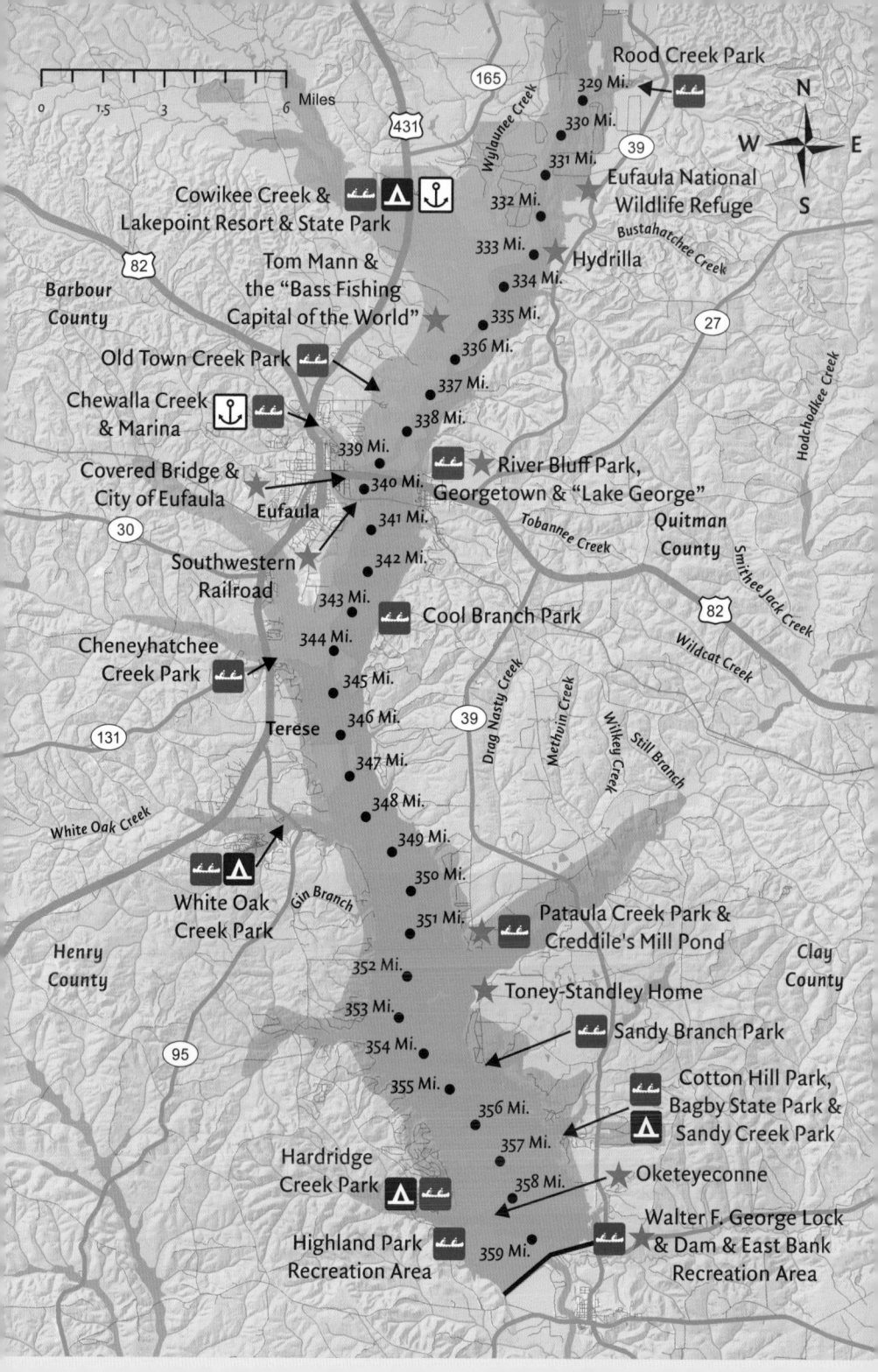

Lake Eufaula

Length 31 miles (Rood Creek to Walter F. George Dam)

Class 1

Time 14+ hours

Minimum Level The lake is navigable year-round. Information on Lake Walter F. George (Eufaula) water levels is at http://water.sam.usace.army.mil/acfframe.htm. Lake levels generally fluctuate less than 2 feet annually, with 188 feet above mean sea level the average operating level.

River Gauge The nearest river gauge is upstream at Ga. 39 near Omaha: http://waterdata.usgs.gov/ga/nwis/uv?site_no=02342881.

Launch Site Rood Creek Park is 0.6 mile off the mainstem of the river. This U.S. Army Corps of Engineers park provides a boat ramp, a dock, restrooms, water, primitive camping, and picnic areas. User fees apply.

DIRECTIONS From the intersection of U.S. 27 and Ga. 39C in Lumpkin, travel west on Ga. 39C for 15.3 miles. Turn left onto Ga. 39 and proceed 3 miles. Turn right onto Rood Creek Landing Road and travel 1.4 miles to the parking area at the boat ramp.

Take Out Site There are multiple access points on Lake Walter F. George (called Lake Eufaula in Alabama, see below), which is operated by the U.S. Army Corps of Engineers. Lake users can create many trips utilizing Corps campgrounds and boat ramps as well as local parks. On the mainstem of the river and just off the mainstem, you'll find at least 13 boat landings in the 30 miles from Rood Creek to the Walter F. George Dam. Most facilities require a nominal parking or user fee; campsites also require fees. Boaters (including canoes and kayaks) may lock through the Walter F. George Dam. Upon locking through, it is 1.4 miles to Franklin Landing, the first take out site below the dam. Lock operations schedules were greatly curtailed in 2012. For lock schedules, call 229-768-0145.

Description Formed in 1964 with the construction of the Walter F. George Lock and Dam, the lake with two names—Walter F. George (the federally designated name) and Eufaula (as it is officially called in Alabama)—is BIG. It spreads over 45,181 acres of the Chattahoochee Valley and encompasses 640 miles of shoreline. At its widest point, it's nearly 3 miles from the Georgia to the Alabama shore. From Rood Creek to the dam is a journey of 31 miles, but multiple U.S. Army Corps of Engineers facilities provide for almost limitless shorter trips and explorations. Filled with alligators, fish, and boaters of all kinds, this recreational paradise hosts nearly 4 million visitors each year. Along its shores you'll find the Eufaula National Wildlife Refuge, Alabama's Lakepoint Resort & State Park, and Georgia's Bagby State Park.

Outfitters The following establishments provide canoe, kayak, or powerboat rentals. Facilities not offering rentals are listed in the main body of this guide.

Lakepoint Resort & State Park in Alabama, 2.5 miles up Cowikee Creek from the mainstem of the river, is a resort providing boat launch-docks, a ship's store, boat gas, powerboat rentals, camping, rental cottages and cabins, a hotel, a restaurant, and golf: 104 Lakepoint Dr., Eufaula, Ala. 36027, www.alapark.com/lakepointresort. Marina & Campground: 334-687-6026; Cottage, Cabin & Hotel Reservations: 334-687-8011.

Bagby State Park in Georgia, 0.6 mile up Sandy Creek from the mainstem of the river, is a resort providing a boat launch and docks, a ship's store, boat gas, canoe rentals, rental cottages, a hotel, a restaurant, picnic areas, and golf: 330 Bagby Pkwy., Fort Gaines, Ga. 39851, 229-768-2571, www.gastateparks.org/GeorgeTBagby.

Points of Interest

MILE 331.1 (31.994087, -85.066980) Eufaula National Wildlife Refuge. Flanking the river here, this wildlife refuge encompasses more than 11,000 acres in Georgia and Alabama. Within the refuge, you'll find bald eagles, ospreys, and an occasional peregrine falcon, but it is best known for its tremendous diversity of waterfowl and migratory birds. Large rookeries of great blue herons, great egrets, snowy egrets, little blue herons, anhingas, and cattle egrets can be found. During the winter, sandhill cranes pay a visit, and during the summer wood storks patrol the refuge wetlands.

MILE 332.7 (31.972465, -85.071400) Hydrilla. The Godzilla of invasive aquatic plants, hydrilla can be seen along the shores here. First found in the lake in 1991, it has spread exponentially. Studies suggest that without controls, the plant—which can root in water as deep as 20 feet—could cover 25,000 of the lake's 45,181 acres. In an effort to stem the green menace, the U.S. Army Corps of Engineers has used herbicides and introduced herbivorous, hydrilla-eating grass carp. The giant mats of hydrilla impede navigation, impact beaches and other recreation areas, and can create large areas of depleted oxygen levels, which can impact fish populations.

MILE 334 (31.981793, -85.105974) Cowikee Creek & Lakepoint Resort & State Park. The large embayment on river right here is Cowikee Creek. Alabama's Lakepoint Resort & State Park is 2.5 miles up this creek. The 1,200-acre park provides a boat ramp, a dock, boat gas, restrooms, water, campsites, cabins, and a 101-room motel. User fees apply. The resort markets Lake Eufaula as the "Bass Capital of the World" and hosts 40 bass tournaments each year.

MILE 335.3 (31.940689, -85.084959) Tom Mann & the "Bass Fishing Capital of the World." Beyond the west bank of the lake here along U.S. 431 is the former site of Tom Mann's Fish World, an aquarium established by the eponymous legendary developer of artificial fishing lures. Mann and his bait company helped make Lake Eufaula into the unofficial "Bass Capital of the World." In his aquarium Mann tested his lures on bass, including the famous "Leroy Brown"—the "smartest fish" Mann ever knew. When Leroy died in 1980, Mann orchestrated a funeral service to coincide with the Alabama Invitational Bass Tournament. More than 1,000 people came to pay respects, filling Brown's tackle box casket with Jelly Worms (a Mann creation) as the Eufaula High School Marching Band played Jim Croce's "Bad, Bad Leroy Brown." Alabama Governor Fob James declared a statewide day of mourning for the fish. Mann, himself, died at age 72 in 2005.

MILE 337.4 (31.918532, -85.120816) Old Town Creek Park. The city of Eufaula park on river right provides a boat ramp, a dock, parking, restrooms, water, and picnic areas. User fees apply.

AMERICAN LOTUS IN EUFAULA NATIONAL WILDLIFE REFUGE, BARBOUR COUNTY, ALA.

MILE 339 (31.892292, -85.109835) River Bluff Park, Georgetown & "Lake George." This U.S. Army Corps of Engineers day-use area on river left provides a boat ramp, a dock, restrooms, water, parking, and a picnic area. User fees apply. Georgetown is the county seat for Quitman, one of Georgia's least-populated counties. In 2010, only one other county had fewer residents than Quitman's 2,513. On this side of the lake, the big federal reservoir is known as Lake George, honoring Georgia's U.S. senator Walter F. George, who was instrumental in securing funding for the dam. Travel to the other side, and Alabama road signs point to "Lake Eufaula"—the name designated by the state legislature honoring the town overlooking the lake. Other names suggested were Lake Chattahoochee, Lake Alaga (combining the states' names), and Lake Henry Clay (combining the names of the Georgia and Alabama counties most inundated by the lake). Congress officially named the lock and dam Walter F. George, but that settled nothing—not along the Chattahoochee, where two states have bickered since the 1830s.

MILE 339.1 (31.906720, -85.143051) Chewalla Creek & Marina. The slough on river right here leads 1.3 miles to this marina that provides boat launches, docks, boat gas, repairs and service, and a store: 580 Chewalla Rd., Eufaula, Ala. 36027, 334-687-5751, www.chewallamarina.com.

MILE 339.7 (31.891223, -85.132136) Covered Bridge & City of Eufaula. Before the construction of the Walter F. George Dam, the bluffs here rose 100 feet above the riverbed and gave the city its nickname, Bluff City. In 1838 John Godwin and his slave Horace King constructed the first bridge to span the river here—a 540-foot covered bridge that sat on 84-foot-high wooden piers to enable the span to reach the top of the bluff. Three years after its completion, it was damaged in a flood and remained in disrepair for almost a decade before the city of Eufaula made repairs. The settlement of Eufaula got off to a similarly rough start. White settlers, ignoring treaties signed between the federal government and the Creek Indians, began building homes, taverns, and a cotton warehouse on the bluff overlooking the river. Federal marshals, in a rare defense of the Creeks' claims to land, arrived to burn the settlement and drive off the squatters, but as soon as they left, the white settlers returned. One of the marshals charged with the action called the people of what would become Eufaula "some of the most lawless and uncouth men" he had ever seen. Today, Eufaula is known for its refinement. Home to the state's second-largest historic district, it is filled with stately antebellum homes, many of which were built with cupolas that allowed their owners to see steamboats arriving on the river from the town's high vantage point.

MILE 340.2 (31.883343, -85.129744) Southwestern Railroad. For Eufaula, this rail line was a critical link to Atlantic Coast markets as it attempted to compete with rival Chattahoochee cotton exchanges like Columbus to the north and Fort Gaines to the south. Completed in 1860, it was built primarily with slave labor,

WALTER F. GEORGE LOCK & DAM, CLAY COUNTY

as were most of the railroads of that era. In 1850, the Southwestern Railroad was the third-largest slave owner in Georgia.

MILE 343 (31.842633, -85.122999) Cool Branch Park. This U.S. Army Corps of Engineers day-use area on river left provides a boat ramp, a dock, restrooms, water, parking, and picnic areas. User fees apply.

MILE 344.2 (31.831641, -85.163619) Cheneyhatchee Creek Park. This U.S. Army Corps of Engineers day-use area at the mouth of the creek on river right, adjacent to the U.S. 431 bridge, provides a boat ramp, a dock, restrooms, and parking. User fees apply.

MILE 348 (31.774443, -85.154172) White Oak Creek Park. This boat ramp operated by the U.S. Army Corps of Engineers is on river right 1.3 miles off the main channel. The park provides a dock, restrooms with showers, water, campsites, a beach, and picnic areas. User fees apply. 334-687-3101.

MILE 351.3 (31.733390, -85.081076) Pataula Creek Park & Creddile's Mill Pond. On river left, the U.S. Army Corps of Engineers boat ramp at Pataula Creek Park is 0.8 mile up Pataula Creek on the north side of the creek. The day-use area provides a boat dock, restrooms, and a picnic area. User fees apply. Near this site on Pataula Creek prior to the construction of the Walter F. George Dam was Creddile's Mill Pond, a gathering and fishing place for local residents in the early and mid-1900s. The original Ga. 39 (a north-south highway running from Fort Gaines to Georgetown) crossed Pataula Creek below the mill dam. When the dam was built, Ga. 39 was relocated farther east.

MILE 352.8 (31.713761, -85.105030) Toney-Standley Home. Just east of the large island here along the shore of the lake sits this historic home believed to have been built in 1803. It is reputed that William Toney played host to Aaron Burr, third U.S. vice president, as Burr traveled through the area in 1804 and again in 1807. Burr is famous for his pistol duel, while serving as vice president, with Secretary of the Treasury Alexander Hamilton, a long-time political enemy. Hamilton died in the incident, but Burr served out his term. The home was saved from being inundated by the lake when it was moved from a low-lying area to this spot in 1959.

MILE 354.4 (31.693058, -85.085266) Sandy Branch Park. This city of Fort Gaines park on river left provides a boat ramp, parking, toilets, water, and a picnic area.

MILE 356.8 (31.669448, -85.060241) Cotton Hill Park, Bagby State Park & Sandy Creek Park. These three facilities are on river left up Sandy Creek. The U.S. Army Corps of Engineers Cotton Hill campground on the north side of the creek provides a boat ramp, parking, restrooms with showers, water, campsites, a swimming beach, and picnic areas: 229-768-3061. Bagby State Park is opposite the campground and features a 30-room lodge and rental cabins as well as a boat ramp, a dock, boat gas, a store, water, and other amenities: 229-768-2571. Sandy Creek Day Use Area is at the mouth of Sandy Creek adjacent to the park. User fees apply.

MILE 358 (31.640762, -85.105077) Hardridge Creek Park. This U.S. Army Corps of Engineers campground provides a boat ramp, parking, restrooms, water, a swimming beach, and picnic areas. User fees apply. The boat ramp is 0.3 mile up the creek on river right. 334-585-5945.

MILE 358.1 (31.640099, -85.084111) Oketeyeconne. Beneath 100 feet of water here are the remains of this Native American village, which was excavated and studied prior to the completion of the Walter F. George Dam. The village was described in 1799 by U.S. Indian Agent Benjamin Hawkins as "situated on good land. . . . They raise plenty of corn and rice and have cattle, horses and hogs." During the War of 1812, Creek Indians from this village took up arms with the British against U.S. forces.

MILE 358.5 (31.631418, -85.098878) Highland Park Recreation Area. This U.S. Army Corps of Engineers day-use area provides a boat ramp, parking, toilets, a swimming beach, and picnic areas. It is the southernmost boat ramp on the Alabama side of the lake, 1 mile upstream of the dam. User fees apply.

MILE 359.7 (31.637949, -85.049579) Walter F. George Lock & Dam & East Bank Recreation Area. Completed in 1962, this dam stretches 2.5 miles across the Chattahoochee and towers 132 feet above the riverbed. The lock, at 88 feet in height and 450 feet in length, is the second-highest lock east of the Mississippi and is made to handle mammoth river barges. Though the lock no longer handles those big boats, recreational boats of any size (including canoes and kayaks) can still use the lock. For the lock schedule, call 229-768-0145. The southernmost boat ramp on the lake is in the East Bank Recreation Area at the end of the dam on the Georgia shore. The park offers parking, restrooms, water, a swimming beach, and picnic areas. User fees apply. For those choosing to lock through the dam, the next take out site is Franklin Landing, 1.4 miles downstream of the dam (see next chapter, "Fort Gaines," for map and location). When construction of the dam began, it was hailed as the beginning of a renaissance for the area, and local leaders hoped that revived river navigation would bring industry and jobs. Such was the excitement that the 1955 groundbreaking ceremonies involved a parade featuring several high school bands, units from Forts Benning and Rucker, and floats from area businesses.

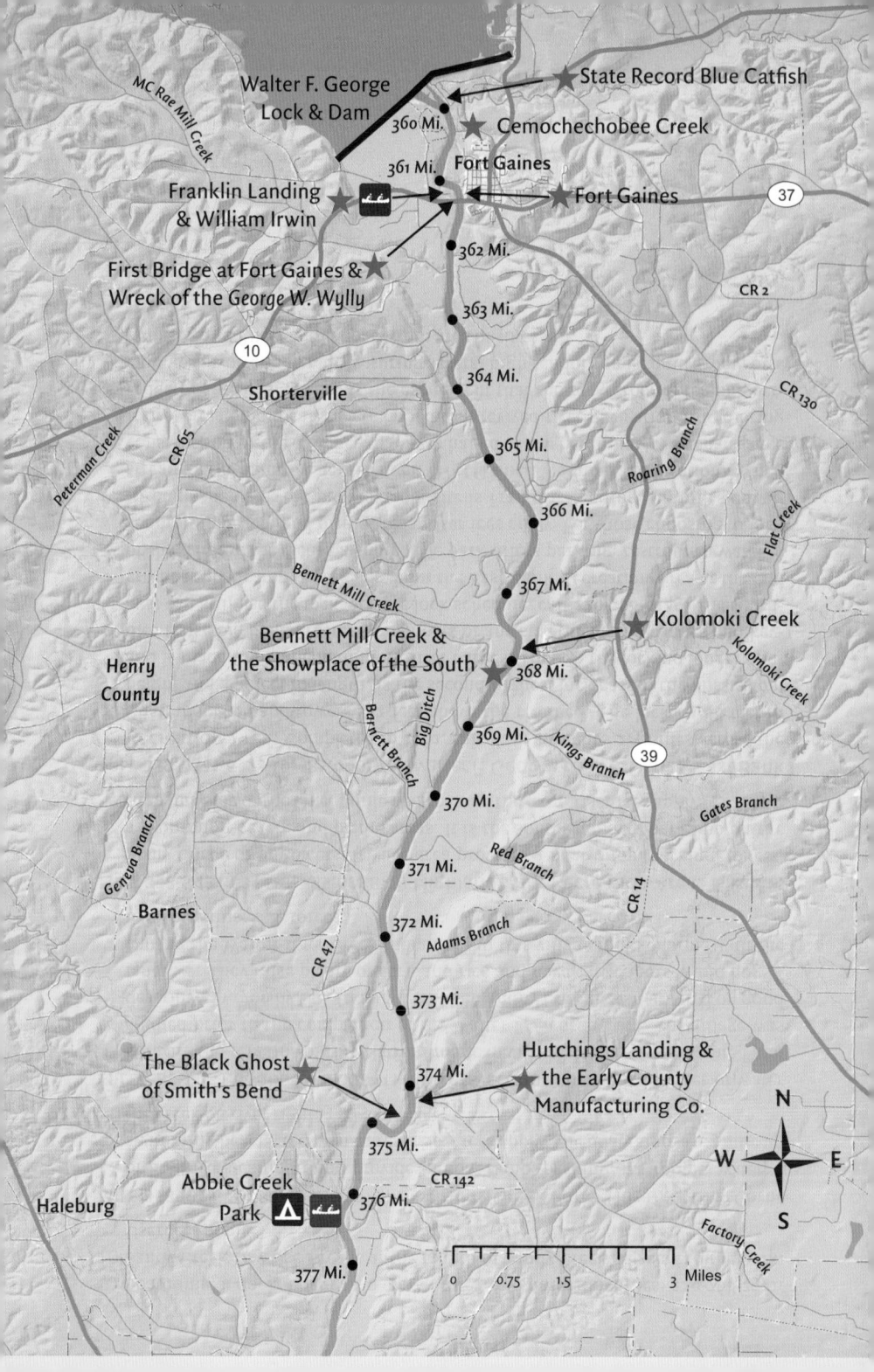

Fort Gaines

Length 17 miles (Walter F. George Dam to Abbie Creek)

Class 1

Time 8–10 hours

Minimum Level The river here is navigable year-round.

River Gauge The nearest river gauge is at the Walter F. George Lock and Dam: http://waterdata.usgs.gov/ga/nwis/uv?site_no=02343241. Boaters should use extreme caution when paddling this section. Hydropower releases from Lake Walter F. George can cause dramatic rises in water levels and flow velocity. Release schedules are issued by the U.S. Army Corps of Engineers daily and can be retrieved at http://water.sam.usace.army.mil/todaySched.htm or by calling 866-772-9542, ext. 244.

Launch Site Unless you are locking through the dam, the nearest launch site to Walter F. George Dam is Franklin Landing, 1.4 miles downstream from the dam on the Alabama side of the river. The landing provides a boat ramp, parking, and pit toilets. User fees apply.

DIRECTIONS From the intersection of Ga. 37 and Ga. 39 in Fort Gaines, travel west on Ga. 37 for 0.8 mile. Turn right onto Powerhouse Road and proceed 0.1 mile. Turn right onto the road leading to the landing and travel 0.2 mile to the parking area.

Take Out Site The take out site at Abbie Creek Park is on river right up Abbie Creek, just off the mainstem of the river. The park provides a boat ramp, parking, camping, pit toilets, and picnic areas.

DIRECTIONS From Franklin Landing, return to Ga. 37 (Ala. 10). Turn right and proceed 3.7 miles to Shorterville. At Shorterville, bear left onto Co. Rd. 65 and proceed 3.6 miles. Turn left onto Co. Rd. 71 and travel 7.3 miles. Turn right onto Co. Rd. 47 and travel 1.1 miles. Turn left onto Co. Rd. 112 and proceed 0.5 mile. Turn left onto Co. Rd. 136 and travel 1.5 miles to the parking area.

Description From the Walter F. George Dam to George W. Andrews Lock and Dam—a distance of 28 miles—the river gives you a taste of what it was before the dams altered the landscape. Flowing through the high Coastal Plain, the river passes beneath tall bluffs like those at Fort Gaines; sandbars become more common, and as always each bend comes with a story from the rich cultural history of the valley.

Outfitters No outfitters operate on this section of the river.

Points of Interest

MILE 359.8 (31.622777, -85.060178) State Record Blue Catfish. Here on February 2, 2010, after a 40-minute battle, Earnest Thompson of Edison, Georgia, landed a 49-inch-long, 80-pound, 4-ounce blue catfish, capturing a new Georgia state record for the fish. Thompson hooked the fish in about 25 feet of water in the tailrace below the dam. He later told reporters: "It looked like a baby elephant with the snout cut off." Thompson donated the fish to the state, and it is displayed at the Albany office of the Georgia Department of Natural Resources. Blue catfish are native to the Coosa River system in North Georgia but have been introduced to the Chattahoochee and other South Georgia rivers.

MILE 360.4 (31.617533, -85.057152) Cemochechobee Creek. "Big Sandy," as the Creek word translates into English, enters on river left here. Near the close of the War of 1812, when U.S. forces battled Great Britain and their Creek Indian allies, the 1814 treaty that General Andrew Jackson signed with defeated Creek warriors designated this creek as the boundary line between U.S. and Creek territories. The treaty forced the Creeks to cede land north of this creek to the United States. Jackson chose this as the boundary because he believed that Creeks from the town of Oketeyeconne (just north of the creek) had allied with the British. Jackson gave orders to build a garrison here to prevent any Creeks from entering the newly acquired territory. "All persons carrying and bringing lies" to the British should be shot, he told his soldiers.

MILE 361.4 (31.606989, -85.057925) Franklin Landing & William Irwin. At river right here is Franklin Landing, the 1814 site of the first white settlement in east Alabama. Settlers of the town endured hostilities with the Creeks for the town's first 20 years but ultimately could not endure the river. After an 1888 flood devastated the town, it was never rebuilt. William Irwin, whose fortunes and death are linked to the river, was one of the town's early merchants. He first arrived in the area in 1819, eventually establishing a large plantation that reportedly encompassed 50,000 acres along the river. In 1825 he was elected to the Alabama state senate, and initially, the city of Eufaula bore his name: Irwinton. In 1850, Irwin was aboard the H. S. Smith on a return voyage from Columbus when the steamer carrying 1,015 bales of cotton caught fire. Irwin, who was reportedly carrying $8,000 in gold coins, jumped off the burning vessel into the river, and drowned. An epitaph on his memorial marker reads: "Roll on, roll on Chattahoochee—mad river! For I thought thou wert created too free to rob others of a brave friend forever and sink all that's dearest to me."

MILE 361.4 (31.604638, -85.055578) Fort Gaines. Atop the bluff on river left here is the city of Fort Gaines. Originally established as a frontier fort during hostilities with the Creek Indians, the town sits atop a 130-foot bluff that provides the perfect (and beautiful) vantage point for observing traffic on the river. During the Civil War, it was repurposed by the Confederacy and outfitted with three cannons to prevent a Union invasion upriver from Apalachicola. During the antebellum era, when river transportation drove commerce, Fort Gaines was

SMITH'S BEND, HENRY COUNTY, ALA.

a bustling town that came to be known as the Queen City of the Chattahoochee, but, as with many river towns, progress bypassed it when railroads (and later interstate highways) were sited elsewhere. In 2010, Clay County ranked as one of Georgia's five least-populated counties and its second-most impoverished county.

MILE 361.5 (31.605630, -85.055859) First Bridge at Fort Gaines & Wreck of the *George W. Wylly*. A bridge has spanned this location on the river since the mid-1800s and has been the site of many a tragedy. The first span was destroyed in an 1855 flood. The second, a covered bridge completed by former slave Horace King in 1869, was similarly damaged by a flood in 1875 and then repaired. In 1883, the bridge was involved in one of the worst steamboat accidents in the river's history. The *George W. Wylly* was steaming downriver in a strong current when she collided with one of its piers, ripping a hole in her stern. Thirteen people died in the wreck, including eight black deckhands and three black passengers. Black steamboat workers, it should be noted, were given the most dangerous jobs. Interestingly, the *Wylly* was the scene of an early attempt by a black man to be treated as "equal." In 1876, a black passenger aboard the steamer took a seat at dinner with white passengers. When asked to leave, he refused, stating that he had paid full fare and deserved the same privileges as others. The clerk of the *Wylly* then took up a knife to threaten the man, grabbed him by the ear, and led him off. Despite the collision with the *Wylly* and being partially damaged in an 1888 flood, the covered bridge spanned the river here until 1925.

MILE 367.9 (31.517237, -85.044507) Kolomoki Creek. From the mouth of this creek on river left, about 7 miles as the crow flies to the southeast, is the site of the largest prehistoric mound complex in Georgia—Kolomoki Mounds. The site includes seven mounds, the largest of which is 56 feet high; archaeologists believe the mounds were built during the Woodland period between 350 and 600 AD. In its time, the village was among the largest dwellings in the Southeast. The creek and the river were likely trade paths for the native peoples who

lived at Kolomoki. By the time the first Europeans arrived, the site had been long abandoned.

MILE 368.3 (31.513762, -85.047793) Bennett Mill Creek & the Showplace of the South. The creek on river right bears the name of the Bennett family that owned land on both sides of the river here. In the 1830s, Colonel James Bennett and his wife, Harriet M. Grace, constructed a mansion on a rise overlooking the river just to the west. Standing three stories tall and with six columns across its facade, the home was visible from the river and among riverboat travelers it came to be known as the Showplace of the South. The Bennetts also ran a ferry near this location to provide access to their Georgia landholdings.

MILE 374.2 (31.433032, -85.064945) Hutchings Landing & the Early County Manufacturing Co. In the mid-1800s this location on river left was the site of a steamboat landing that serviced the Early County Manufacturing Co. Built in 1855 by Anthony Hutchins and other investors, the brick textile mill produced cotton thread that was shipped upriver to Columbus. Six years after the establishment of the mill, Hutchins and his brothers were off to war. He would be the only one to return from the Civil War alive, discharged with tuberculosis in 1862. Though the mill operated until 1876, the region was ravaged by the war, and life back home was not what it had been. With much hard work, he and his wife, Sarah Rebecca, slowly rebuilt their lives. W. H. Andrews, an overseer on Early County plantations before the war, referenced the resilient Sarah in his recollections published in the *Early County News* in 1916: "How was that for a bride who had graduated at the Wesleyan Female College and had never soiled her hands in a pan of dough?" A short journey up Factory Creek leads to a picturesque waterfall.

MILE 374.9 (31.4277754, -85.071501) The Black Ghost of Smith's Bend. This beautiful bend is home to a large sandbar that is a favorite of recreational boaters. It is also home to one of the river's best ghost stories, recorded in Lynn Willoughby's *Flowing through Time: A History of the Lower Chattahoochee*: "In the days before the Civil War, an old black man lived in a hut [here]. Recent hunters had discovered his body, lying in a heap with his five pet alligators and a dog, all of them dead. Some months afterward, just as the roosters were crowing for midnight, a witness saw the old man sitting stiff and motionless in his bateau, which was being drawn to the river by the shadowy forms of five alligators, yoked two abreast, and in the lead crouched in the neck of the leading reptile was the form of a dog with phosphorescent insects lighting his eye sockets. The entourage glided into the water, then eventually veered back to the old man's hut, a fish tail protruding from each gator's mouth."

MILE 376.1 (31.411514, -85.079183) Abbie Creek Park. Near the mouth of Abbie Creek on river right is the boat ramp leading to this park that provides parking, pit toilets, camping, and picnic areas.

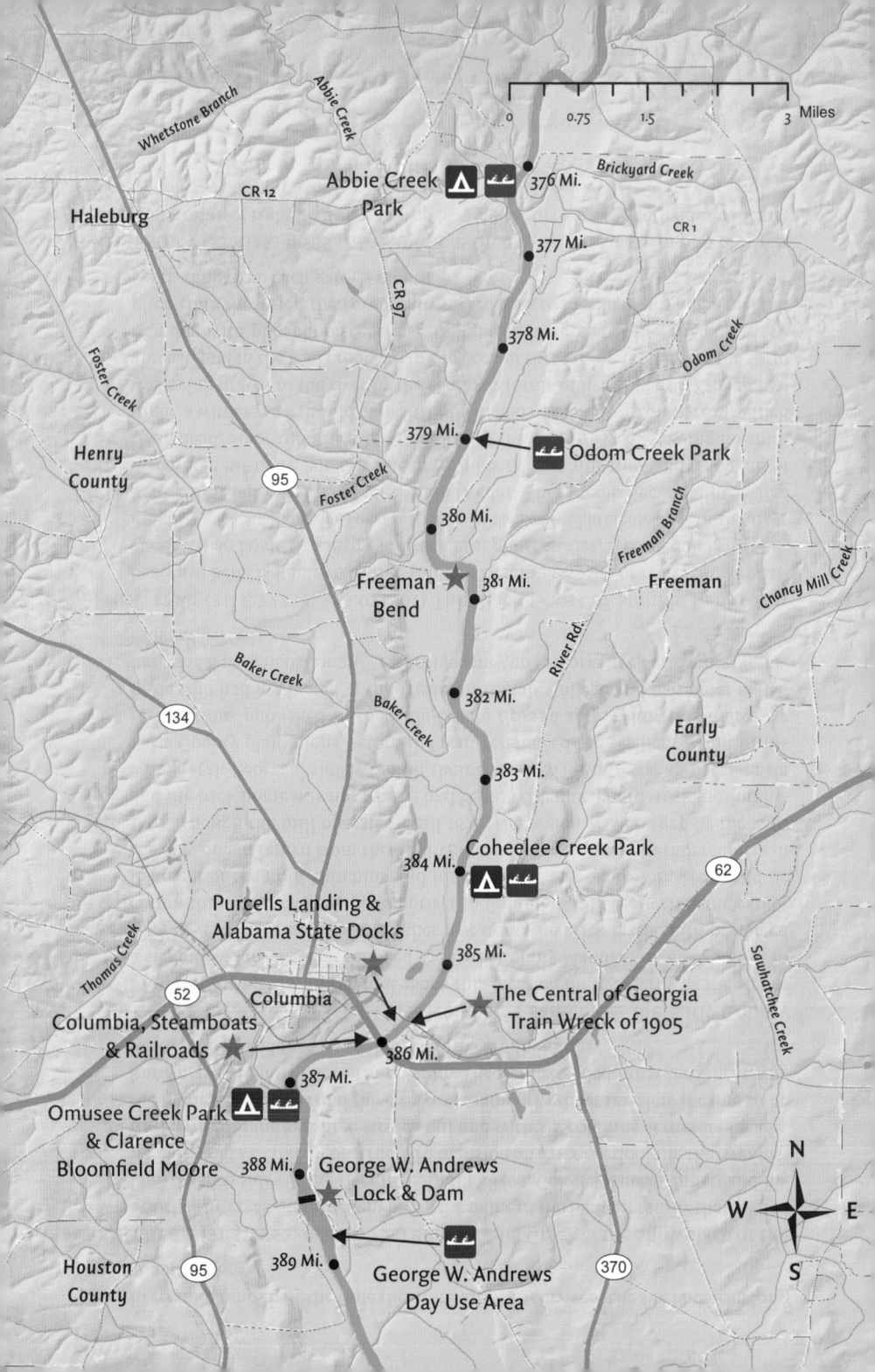

Whetstone Branch

Abbie Creek

0   0.75   1.5   3   Miles

Brickyard Creek

Abbie Creek Park   376 Mi.

Haleburg

CR 12

CR 1

CR 97

377 Mi.

378 Mi.

Odom Creek

379 Mi.   Odom Creek Park

Foster Creek

95

Henry County

Foster Creek

380 Mi.

Freeman Branch

Freeman

Freeman Bend   381 Mi.

134

Baker Creek

Baker Creek

382 Mi.

River Rd.

Early County

Chancy Mill Creek

383 Mi.

Coheelee Creek Park

384 Mi.

62

Purcells Landing & Alabama State Docks

385 Mi.

Sawhatchee Creek

Thomas Creek

52

Columbia

The Central of Georgia Train Wreck of 1905

Columbia, Steamboats & Railroads

386 Mi.

387 Mi.

Omusee Creek Park & Clarence Bloomfield Moore

388 Mi.

George W. Andrews Lock & Dam

Houston County

95

389 Mi.

George W. Andrews Day Use Area

370

N
W   E
S

Coheelee

Length 12 miles (Abbie Creek to George W. Andrews Dam)

Class 1

Time 5–7 hours

Minimum Level The river here is navigable year-round.

River Gauge The nearest river gauge is at the Walter F. George Lock and Dam: http://waterdata.usgs.gov/ga/nwis/uv?site_no=02343241. Boaters should use extreme caution when paddling this section. Hydropower releases through the Walter F. George Dam can cause dramatic rises in water levels and flow velocity. Release schedules are issued by the U.S. Army Corps of Engineers daily and can be retrieved at http://water.sam.usace.army.mil/todaySched.htm or by calling 866-772-9542, ext. 244.

Launch Site The launch site at Abbie Creek Park is at the mouth of Abbie Creek on the west bank of the river. The park provides a boat ramp, parking, camping, pit toilets, and picnic areas.

DIRECTIONS From the intersection of Ala. 10 and Ala. 95 in Abbeville, Alabama, take Ala. 95 South for 0.6 mile. Turn left onto East Alabama Street and then immediately right onto Ala. 95. Continue on Ala. 95 for 13.3 miles into Haleburg. Turn left onto Davis Street (Co. Rd. 47) and proceed 2.2 miles. Turn right onto Co. Rd. 112 and travel 0.5 mile. Turn left onto Co. Rd. 136 and proceed 1.5 miles to the parking area.

Take Out Site The take out site is below the George W. Andrews Lock and Dam on river left. Adjacent to the lock and dam, the site provides a boat ramp, parking, restrooms, and water.

DIRECTIONS From Abbie Creek Park, return to Co. Rd. 112. Turn left and proceed 3 miles. Turn left onto Ala. 95 and travel 5.4 miles to Columbia. Turn left onto Ala. 52 and proceed, crossing the river, for 1.4 miles into Georgia. Turn right onto Co. Rd. 81 and proceed 1.3 miles. Turn right onto Co. Rd. 27 (Andrews Dam Rd.) and proceed 0.8 mile to the parking area.

Alternative Take Out Sites To create shorter trips on this section of the river, boaters can utilize three access points between Abbie Creek Park and the George W. Andrews Day Use Area: Odom Creek (3 miles), Coheelee Creek (8 miles), and Omusee Creek (11 miles).

DIRECTIONS TO ODOM CREEK From Abbie Creek Park, return to Co. Rd. 112. Turn left and proceed 3 miles. Turn left onto Ala. 95 and travel 5.4 miles to Columbia.

Turn left onto Ala. 52 and proceed, crossing the river, for 3.4 miles. Turn left onto Old River Road and proceed 7.2 miles. Turn left onto Odom Creek Park Drive and proceed 2.3 miles to the boat ramp.

DIRECTIONS TO COHEELEE CREEK PARK From Abbie Creek Park, return to Co. Rd. 112. Turn left onto Co. Rd. 112 and proceed 3 miles. Turn left onto Ala. 95 and proceed 5.4 miles to Columbia. Turn left onto Ala. 52 and proceed, crossing the river, 3.4 miles. Turn left onto Old River Road and proceed 1.5 miles. Turn left into the entrance to Fannie Askew Williams Park and proceed 0.8 mile to the boat ramp.

DIRECTIONS TO OMUSEE CREEK PARK From Abbie Creek Park, return to Co. Rd. 112. Turn left and proceed 3 miles. Turn left onto Ala. 95 and travel 5.4 miles to Columbia. Turn right onto Ala. 52 and proceed 1.3 miles. Turn left onto Ala. 95 and travel 1.3 miles. Turn left onto Omusee Creek Road and proceed 0.4 mile. At the fork at 0.4 mile, continue to the left on Omusee Creek Road and travel 0.4 mile to the boat ramp.

Description This 12-mile run from Abbie Creek takes a direct route south, with just a few crooks and bends, as the river flows to the George W. Andrews Lock and Dam. A run-of-the-river dam, it does little to widen the river or slow the current. Boaters choosing to take out below the dam are treated to a ride through the 450-foot-long, 82-foot-wide lock that drops 25 feet from the lake level to the river bed. Public boat ramps and recreation areas dot the river's course, with Odom and Coheelee Creeks as highlights. Short journeys up these creeks lead to picturesque waterfalls and, at Coheelee Creek, to one of Georgia's remaining covered bridges.

Outfitters No outfitters operate on this section of the river.

Points of Interest

MILE 379 (31.374245, -85.086252) Odom Creek Park. A 0.4-mile journey up this creek leads to a series of small but picturesque falls. A boat ramp at the mouth of the creek provides access to parking, pit toilets, and picnic areas.

MILE 380.7 (31.354494, -85.085887) Freeman Bend. This sharp bend in the river as well as the creek on river left just downstream of the bend bear the name of James Freeman, one of Early County's first white settlers, who operated a plantation along the river here. In 1860, he and his family worked the land with 49 slaves.

MILE 384 (31.308673, -85.087282) Coheelee Creek Park. A half-mile journey up the creek on river left takes you to the Coheelee Creek Covered Bridge, one of 15 surviving covered bridges in Georgia. Believed to be the southernmost historic covered bridge in the United States, this 121-foot-long bridge spans a beautiful section of the creek where it spills over a series of rock shelves. The bridge was built in 1891 at a cost of $490. Fannie Askew Williams Park, owned by Early County, surrounds the covered bridge. A boat ramp at the mouth of the creek provides access to Early County's Coheelee Creek Park, which has parking, pit toilets, water, and camping.

MILE 385.4 (31.286836, -85.09511) The Central of Georgia Train Wreck of 1905. A trestle first spanned the river here in 1889 when the Central of Georgia extended a line from Blakeley, Georgia, to Columbia, Alabama. Six years later, tragedy struck here. On February 20, 1905, the steamer *Queen City* had just passed through the 6-year-old drawbridge, but before the span could be moved back into place the westbound train from Blakely barreled across the bridge and plunged into the river. Three crew members on the train drowned in the incident, despite the efforts of the crew of the *Queen City* to rescue them. The bodies proved difficult to recover. One was not found until 10 months later, lodged against a lumber raft in Apalachicola Bay more than 150 miles down river. The modern bridge here was built to allow clearance of river barges.

MILE 385.7 (31.285570, -85.096787) Purcells Landing & Alabama State Docks. On river right in the 1800s and through the early 1900s this was a bustling spot along the river—the site of Purcells Landing. During the days when the river and steamboats drove commerce, local residents would often ride their wagons to this location and camp so as not to miss the boat. Later, as the U.S. Army Corps of Engineers built the river's locks and dams, the state of Alabama established an inland port here on 50 acres, but as commercial navigation dried up, so did activity at the state docks. The Alabama Farmers Cooperative still operates a grain facility here, but none of the commodity leaves via the river.

MILE 386 (31.283590, -85.099598) Columbia, Steamboats & Railroads. One mile west of this bridge on Ala. 52 is Columbia, the oldest continuously occupied town in southeast Alabama. First settled in 1820, for 11 years it was the county seat, and with its strategic location along the river became the center of culture in the region. Steamboats coming and going on the Chattahoochee, servicing the town's three boat landings, made it so. The railroad from Blakely arrived in 1889 with much fanfare. A ceremony was organized for townspeople to witness the drawbridge swing into place for the first time. At the ceremony, one witness quipped: "This was the first time in the history of this place when anyone walked across the river at this point without getting wet." Locals predicted that the new railroad would take the "whole trade of Columbia" to the Savannah cotton markets. Indeed, steamboat trade on the river—and the importance of the town's location by the river—steadily declined. After a second railroad bypassed Columbia to connect with Dothan instead, the town never regained its position as a commercial and cultural center.

COHELEE CREEK, EARLY COUNTY

MILE 387.2 (31.276163, -85.113889) Omusee Creek Park & Clarence Bloom-field Moore. On river right here at the mouth of Omusee Creek, a boat ramp provides access to this park with campsites, restrooms, and a picnic area. This is also a site visited by Clarence Bloomfield Moore. After accumulating a personal fortune at his family paper company in the late 1800s, the Harvard-educated Philadelphian and lifelong bachelor left his business to managers and devoted the next three decades of his life to exploring the Southeast's Native American archaeological sites. In 1905, he plied up the Chattahoochee in his steamer, the *Gopher*, stopping at prospective sites and prodding farmers for permission to dig. By the end of his 155-mile voyage, he'd investigated 21 sites, including a mound near Omusee Creek that stood on a "high bluff above the river" and was one of the largest platform mounds in the region. Like many snowbirds to follow him, Brown usually spent the fall, winter, and spring exploring the South and then in summer returned to Philadelphia's relatively cooler climes to write the reports of his digs.

MILE 388.3 (31.259381, -85.111014) George W. Andrews Lock & Dam. In operation since 1963, this lock was to be another key to turning the Lower Chattahoochee into an industrial center driven by river naviga-tion, but by 2003 lock operators rarely accommodated river barges. Because of lack of demand, in 2012 the lock began operating on an "appointment-only basis" for commercial boats. Recreational boat-ers can still lock through and take out at the day-use area just downstream of the lock and dam. Securing federal funds for the development of the Chattahoochee, and other Alabama rivers, was one of Senator George W. Andrews's crowning achievements. It is perhaps fitting that this unused multimillion-dollar federal project bears his name, for in other are-

GEORGE W. ANDREWS LOCK &
DAM, EARLY COUNTY

nas of politics, he cannot be considered visionary. After the U.S. Supreme Court ruled that segregated public schools were unconstitutional, in 1957 Senator Andrews proposed a bill to create a Commission on Human Resettlement that would provide financial assistance to allow African Americans in Alabama to move to states that supported integration.

MILE 388.7 (31.254313, -85.107717) George W. Andrews Day Use Area. Located on river left, just below the dam, a boat ramp provides access to parking, rest-rooms, water, and views of the lock-and-dam operation.

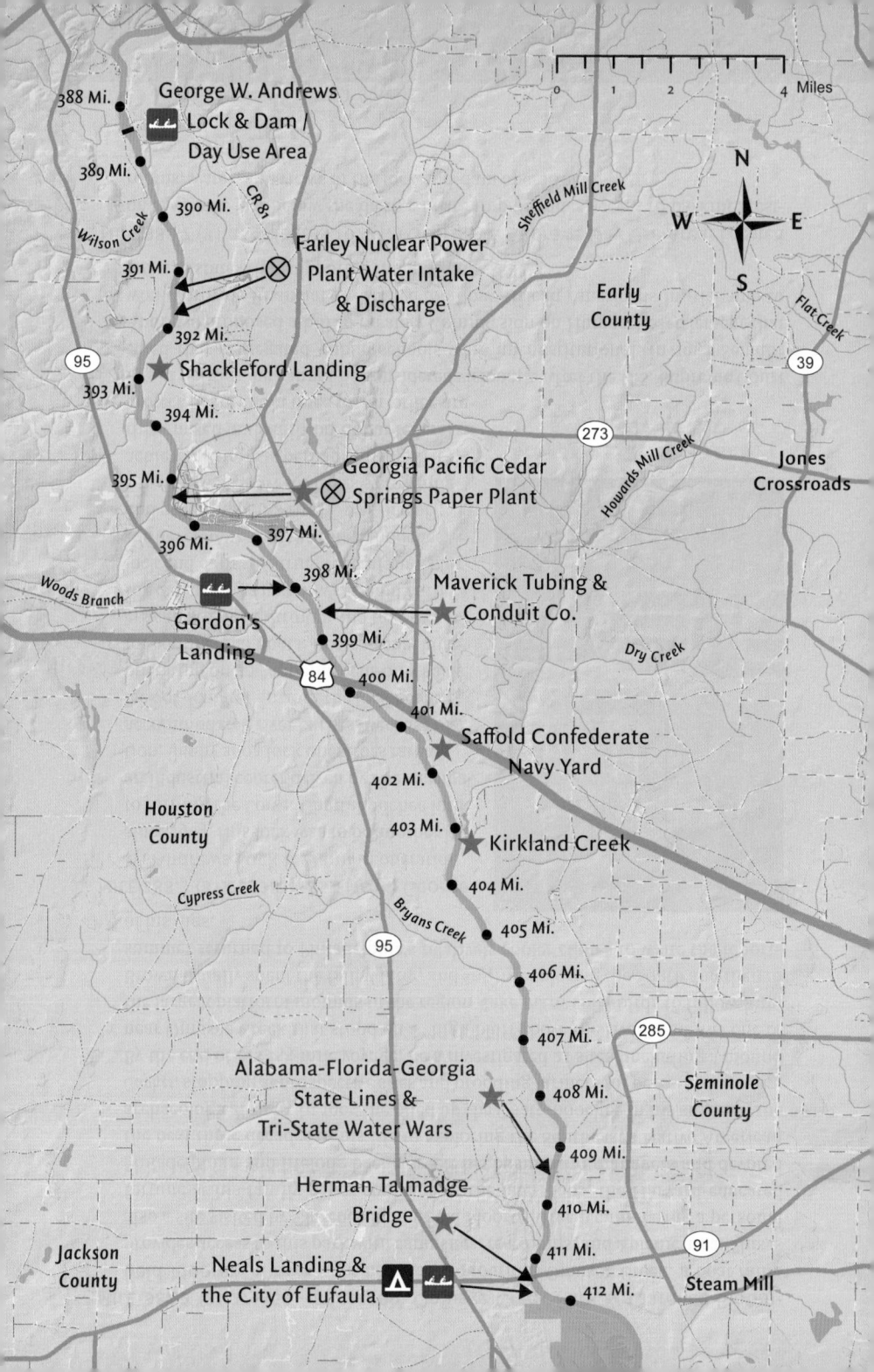

Alaga

Length 23 miles (George W. Andrews Dam to Ga. 91)

Class 1

Time 10–13 hours

Minimum Level The river here is navigable year-round.

River Gauge The nearest river gauge is at the George W. Andrews Dam: http://waterdata.usgs.gov/ga/nwis/uv?site_no=02343805. Release schedules for the Walter F. George Dam that impact water levels and flow volumes in this section of the river are issued by the U.S. Army Corps of Engineers daily and can be retrieved at http://water.sam.usace.army.mil/todaySched.htm or by calling 866-772-9542, ext. 244.

Launch Site The launch site is below the George W. Andrews Lock and Dam on the east bank of the river. It provides a boat ramp, parking, restrooms, and water.

DIRECTIONS From the intersection of Ala. 52 and Ala. 95 in Columbia, travel east on Ala. 52 for 1.4 miles. In Georgia, turn right onto Co. Rd. 81 and proceed 1.3 miles. Turn right onto Co. Rd. 27 (Andrews Dam Rd.) and travel 0.8 mile to the parking area.

Take Out Site Neals Landing Campground is 0.2 mile downstream of the Ga. 91 (Fla. 2) bridge and provides parking, restrooms with showers, water, picnic areas, and campsites.

DIRECTIONS From the George W. Andrews Lock and Dam, return to Co. Rd. 81. Turn right and proceed 2.7 miles. Turn right onto Ga. 370 and travel 7.5 miles. Turn right onto Ga. 363/370 and proceed 1.5 miles. Turn left onto U.S. 84 and travel 2.9 miles. Turn right onto J. Q. Harvey River Road and proceed 7.8 miles. Turn right onto Ga. 91 and travel 2.1 miles to the campground entrance on the left.

Alternative Take Out Site To create a 9-mile trip, boaters can utilize Gordon's Landing.

DIRECTIONS TO GORDON'S LANDING From the George W. Andrews Lock and Dam, return to Co. Rd. 81. Turn right and proceed 2.7 miles. Turn right onto Ga. 370 and travel 7.5 miles. Turn right onto Ga. 363/370 and proceed 1.5 miles. Turn right onto U.S. 84 and travel 2.5 miles. Turn right onto Ala. 95 and proceed 1 mile. Turn right onto Boat Landing Road and travel 0.7 mile. Turn left onto Jowers Road and proceed 0.2 mile to the boat ramp on the right.

Description   This 23-mile run spans three states (passing by the state-line community of Alaga), visits a nuclear power plant, and slips by a paper plant. With the exception of these intrusions by modern industry, the river remains wild and its banks wooded, with numerous sandbars and blue-hole springs on tributaries. It also flows through a landscape rich with antebellum and Civil War history, passing by the Confederate Navy shipyard, where the ill-fated gunboat *Chattahoochee* was constructed.

Outfitters   No outfitters operate on this section of the river.

Points of Interest

MILE 391.3 (31.219229, -85.098287) Farley Nuclear Power Plant Water Intake. At river right here is the water intake for this Alabama Power Co. nuclear power plant. Completed in 1977 at a cost of $1.57 billion, the plant's two nuclear reactors generate about 20 percent of the electricity that the company sells (enough for 800,000 households). This, and other power plants, also demand a lot of water, accounting for nearly 50 percent of surface water withdrawals in the United States. With a growing population demanding more water and energy, environmental advocates now call for the conservation of both. Water is used to produce electricity; meanwhile, electricity is used to treat and deliver water. The U.S. Environmental Protection Agency estimates that if 1 percent of U.S. homes were retrofitted with water-efficient fixtures, about 100 million kilowatt-hours of electricity per year could be saved. Likewise, it takes on average 21 gallons of water to produce 1 kilowatt hour of electricity at our nation's power plants. Thus, reducing demand for electricity can also reduce the need for additional withdrawals from our rivers at new and existing power plants like this one.

MILE 391.7 (31.214017, -85.098158) Farley Nuclear Power Plant Water Discharge. At river right is the water discharge from this facility. Each day it discharges around 100 million gallons of cooling water to the river—at a slightly elevated temperature than the temperature of the river itself. The water is used for two purposes at the plant: to cool the steam used to turn electric turbines and to keep the reactor core and used fuel rods cool.

MILE 392.8 (31.199674, -85.106741) Shackleford Landing. Located on the east bank of the river, in the 1800s this was the river gateway to the Pines, a plantation owned by the Shackleford family. With 217 slaves, the Shacklefords were the largest slave owners in Early County in 1860. The Pines and Mr. Shackleford's daughters drew the attention of Confederate sailors stationed nearby aboard the gunboat *Chattahoochee*, and a visit to the Pines was a welcome distraction from the monotony of their post on the river. Lieutenant George Gift would marry one of the Shackleford daughters, and his account of a visit to the plantation, recorded in Maxine Turner's *Navy Gray*, attests to the opulent lifestyle of the Southern aristocracy: on his arrival at the Pines, Gift was "ushered to a room where a body servant prepared his bath and laid out fresh linen and his uniform. Downstairs, candles and an open fire illuminated a large room with French windows opening onto a verandah. There were comfortable chairs . . . a secretary for writing, a piano piled high with music."

MILE 395.4 (31.167687, -85.099547) **Georgia Pacific Cedar Springs Paper Plant.** The sprawling facility on river left is considered one of the largest containerboard operations in the world. The plant employs about 500 people and uses up to 115 million gallons of water a day to transform wood chips into 100 million tons of containerboard annually. It holds permits from the state to discharge treated wastewater into the river and ranks as one of the state's biggest polluters. In 2011, the facility released more than 2 million pounds of pollutants into the air and water. The visually dramatic wastewater discharge is on river left just around the bend.

MILE 398 (31.147325, -85.068892) **Gordon's Landing.** This public boat ramp and parking area provide an alternative take out, the last public facility until Neals Landing 13 miles downstream.

MILE 398.4 (31.143386, -85.063683) **Maverick Tubing & Conduit Co.** This facility on river left manufactures steel electrical conduit and holds permits from the state that allow the facility to discharge pollutants into both the air and water. In 2012, more than 300,000 pounds of nitrates and 600 pounds of zinc were discharged to the water here. Nitrates can facilitate algal growth in streams and potentially deplete oxygen levels affecting aquatic wildlife. Excessive exposure to zinc is associated with anemia and pancreas damage in humans.

MILE 401.7 (31.104042, -85.033903) **Saffold Confederate Navy Yard.** Here on river left in October 1861, David S. Johnston of Saffold began building the *Chattahoochee*, a 130-foot-long, 30-foot-wide gunboat outfitted with five cannons. Like much of the Confederate Navy's efforts on the river, this vessel was ill fated—a perfect storm of a controversial Confederate strategy, questionable design, and a predictably uncooperative river. Built to steam downriver and break the Union blockade of Apalachicola, the *Chattahoochee* and her mission were seriously hampered by the Confederate decision to build obstructions on the Apalachicola to prevent an upriver assault by Union forces. In January 1863 after floods partially opened the obstructions, the landlocked *Chattahoochee* steamed downriver with hopes of reaching Apalachicola, but within two hours of leaving Saffold, she ran aground—a result of the shallow river and the gunboat's deep draft. She sprang a leak and the steamboat *Uchee* was summoned to tow the wounded boat further downstream to the town of Chattahoochee along the Georgia-Florida state line.

After repairs were completed, in May the crew continued toward Apalachicola only to find the obstruction still impassable. When they began their journey back upriver, the boat's boilers exploded, killing 14 men and leaving the vessel partially sunk. Demoralized and frustrated, two crew members deserted and fled to Apalachicola to join the Union Navy. Later that year, the *Chattahoochee* was raised, towed to Columbus, and repaired. In April 1865, when the Union cavalry captured Columbus, Confederate soldiers set fire to the boat and cut its moorings loose. The boat drifted downstream for 20 miles before sinking. It never fired a shot on the enemy. In 1964 it was recovered from the river, and now a 30-foot section of the *Chattahoochee*'s stern and steam engines are on display at the National Civil War Naval Museum in Columbus.

MILE 403.3 (31.083554, -85.025357) Kirkland Creek. A 0.2-mile journey up this tributary on river left leads you to a beautiful "blue hole"—a spring issuing forth clear, cold water from the Upper Floridan aquifer. This vast underground "lake" provides much of the irrigation water used for agriculture in southwest Georgia, the bread basket of the state. Excessive pumping from this aquifer that feeds South Georgia waterways, especially the Flint River to the east, threatens adequate flows and endangered species—and has exacerbated water conflicts with Florida.

MILE 409.6 (31.000598, -85.001480) Alabama-Florida-Georgia State Lines & Tri-State Water Wars. At this spot, Georgia, Alabama, and Florida share a state line, with Alabama and Florida separated by a boundary extending due west. Georgia and Florida—unlike Georgia's circa-1802 arrangement with Alabama—share the river and from here to Jim Woodruff Dam, the center of the river's channel is the boundary between the two states. In 1990, after Metro Atlanta communities petitioned the U.S. Army Corps of Engineers to withdraw more water from Lake Lanier and the Chattahoochee, the state of Alabama filed suit to prevent this reallocation of water, claiming that it needed sufficient flows to ensure economic development. Florida soon joined the suit, bringing concerns about reduced flows impacting industry and Apalachicola Bay's commercial seafood harvest that depends on adequate freshwater flows. Between 1992 and 1997, the three states and federal government spent $15 million studying the river with the intention to develop a water sharing agreement. Those efforts failed and in 2013, the states were still facing off in court, the river's fate still in the balance.

MILE 411.3 (30.977347, -85.006115) Herman Talmadge Bridge. Built in 1956, this bridge is named in honor of Herman Talmadge, the son of Georgia Governor Eugene Talmadge. When his father died shortly after being elected to a fourth term in office in 1946, the young Talmadge was voted into the office by the Georgia General Assembly. At the same time, newly elected lieutenant governor Melvin Thompson claimed the office of governor, and outgoing governor Ellis

Arnall refused to leave office. The Georgia Supreme Court settled the bizarre three-governor controversy, calling for a special election that Talmadge won later that year . . . but not before Talmadge and Arnall simultaneously occupied the governor's office. Arnall even set up an office in exile at an information kiosk in the capitol.

MILE 411.5 (30.973998, -85.005128) Neals Landing & the City of Eufaula. On February 11, 1921, the steamer *City of Eufaula* caught fire here, drifted downriver 4 miles, and sank. The 45 passengers onboard escaped, but the loss of this steamer prompted Columbus's W. C. Bradley to get out of the steamboat business. He offered to give his remaining ships to the city of Columbus. The *City of Eufaula*'s cargo during her last months in service attest to the river's decline in importance. That year she moved mostly beehives for apiaries on the Apalachicola and carried barrels of turpentine—gone were the days of decks filled with cotton. The boat ramp at Neals Landing leads to campsites, restrooms with showers, water, and picnic areas.

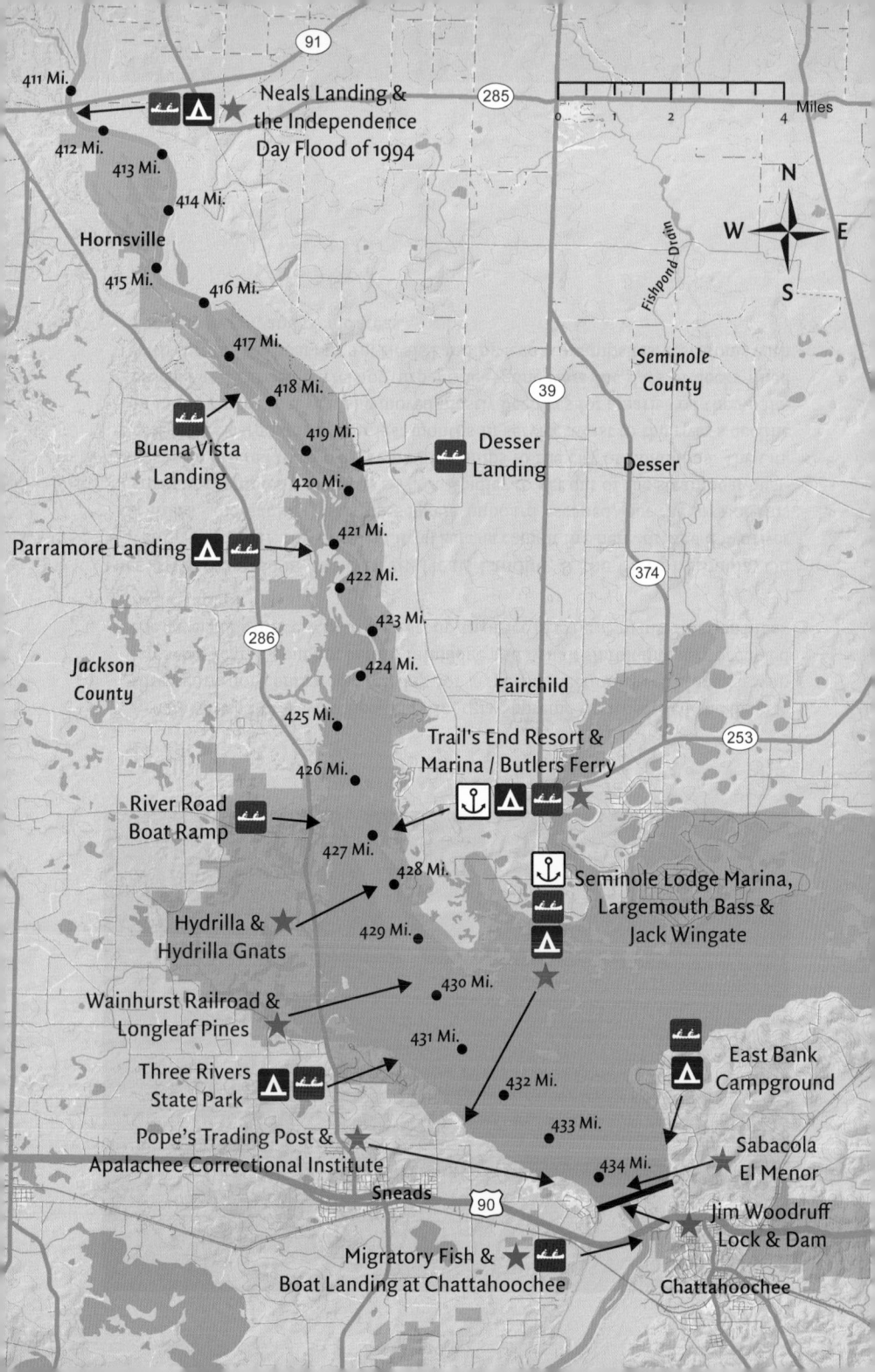

411 Mi.

91

285

Miles
0 1 2 4

Neals Landing & the Independence Day Flood of 1994

412 Mi.

413 Mi.

414 Mi.

Hornsville

415 Mi.

416 Mi.

417 Mi.

418 Mi.

Buena Vista Landing

419 Mi.

Desser Landing

39

Seminole County

Desser

420 Mi.

421 Mi.

Parramore Landing

422 Mi.

286

423 Mi.

374

Jackson County

424 Mi.

Fairchild

425 Mi.

426 Mi.

253

Trail's End Resort & Marina / Butlers Ferry

River Road Boat Ramp

427 Mi.

428 Mi.

Seminole Lodge Marina, Largemouth Bass & Jack Wingate

Hydrilla & Hydrilla Gnats

429 Mi.

430 Mi.

Wainhurst Railroad & Longleaf Pines

431 Mi.

East Bank Campground

Three Rivers State Park

432 Mi.

Pope's Trading Post & Apalachee Correctional Institute

433 Mi.

Sabacola El Menor

434 Mi.

Sneads

90

Jim Woodruff Lock & Dam

Migratory Fish & Boat Landing at Chattahoochee

Chattahoochee

Fishpond Drain

N
W   E
S

Lake Seminole

Length 24 miles (Ga. 91 to Jim Woodruff Dam)

Class 1

Time 11+ hours

Minimum Level The lake is navigable year-round. Information on Lake Seminole water levels is at http://water.sam.usace.army.mil/acfframe.htm. Lake levels generally fluctuate less than 2 feet annually, with 77 feet above mean sea level the average operating level.

River Gauge The nearest river gauge is at George W. Andrews Dam: http://water data.usgs.gov/ga/nwis/uv?site_no=02343805.

Launch Site The launch site is Neals Landing Campground, which provides parking, restrooms with showers, water, picnic areas, and campsites.

DIRECTIONS From the intersection of Ga. 39 and Ga. 91 in Donalsonville, travel west on Ga. 91 for 8.9 miles to the campground entrance on the left.

Take Out Site There are multiple access points on Lake Seminole, which is operated by the U.S. Army Corps of Engineers. Lake users can create many trips utilizing Corps campgrounds and boat ramps as well as local parks. On the mainstem of the river, you'll find at least 10 boat landings in the 24 miles from Neals Landing to Jim Woodruff Lock and Dam. Those wishing to finish their journey on the Apalachicola can lock through Jim Woodruff Dam and use a boat ramp 0.6 mile downstream of the lock. Most facilities require a nominal parking or user fee; campsites also require fees.

Description The Chattahoochee's final 24 miles traverse the backwaters and main body of Lake Seminole, perhaps the most unique of the river's many lakes. Shallow and swampy, especially in the backwaters, the lake covers 37,500 acres and has 376 miles of shoreline. Alligators are common; hydrilla, the invasive aquatic plant, is even more common. Sloughs, some blanketed in lotus and water lily, offer endless off-river exploration opportunities.

Outfitters Three Rivers State Park, in Florida on the west bank of the lake, provides camping, cabin rentals, canoe rentals, picnic areas, restrooms, and water: 7908 Three Rivers Rd., Sneads, Fla. 32460, 850-482-9006, www.floridastateparks .org/threerivers.

Points of Interest

MILE 411.5 (30.974008, -85.005493) Neals Landing & the Independence Day Flood of 1994. In the campground at Neals Landing on river right are markers designating the high-water mark during the flood of 1994. This, and another flood in 1998, rank as the worst floods on the Lower Chattahoochee since the river's major dams were built in the 1950s and 1960s. On July 10, 1994, after Tropical Storm Alberto stalled over central Georgia during Fourth of July celebrations, flows at the Jim Woodruff Dam where the Flint and Chattahoochee Rivers join to form the Apalachicola River reached 206,000 cubic feet per second (cfs); average discharge is 32,900 cfs. As much as 21 inches of rain fell on some locations in 24 hours; the flood killed 33 people and caused $750 million in damages.

MILE 417.8 (30.904853, -84.960029) Buena Vista Landing. This slough on river right here leads 0.2 mile to a Jackson County park that provides a boat ramp, parking, and picnic areas.

MILE 419.6 (30.889064, -84.934752) Desser Landing. This slough on river left leads 0.2 mile to this landing with a boat ramp and parking area.

MILE 421 (30.869340, -84.943872) Parramore Landing. A slough on river right here leads 0.4 mile to this landing that provides a boat ramp, a dock, a restaurant, a bait shop, campsites, restrooms, and water. User fees apply.

MILE 426.9 (30.800156, -84.920966) Trail's End Resort & Marina / Butlers Ferry. The slough at river left leads 0.5 mile to this marina that provides a boat ramp, parking, restrooms, water, a restaurant, camping, cabin rentals, boat gas, and a store. From the 1870s until the 1940s a ferry operated here on the river, and during the days of steamboats this site also served as a landing. Emanuel Turnage established the ferry and landing, selling wood cut from his land as fuel for the steamboats. His son sold the ferry to L. C. Butler in 1923, and the spot soon came to be known as Butlers Ferry. Marina information: 3371 Ga. Hwy. 253 South, Bainbridge, Ga. 39845, 229-861-2000.

MILE 427 (30.804722, -84.943107) River Road Boat Ramp. Directly opposite the slough leading to Trail's End Marina is a slough on the Florida side of the lake that leads 1.6 miles to a boat ramp along River Road.

MILE 428 (30.786834, -84.923817) Hydrilla & Hydrilla Gnats. Along the margins of the lake here are large mats of hydrilla, a nonnative invasive aquatic plant that has taken over Lake Seminole. First introduced in the late 1960s, by 1992 the plant covered 70 percent of the lake. Since then, the U.S. Army Corps of Engineers has found ways to tame the aquatic nuisance using herbicides, grass-eating carp, and an imported insect—the Asian Hydrilla Leaf Mining Fly. Push your vessel into a mat of hydrilla and you will likely be swarmed by these tiny, gnat-like critters. The insects are so prolific that a local Bass Anglers Sportsman Society (BASS) calls itself the Hydrilla Gnats (bass are known to patrol the margins of the hydrilla beds for food, thus the anglers are also found there). These insects bore into the hydrilla, weakening the plant and helping control its spread.

MILE 429.8 (30.762519, -84.916446) Wainhurst Railroad & Longleaf Pines. During the logging boom of the early 1900s, this railroad terminated along the east bank of the river here. The 40-mile line ran from here to Brinson with connections to Donalsonville and Bainbridge and was used to access the once-vast stands of longleaf pines. Prior to European settlement of the Southeast, long-leaf pine forests stretched across 90 million acres from North Carolina to Texas. Today, less than 4 percent remain. More than half of Georgia was covered by pine forest typified by towering longleafs (100 feet tall or more) above an understory of shrubs and grasses that gave the forest a manicured, parklike appearance. Beginning in the 1800s, longleafs around the Chattahoochee were tapped for tar, pitch turpentine, and rosin, and then during the late 1800s and early 1900s they were cut for timber. Dependent on frequent fires to squelch competition from hardwoods, the ancient pine forests were further diminished by fire suppression efforts in the 1900s. With the loss of longleafs, species dependent

AMERICAN LOTUS, SEMINOLE COUNTY

LAKE SEMINOLE, SEMINOLE COUNTY

NEAR EAST BANK CAMPGROUND, SEMINOLE COUNTY

on them like the federally protected red-cockaded woodpecker, flatwoods sala-manders, and indigo snake also began disappearing. Efforts are now underway across the Southeast to restore these forests—part of which were hauled away on the Wainhurst Railroad.

MILE 430.9 (30.743158, -84.920900) Three Rivers State Park. A boat ramp on river right provides access to this Florida state park with camping, cabin rentals, canoe rentals, picnic areas, restrooms, and water.

MILE 432 (30.725167, -84.904030) Seminole Lodge Marina, Largemouth Bass & Jack Wingate. A cove on river right leads to this marina that provides a boat ramp, a dock, camping, hotel rooms, a bait shop–store, restrooms, and water: 2360 Legion Rd., Sneads, Fla. 32460, 850-593-6886, www.seminolelodge.com. The lodge is one of many businesses that has grown up around Lake Seminole's excellent reputation for its bass fishery. In 2008 *Bassmaster* magazine ranked it among its 35 most historically significant lakes in the nation because of its importance in promoting the sport of bass fishing. The lake's stature is due, in large part, to the work of the legendary Jack Wingate, known as the Sage of Seminole, who operated a fish camp and lodge on the Flint River arm of the lake. He was instrumental in bringing the first-ever Bass Anglers Sportsman Society tournament to the lake in 1968. In 2011, he died at the age of 82, but Wingate's Lunker Lodge is still synonymous with Lake Seminole.

MILE 433.8 (30.720705, -84.852980) East Bank Campground. A boat ramp on river left provides access to this U.S. Army Corps of Engineers campground with parking, restrooms, water, camping, and picnic areas. It is located one mile northeast of the dam. 229-662-9273.

MILE 433.8 (30.715780, -84.879630) Pope's Trading Post & Apalachee Correctional Institute. The fenced facility on the high ground along the west bank of the lake near the dam is Florida's Apalachee Correctional Institute, which houses more than 2,000 state prisoners. In 1821 this site along the banks of the river (now under the surface of the lake) was settled by William S. Pope, who established a healthy trade with local Native Americans. As a U.S. subagent to the Native Americans, in 1833 he negotiated a treaty in which the Indians with whom he traded ceded their lands to the United States.

MILE 434.4 (30.711481, -84.864824) Sabacola El Menor. Lying beneath the water of the lake at the confluence of the Flint and Chattahoochee Rivers here is the site of this Spanish mission, established in 1675. The Spanish had hoped to control the Chattahoochee Valley, but their New World rivals, England, proved more savvy in dealing with the Natives. While the Spanish offered Catholicism (and sometimes brutal suppression of the native population), the English offered goods in exchange for deer pelts and other commodities. When the Spanish mission at Apalachicola (upriver in present-day Alabama) failed, the remaining Spanish and their Indian allies retreated to this stronghold. Later, in 1717, pro-Spanish Indians fortified this location, and finally in 1724, a pro-English band of Indians raided the site and it was abandoned. This area of what was then colonial Florida was lost twice by the Spanish, first in 1763 to the British, and then again in 1821 to the United States.

MILE 434.5 (30.708414, -84.864213) Jim Woodruff Lock & Dam. Named for the Columbus businessman who probably did more than anyone to promote navigational improvements to the Chattahoochee, the dam stretches 7,000 feet across the Apalachicola River about 1,000 feet downstream of the confluence of the Chattahoochee and Flint Rivers. It was the first of the Lower Chattahoochee's dams completed in 1957 with hopes of transforming the region into a thriving industrial complex. Woodruff, who formed the Chattahoochee Valley Chamber of Commerce in 1935 to promote river improvements, was a frequent visitor to Washington to lobby for river dams. Though Woodruff's vision of inland ports and industrial facilities lining the river never came to fruition, Lakes Seminole and Walter F. George have transformed the landscape and the economy of the region. The lock is 82 feet wide and 450 feet long, with a 33-foot drop from lake level to riverbed. It provides service to all size boats—both motorized and nonmotorized. For operation hours, call 850-663-4692.

BACKWATERS LAKE SEMINOLE, JACKSON COUNTY, FLA.

APALACHICOLA MILE 435.3 (30.700583, -84.857679) Migratory Fish & Boat Landing at Chattahoochee. Less than 1 mile below Jim Woodruff Lock and Dam on river left is a public boat landing that provides a final take out for those locking through the dam. While the lock has seen decreased use by commercial and recreational boaters through the years, it has recently been employed in an innovative effort to restore populations of migratory Alabama shad and striped bass in the Chattahoochee. When the gates of Jim Woodruff closed in 1957, anglers in Columbus saw an immediate reduction in the historic runs of striped bass, because the dam blocked passage of the anadromous fishes. In 2005, the Nature Conservancy began working with the U.S. Army Corps of Engineers to open the locks during spawning periods, thus allowing fish passage through the dam. The result: a nearly five-fold increase in Alabama shad in the Chattahoochee. The hope is to restore some of the river's historic spawning grounds for not only shad and striped bass, but also the federally threatened Gulf sturgeon and other species.

Animals and Plants along Georgia Rivers

Species are arranged, as best as possible, into groups similar to one another. Mammals move from aquatic toward terrestrial; birds from water birds to birds of prey and wild turkey; fish from cold-water to warm-water species; reptiles and amphibians from smallest (frogs) to largest (alligators), with snakes and turtles grouped together; and plants from largest to smallest, with large trees first, then smaller flowering trees, shrubs, understory vegetation (ferns, canes, wildflowers), and finally aquatic vegetation.

Mammals

Beaver (*Castor canadensis*)

Reaching lengths of up to 4 feet (including the iconic paddle-shaped tail) and weights of up to 60 pounds, beavers are North America's largest rodents. On Georgia rivers they usually live in burrows in the banks, rather than in constructed dens. They are rarely seen during daylight hours, but along the shore, "bleached" sticks that they have stripped of bark are a sign of beaver activity. Beavers are keystone species for clean water, as the wetlands they construct serve as natural filters that capture sediment and other pollutants and provide habitat for many other species.

Muskrat (*Ondatra zibethica*)

This common aquatic rodent grows to lengths of 2 feet (including its foot-long, hairless tail). Though primarily nocturnal, muskrats can sometimes be seen foraging for food during the day. Its riverbank dens are concealed via an underwater entrance. Among its more notable attributes: lips that close behind its teeth to allow underwater feeding, and a prodigious reproductive cycle. They commonly bear four litters of five to seven young each year. They eat primarily plants but also consume mussels, frogs, and crayfish. If you come across a pile of small mussels, it's likely the site of a muskrat feast.

Otter (*Lutra canadensis*)

Reaching lengths of over 4 feet (including its long fur-covered tail), river otters are long and slender compared to muskrats and beavers. They commonly commandeer abandoned muskrat or beaver dens for their homes, but unlike their aquatic neighbors they are carnivores, using their swimming skills to capture fish, crayfish, frogs, salamanders, snakes, and turtles. They also partake of mussels and even birds. Although they are rarely seen during the day, you sometimes hear their barks and squeals and see them in the early morning or at twilight.

Groundhog (*Marmota monax*)

Often mistaken for an otter or beaver, groundhogs (also known as woodchucks) frequent areas where woodlands meet open spaces—like along rivers—where they forage on grasses, plants, fruits, and even tree bark. Yes, woodchucks do chuck wood. Though they are not aquatic, they do swim . . . and climb trees, but den in the ground, lending them their common name. Groundhogs grow to about 2 feet in length and have a short (7–9 inches) furry tail.

Raccoon (*Procyon lotor*)

Known for its black mask and black-ringed tail, raccoons are riverside foragers. While they are highly adaptive and opportunistic, they prefer habitats near water (for food) that are filled with mature hardwoods (for shelter). The Latin *lotor* means washer—a reference to the raccoon's penchant for washing its food before eating. Theories abound about this practice, but to date scientists have not reached any conclusions. Raccoons feed on crayfish, fiddler crabs, fish, and even some snakes as well as fruits and acorns. They grow to lengths of 3 feet and can weigh as much as 20 pounds.

Opossum
(*Didelphis virginian*)

About the size of your average house cat, opossums are North America's only marsupial. After birth (following a gestation period of just 12 days), infants crawl into a pouch on their mother's abdomen, where

they are suckled for about 70 days. They are unique for additional reasons . . . they have more teeth (50) than any other land mammal in the world, and they are immune to snake venom and kill and eat venomous snakes.

Coyote (*Canis latrans*)

A nonnative species to Georgia, coyotes have filled the ecosystem niche vacated by the red wolf, which is a critically endangered species. In the late 1960s, coyotes were reported in only 23 Georgia counties, but in 2010 they could be found in all 159 counties. Their success in the state is attributable to their adaptability: they'll eat anything and live anywhere.

Armadillo (*Dasypus novemcinctus*)

Originally restricted to Texas, nine-banded armadillos have pushed steadily east during the past century and are now found throughout Georgia except in the far north. Their preferred habitat is along streams, and they cross water either by swimming or by walking on the stream bottom while holding their breath. Their

primary food is insects, which they forage from the ground, employing a sensitive nose, a sticking tongue, and feet adapted for digging.

Gray Squirrel (*Sciurus carolinensis*)

The most commonly seen native mammal in Georgia, adaptable gray squirrels survive in many habitats but prefer hardwood forests, where nuts and acorns provide the bulk of their pound-a-week dietary requirements. Cracking the forest masts requires specialized equipment—namely incisor teeth that are continuously ground down but also continuously grow—up to 6 inches per year. Fossil records show that the gray squirrel roamed North America 50 million years ago.

White-tail Deer (*Odocoileus virginianus*)

A species nearly lost to Georgia, white-tailed deer survive now because of restocking and wildlife management programs initiated during the mid-20th century. In 2002, Georgia's Department of Natural Resources estimated the state's deer population at 1.2 million. Hunting season in Georgia for white-tail deer runs from September to January, depending on the area.

Black Bear (*Ursus americanus*)

Prior to the 19th century, black bears were abundant in Georgia, but habitat loss and overhunting dramatically reduced their population. Restrictions on hunting and other management practices implemented during the 20th century have allowed the species to recover. Georgia's Department of Natural Resources estimates a population of more than 5,000. Their range is mostly restricted to the North Georgia mountains, the bottomland forests along the Ocmulgee River, and the Okefenokee Swamp. Reaching weights of up to 500 pounds, black bears are the state's heftiest land mammals, but their weight doesn't slow them down. They are excellent climbers, swim well, and can run at speeds up to 30 miles per hour.

Red Fox (*Vulpes vulpes*) and Gray Fox (*Urocyon cinereoargenteus*)

The gray fox is Georgia's only remaining native member of the canine family, but along Georgia rivers you're more likely to encounter the red fox, a species introduced from Europe by early settlers. That's because the red fox is more common along forest edges, fields, and river bottoms, whereas the gray stays primarily in wooded areas. Grays are distinguished by a mottled gray coat, a black-tipped tail, and the unique ability (for canines) to climb trees. Reds have a rust-colored coat and a white-tipped tail.

Birds

Kingfisher (*Megaceryle alcyon*)

A slate-blue back, wings, and breast belt along with a white belly and crested head distinguish this patroller of riverbanks. Feeding mostly on fish, the kingfisher spends its time perched in trees over the water. In the spring, they construct nest burrows in riverbanks, and mating pairs produce five to eight offspring. Kingfishers, which have a distinctive cry (a loud, harsh rattle usually delivered in flight), are among the most common birds sighted along Georgia rivers.

Great Blue Heron (*Ardea herodias*)

The largest North American heron, great blues grow to almost 4 feet in length and have a 6-foot wingspan. Silent sentinels along riverbanks, they wade slowly but strike with their bill with lightning quickness, feeding mostly on fish, frogs,

and crustaceans, which they swallow whole. Herons engage in elaborate courtship displays and nest in colonies located high up in trees along rivers and lakes. When disturbed, they sometimes let out a loud, distinctive squawk as they flee.

Green Heron (*Butorides virescens*)

A small, stocky wading bird reaching lengths of 18 inches, the green heron is one of the few tool-using birds. It commonly drops bait onto the surface of the water and grabs the small fish that are attracted. It uses a variety of baits and

lures, including crusts of bread, insects, earthworms, twigs, or feathers. It feeds on small fish, invertebrates, insects, frogs, and other small animals.

Great Egret (*Ardea alba*)

Like the great blue heron, this large wading bird reaches lengths of close to 4 feet, but it is distinguished by its all-white plumage and black legs and feet. It is more commonly seen along the Georgia coast. It has the distinction of being the symbol of the National Audubon Society because when the society was founded in 1905, the egrets were being hunted into extinction for their plumes, which were used to decorate hats and clothing.

Osprey (*Pandion haliaetus*)

Known as fish hawks because they feed almost exclusively on live fish, ospreys glide above open water and then dive-bomb their prey, sometimes completely submerging themselves to secure their quarry. Studies have shown that ospreys catch fish on at least 25 percent of their dives, with some kill rates as high as 70 percent. The average time they spend hunting before making a catch is about 12 minutes. Ospreys have a wingspan of 4–6 feet and can be con-

fused with bald eagles because of their white head and brown wings. In flight, however, the white underside of their wings gives them away as eagle imposters. They build large nests of sticks in trees and artificial platforms high above open water.

Bald Eagle
(Haliaeetus leucocephalus)

The bald eagle has been emblazoned on the Great Seal of the United States since 1782 and has been a spiritual symbol for Native people far longer than that. Once endangered by hunting and pesticides, bald eagles have flourished under federal protection. Though regal-looking birds, their behavior is often less than noble. While they do hunt and capture live prey, they more often obtain their food by harassing and stealing it from other birds (like the osprey) or by dining on carrion. They can be found on rivers throughout Georgia.

Turkey Vulture (Cathartes aura)

This large, black bird with a bald, red head can often be seen along Georgia rivers feeding on carrion that has washed onto sandbars or become stranded on strainers. Turkey vultures soar to great heights searching for food, and unique among birds, they have a strong sense of smell, which helps them locate it. They have a wingspan of 4–6 feet and are easily identified in flight by their two-toned wings—silvery to light gray flight feathers with black wing linings.

Wild Turkey (*Meleagris gallopavo*)

Wild turkeys were almost hunted to extinction by the 20th century, but conservation efforts implemented after the 1930s have resulted in a dramatic increase in populations. Benjamin Franklin lobbied for the wild turkey to be featured in the national emblem instead of the bald eagle. He thought the turkey a more noble and beautiful bird than the thieving, carrion-eating bald eagle. Turkeys feed on nuts, seeds, fruits, insects, and salamanders and are commonly seen in floodplain forests along the river. And, they do fly . . . on wingspans of more than 4 feet.

Fish

Brook Trout (*Salvelinus fontinalis*)

The East Coast's only native trout species, brookies require cold, clear water to survive and as such are found only in the highest headwaters of the North Georgia mountains. Aquatic insects, like mayflies, caddisflies, and stoneflies, as well as fish and crayfish make up the bulk of their diet. There are 5,400 miles of trout streams in Georgia. Nonnative rainbow and brown trout can be found in all those streams, but only 142 miles support native brook trout.

Longnose Gar (*Lepisosteus osseus*)

This prehistoric fish is known for its long, cylindrical body and pointed snout filled with many sharp teeth. Little changed since the day of the dinosaur, its body is armored in thick hard scales that Native Americans employed as arrowheads. Its evolutionary longevity might be attributed to its unique ability to acquire oxygen from air. During summer months, when oxygen levels in water decrease, it can often be spotted just beneath the surface and surfacing to "gulp" air—a trait that makes it well adapted for surviving in warm, shallow water.

Striped Bass (*Morone saxatilis*)

Easily identified by rows of dark horizontal lines on their flanks, striped bass are one of Georgia's native anadromous fishes, meaning they move from saltwater to freshwater to spawn. Female stripers can carry as many as 4 million eggs. Once fertilized by males, the eggs need at least 50 miles of free-flowing river to hatch. Less than 1 percent survive to adulthood. Dams have interrupted most migratory routes along the Atlantic and Gulf Coasts, but stocking programs maintain populations on inland lakes and rivers.

Channel Catfish (*Ictalurus punctatus*)

One of 20 catfish species found in Georgia, channel cats are the most commercially important catfish species in North America and are commonly raised in large aquaculture operations.

In the wild they are nighttime hunters, feeding on everything from small fish to algae and insects. They aren't fazed by low-visibility situations thanks to their distinctive whiskers and skin being covered in "taste buds." These external sensors help them locate food by taste rather than sight.

Reptiles and Amphibians

Green Tree Frog (*Hyla cinerea*)

Georgia's official state amphibian, the green tree frog primarily resides along South Georgia rivers. A green back, a white belly, and a white, yellow, or iridescent stripe down each flank distinguish this frog among the state's 30 native species. Protecting riparian vegetation along water bodies helps ensure the survival of this and other frogs.

Snapping Turtle (*Chelydra serpentine*)

Snapping turtles are not commonly seen on Georgia rivers because they rarely bask. Instead, they spend much of their lives on the river bottom under cover of vegetation and mud, where they feed on aquatic vegetation and ambush fish, crayfish, frogs, and anything else that happens to cross their paths. They are most often spotted from May to June, when females leave the water to lay eggs in nearby sandbars or loamy soil. Young hatch out from August through October.

River Cooter (*Pseudemys concinna*)

The consummate baskers of Georgia rivers, you may often spot river cooters sunning themselves on logs or rocks. At the first sign of danger, they plunge into the water, often creating loud splashes. They grow to 12 inches in length, feed mostly on aquatic vegetation and algae, and lay their eggs in sandbars along riverbanks. A pile of broken white shells on a sandbar in August and September is a likely indication of a cooter nest. Georgia limits the wild harvest of river cooters and other turtles that have come under increasing pressure due to demand in Asian food markets.

Spiny Softshell Turtle
(*Apalone spinifera*)

Sometimes described as a pancake with legs, the spiny softshell turtle sports a flat leathery shell. Males and young have dark spots on the shell that are absent in females, which can grow to lengths of 17 inches (males top out at 9 inches). Unique in the turtle world, softshells have the ability to obtain oxygen from adaptations on their throats and anuses, enabling them to remain submerged for up to 5 hours. They are carnivorous, ambushing unsuspecting prey while lying partially covered on the river bottom.

Banded Watersnake (*Nerodia fasciata*)

The most common snake of Georgia's Coastal Plain rivers, streams, lakes, and wetlands, banded water snakes are often spotted basking on rocks, logs, and limbs overhanging the water's edge. They vary in color from light brown or reddish to black in ground-color with darker crossbands, and hunt for fish and amphibians in shallow water. A similar species, the northern watersnake (*Nerodia sipedon*) is restricted to North Georgia.

Water Moccasin
(*Agkistrodon piscivorous*)

Georgia is home to 11 species of water snakes; only the water moccasin is venomous. Unfortunately, five species of water snakes are similar in appearance to water moccasins, making positive identification of moccasins tricky. Moccasins are best differentiated from other snakes by their behavior and habitat preference. They are restricted to Georgia's Coastal

Plain and southern portions of the piedmont. In these regions, they bask on land, stumps, or logs near the water's surface and prefer slow-moving streams, swamps, and backwaters. Common water snakes, on the other hand, bask on limbs and shrubs overhanging the water and prefer large, open reservoirs and rivers. Finally, swimming moccasins hold their heads above the water and their bodies ride on the surface of the water; water snakes swim below the surface. It is illegal to kill nonvenomous snakes in Georgia.

Alligator (*Alligator mississippiensis*)

The largest predator in the state, alligators can grow to 16 feet in length and weigh as much as 800 pounds. They are found only in South Georgia, below the fall line running from Columbus to Augusta. Once a federally protected species, alligators have rebounded in population, and they are now common within their range. During warm weather, they can be spotted basking along riverbanks or patrolling the water with only their snouts visible above the water's surface. Since 1980, there have been only nine confirmed alligator attacks on humans in Georgia, only one of which was fatal.

Macroinvertebrates

This group of animals includes mollusks (mussels and snails), arthropods (crayfish and sowbugs), and aquatic insects (mayflies, stoneflies, etc.). Though usually small, they form the base of the aquatic food chain and play critical roles in clean water. Their life cycles and adaptations are among the most interesting in nature, and their presence, or lack thereof, can be an indicator of the health of a water body.

Native Freshwater Snails

Georgia is home to 67 species of freshwater snails that range in size from 0.1 inch to more than 1 inch in length. Easily overlooked because they dwell on the river bottom, they play an important role in river ecosystems. They scour rocks and other debris of algae, helping maintain healthy water and providing suitable habitat for aquatic insects. Snails, in turn, are an important food source for other wildlife.

Native Freshwater Mussels

Historically, Georgia was home to 126 species of freshwater mussels. However, many have become extinct due to habitat changes wrought by the construction of dams and water pollution. The state is currently home to 14 federally protected species. Because they are filter feeders, meaning they remove nutrients from the water, they play a critical role in clean rivers. They come in various colors, shapes, and sizes, with some species growing to the size of dinner plates. Because their unique life cycle involves fish carrying young mussels on their gills, the loss of some fish species has contributed to declining mussel populations.

Asian Clams
(Corbicula fluminea)

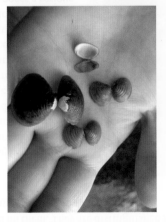

This nonnative, invasive clam is the most commonly seen mollusk in Georgia rivers. Corbicula entered the United States in the Pacific Northwest and are now found in 38 states. Prolific reproducers and adaptable to many habitats, corbicula have flourished where native mussels have struggled. In doing so they have filled a food void. Numerous species of fish as well as crayfish, raccoons, muskrats, and otters feed on them. They are distinguished from native mussels by their size, rarely growing to more than 1 inch in length.

Crayfish

Georgia is home to 73 species of crayfish, many of which are restricted to isolated populations in specific regions of the state. On Georgia rivers, you'll find them beneath rocks and debris on the river bottom, though some species create extensive burrows in the soil near wetlands areas. They are protected by a hard exoskeleton that, as adults, they outgrow and molt once or twice each year. In combination with diminishing stream health because of pollution, the introduction of nonnative crayfish used as bait by anglers poses a serious threat to Georgia's native crayfish.

Hellgrammite (Dobsonfly Larvae)

Flip over a rock in a healthy to moderately healthy stream in Georgia, and you'll find these frightening-looking creatures that are distinguished by two large mandibles. Reaching up to 3 inches in length, the hellgrammite is a predator of other

aquatic insects and is a favorite food of popular game fish species. Dobsonfly larvae develop for one to three years in the water, crawl from the water, dig a cavity to pupate, and emerge 14–28 days later as adults. The adults survive just long enough to mate and lay eggs. The females deposit their eggs, encased in a white covering, on overhanging leaves, logs, tree trunks, or rocks so that when the larvae hatch they fall into the water.

Dragonfly Nymphs

While adult dragonflies are always associated with water, by far most of a dragonfly's life is spent in the water, not hovering above it. Dragonfly nymphs live in the water for up to four years before crawling out for their final molts and becoming adults. The skin (exuvia) left on rocks  and plants along the water can be found long after the molt has occurred. Adult dragonflies generally survive less than two months. Dragonflies are appreciated for their efforts in mosquito control. Nymphs eat mosquito larvae from the water, while adults can consume hundreds of flying mosquitos daily, earning them the moniker "mosquito hawks."

Mayfly Nymphs

Because all mayfly nymphs in an area commonly transform to adults at the same time, mayflies are known for their massive swarms that occur during the summer months. Their life underwater in Georgia rivers consists of clinging to the underside of rocks, where they feed mostly on algae. After a prolonged period (in some cases more than two years), they crawl out of the water to transform into adults. Nymphs are easily identified by their three hairlike tails (though sometimes only two). With fossil evidence confirming their existence more than 300 million years ago, they are believed to be the oldest living winged insects.

Trees and Plants

Sycamore (*Platanus occidentalis*)

A dominant deciduous tree of river corridors, sycamores are easily identified by their dark-brown to gray bark that peels and flakes, revealing a white inner bark. Sycamores also sport large, multilobed leaves that turn yellow and then tan in the fall, as well as conspicuous fruits—a round woody ball that in the winter breaks into many soft, fluffy seeds. Native Americans fashioned the large trunks of sycamores into dugout canoes; beaver, squirrel, and muskrat eat the fruits; juncos and finches eat the seeds. They grow to 80–100 feet tall with a spread of 40–50 feet.

River Birch (*Betula nigra*)

The deciduous river birch is known for its reddish brown to cinnamon-red bark that peels back in tough papery layers, giving the trunk a ragged appearance. In the winter, its fruits and flowers are conspicuous. Male flowers, dangling woody tubes (catkins) that are 1–3 inches long, can be seen on the ends of stems, along with the remnants of the previous year's fruit—1-inch woody cones. In the spring, the male flowers release pollen, fertilizing the emerging female flowers that produce the fruit. Growing to heights of 80 feet, birch play an important role in stabilizing stream banks with their extensive root system. Extracts from the tree are used in herbal treatments for gout, rheumatism, and kidney stones.

Black Willow (*Salix nigra*)

The deciduous black willow is a dominant tree of Georgia's Coastal Plain rivers, especially along sandbars. Distinguished by its long, lance-like leaves, willows are perhaps most conspicuous in the midsummer, when their cottony seeds are borne on the wind, falling to the river and sometimes forming large floating mats of white fluff. Their fibrous roots play a critical role in stabilizing stream banks, and a compound derived from their bark is known for its fever-reducing and pain-killing effects. A synthetically produced variety is found in modern aspirin. Willows can attain heights of up to 60 feet.

Black Walnut (*Juglans nigra*)

Because it thrives in full sunlight, the black walnut is often found in the open, well-lit spaces afforded by riverbanks. In the fall, after dropping its leaves it then drops its golf-ball-sized fruits, and it is not uncommon to find them floating down the river. After removing their husk (which stains hands and clothes), the hard, brown corrugated nut can—with considerable work—be broken to obtain the meat. Walnuts are high in antioxidants and beneficial fats and have more protein than any other nut—thus they are prized by squirrel, deer, and people. Walnuts typically grow to 60–70 feet, but specimens over 100 feet are common.

Red Maple (*Acer rubrum*)

Aptly named because its buds, winged seeds, leaf stems, and leaves (in the fall) are all brilliant red, the red maple is one of the earliest flowering trees of the spring. Its buds sprout long before vegetation appears, and once pollinated, these buds mature to bright red, winged seeds that twirl off, helicopter-like, in the wind. Red maples also change color in the fall long before other trees have begun their transformation. Because of its tolerance for moist soils, it is commonly referred to as swamp maple.

Water Oak (*Quercus nigra*)

A dominant oak of bottomland forests and riparian buffers, water oaks sport leaves that resemble a small kitchen spatula—narrow at the base and widening at a lobed end. Though deciduous, young water oaks are known to hold their leaves through the winter, while leaves on older specimens persist well into the winter. The tree's acorns are important food for squirrel, deer, and wild turkey. They commonly grow to a height of 50–80 feet.

American Hornbeam (*Carpinus caroliniana*)

A tree of the bottomland forest understory, hornbeams grow to 20–30 feet in height and thrive in the shade beneath larger trees. Leaves are egg-shaped with distinct veins radiating from the main stem, ending in toothed leaf edges. The tree's fruit is conspicuous, as the nutlets are contained within a three-winged, narrow, leaflike bract. The leaves turn yellow, orange, and red in the fall and sometimes persist on the tree into the winter, causing confusion with the beech tree, which also holds its leaves in the winter.

Tag Alder (*Alnus serrulata*)

Fibrous roots and flexible stems make this a favorite species for stream bank restoration projects. A shrub-like tree, it grows to heights of 8–12 feet and tends to form thickets along rivers and streams. Like river birch, during the winter months it is easily identified by the pres-

ence of last year's fruit (0.5-inch woody cones) and dangling catkins, which though brown in the winter bloom bright yellow in the early spring. The bark and leaves of the alder have historically been used as an astringent to treat internal bleeding as well as external wounds.

Catalpa (*Catalpa bignonioides*)

Perhaps the showiest bloomer of Georgia's river corridors, the catalpa produces large clusters of white bell-shaped blossoms with purple spots and two large orange markings at the throat. In the summer, these fertilized blooms produce long (up to 16 inches) bean-like pods that hang beneath the tree's heart-shaped leaves. The pods ripen and turn brown in the fall, eventually splitting to release paper-thin fringed seeds that float off in a breeze. Catalpas are best known as the sole host for catalpa sphinx moth larvae—a black-and-yellow, horned caterpillar highly prized by anglers as fish bait.

Mountain Laurel (*Kalmia latifolia*)

A showy shrub of the Georgia mountains and piedmont (and occasionally the Coastal Plain), mountain
laurel produces abundant clusters of white-to-pink
honeycomb-shaped blooms in the early spring. It
is commonly seen along Georgia rivers at rocky
outcroppings. Its evergreen leaves are conspicuous in
the winter, but can be confused with rhododendron,
another evergreen, flowering shrub. Rhododendron
leaves are larger and more elongated. The leaves of
the mountain laurel, as well as those of rhododendron
and azalea, are toxic if consumed in quantity.

Piedmont Azalea (*Rhododendron canescens*)

In 1979, the Georgia General Assembly designated
wild azaleas as the state wildflower, and with good
reason: Georgia is home to 10 of North America's
16 native azalea species. Almost all are partial to
moist woodlands and stream banks, thus traveling
Georgia's rivers you are likely to encounter many,
from the hammock sweet azalea on the coast to the
sweet azalea of the mountains. Piedmont azalea is
among the most common. Its pink-to-white flowers
appear from March through early May and emit a
sweet, musky fragrance. Azaleas are considered
shrubs and rarely grow taller than 15 feet.

Dogwood (*Cornus florida*)

Perhaps the best known of North America's native flowering trees, dogwoods are common understory trees in floodplain forests along Georgia's rivers. The iconic four-petal, white flower blooms from March through April. In the fall the leaves turn scarlet red and the red berries become very conspicuous. Songbirds, wild turkeys, and a host of mammals—from chipmunks to bears—feed on these berries. Historically, humans have employed the root bark as an antidiarrheal agent, fever reducer, and pain reliever. Dogwoods grow up to 20 feet in height with a spread of up to 30 feet.

Persimmon (*Diospyros virginiana*)

A lover of bottomland forests, persimmons can be found growing along streams and rivers in Georgia, and occasionally the prized fruit can be plucked from branches overhanging the water in the late fall. The plum-sized pulpy fruit filled with large seeds is very sweet, but only after it is fully ripe (usually after a hard frost). Unless the fruits are fully orange to black—and soft—avoid them. Unripe persimmons can leave you puckering and longing for a drink of water. Birds, deer, and hogs eat the fruits and thus help distribute the seeds throughout the forest. Persimmons can grow to 80 feet in height.

Dog Hobble (*Leucothoe fontanesiana*)

Like its close relatives rhododendron and mountain laurel, this member of the heath family is an evergreen shrub, making it easy to identify during the winter. In the spring, it produces showy clusters of small, white bell-shaped blossoms that are often concealed beneath the leaves. Its common name is derived from its dense tangle of arching branches that make traveling through it a chore. Hunters say that bears run through stands of dog hobble to distance themselves from pursuing hounds. The leaves and flower nectar are poisonous to both humans and animals.

Yellowroot (*Xanthorhiza simplicissima*)

A streamside dweller throughout the state, this unique shrub derives its common name from the color of its roots and inner bark. In the early spring before its leaves appear, it puts out 2-to-4-inch clusters of purple star-shaped flowers. The leaves are unique; their deeply toothed edges giving them a lacey appearance. In the fall they turn yellow, bronze, or red. It has long been recognized for its medicinal properties in treating ulcers of the mouth and stomach. It tends to grow in dense thickets and reaches no more than 3 feet in height.

Elderberry (*Sambucus nigra*)

Common along streams, springs, and swamps, the elderberry is a favorite of songbirds and humans thanks to its abundant purple berries that appear in the late summer and early fall. More than 50 birds are known to feed on elderberries, and humans transform the berries into wines, jellies, and pies. The plant was an important food and medicinal source for Native Americans, who also fashioned the stems into flutes and arrow shafts. Elderberries tend to form thickets that commonly reach heights of 12–15 feet. The flower and berry clusters sit conspicuously at the top of the foliage.

River Cane (*Arundinaria gigantean*)

Arundinaria is the only genera of bamboo native to North America. Growing in expansive, dense stands known as canebrakes, it was once the dominant plant along Georgia's rivers, but today scientists believe that it occupies less than 5 percent of its original range due to agriculture, grazing, fire suppression, and urbanization. It propagates primarily through rhizomes, with these spreading roots leading to the impenetrable canebrakes. The demise of river cane has likely contributed to the pollution of our streams, as it plays a critical role in slowing stormwater and filtering pollutants. Native Americans used the plant for nearly everything, fashioning it into spears, arrows, baskets, homes, mats, knives, torches, rafts, tubes, and drills.

River Oats
(*Chasmanthium latifolium*)

This 2-to-4-foot-tall native grass is distinguished by its seed head clusters that resemble flattened oats. In the summer, these clusters are bright green, but with the fall they turn brownish tan along with the plant's grasslike leaves. Like other riparian vegetation, it plays a critical role in stabilizing stream banks and minimizing erosion. It also serves as food for many songbirds.

Sensitive Fern (*Onoclea sensibilis*)

This shade-loving fern is found in floodplain forests along rivers and streams as well as in swamps and marshes. To the untrained eye, the fronds of this fern may look very unfernlike because of the generous space between lobes. By late summer, fertile fronds arise that resemble an elongated cluster of dark brown beads on a stalk. Like many ferns, the leaves of the sensitive fern contain toxins that dissuade grazing by deer.

Cinnamon Fern (*Osmunda cinnamomea*)

Cinnamon fern flourishes where its roots remain wet; thus it is a common fern along the river's edge. A large fern, it sends up several fronds in a palmlike whorl that reach 5 feet in length. The fertile fronds (cinnamon-colored stalks bearing the plant's spores) rise from the center of the whorl. In early spring, the young, hairy fiddleheads are a culinary treat for both humans and beasts, and hummingbirds are known to line their nests with the "hair" that covers this early growth. Fossilized fern specimens resembling cinnamon ferns date back 220 million years.

Privet (*Ligustrum sinense*)

Next to kudzu, perhaps no other invasive plant has done more to alter Georgia's woodlands. A native of China, privet was introduced into the United States in 1852 for use as an ornamental shrub. By the mid-20th century, it had escaped domestic cultivation and spread throughout Georgia. It can grow to 30 feet in height and, owing to its ability to spread via seeds and sprouts, it forms dense thickets, outcompeting native species like river cane. Once established, it is very difficult to remove.

Its berries are eaten by many songbirds (which unfortunately further disperse the seeds), and beavers like the bark. Privet sports sickly-sweet-smelling white blooms in the spring and summer, which produce blue-black berries that persist on the plant into the winter.

Cardinal Flower (*Lobelia cardinalis*)

From July through September, it is difficult to find a Georgia river that does not have the tall slender green stalks of cardinal flower topped by a cluster of brilliant red blooms along its banks. The stalks can grow to up to 4 feet in height and are common along the base of the riverbank. A lover of moist soils, some have even been seen growing in cavities of partially submerged logs. Their common name is derived from the colored vestments worn by cardinals of the Roman Catholic Church. That color makes the plant irresistible to hummingbirds, which, along with bees and butterflies, are the flower's primary pollinators.

Aquatic Plants

Riverweed/Threadfoot (*Podostemum ceratophyllum*)

This inconspicuous and highly specialized aquatic plant grows on rocks and boulders on the river bottom in swift-moving shoals, rapids, and waterfalls of Georgia rivers above the fall line. Its threadlike masses have an unusual rubbery, seaweed-like texture sporting many narrow olive-green leaves. It plays an important role in stream ecology by providing habitat and food for aquatic insects that form the base of a river's food chain.

Water Willow (*Justicia americana*)

This perennial aquatic wildflower is common along river, stream, and lake margins and is often seen in large, dense colonies. Grasslike, its has leaves very similar to those of the black willow tree, but its white-to-pale-purple orchidlike blooms with purple streaks on the lower petals make this plant easy to identify. The blooms that appear throughout the summer are borne at the top of long (up to 3 feet) slender stems. Another important plant for the river's macroinvertebrate community, mammals also make use of it. Deer browse the leaves, while beavers and muskrats consume the plant's rhizomes.

Pennsylvania Smartweed (*Polygonum pensylvanicum*)

There are more than a dozen native species of smartweed in Georgia, with Pennsylvania smartweed being one of the most important for waterfowl, songbirds, and mammals. Stands of smartweed provide cover for young waterfowl, and the shiny black seeds produced in the late summer provide food for those waterfowl and dozens of other birds. Muskrats, raccoons, and fox squirrels also feast on the seeds and the plants themselves. The white-to-light-pink blooms of smartweed are borne on spikes at the end of stems.

Aquatic Species of Interest in the Chattahoochee River

Greater Jumprock (*Moxostoma lachneri*)

Found only in the Apalachicola-Chattahoochee-Flint River system (and nowhere else on earth), the jumprock is a lover of fast-moving currents and rocky river bottoms and is thus found in the Upper Chattahoochee and its larger tributaries.

A member of the sucker family, it has a long cylindrical body and narrow head. It reaches lengths of up to 17 inches.

Broadstripe Shiner (*Pternotropis euryzonus*)

Found in small, clear streams of the Lower Chattahoochee from Columbus downstream to Lake Seminole (and nowhere else in the world), this 2-inch endemic minnow usually inhabits cover around woody debris and aquatic plants where it feeds on adult and larval insects and other detritus. It gets its name from the broad, blue-gray band that runs along its flank from its nose to the tail fin. That band is bordered above by a narrow orange stripe.

Chattahoochee Sculpin (*Cottus chattahoochee*)

There are more than 700 species of sculpins in the world, but this one is unique to the Chattahoochee and its tributaries above the fall line. With oversized pectoral fins, a flattened body, a narrow tail, and a mottled camouflaged back, sculpins are specialized for life on the bottom of rivers and streams in swift-moving water. The Chattahoochee variety, first described in 2007, appears to be highly sensitive to temperature changes and is found primarily in streams draining heavily forested areas. Although dams on tributaries have eliminated much of this fish's habitat, Buford Dam on the mainstem of the Chattahoochee has created suitable habitat because of the cold water issuing forth from Lake Lanier.

Halloween Darter (*Percina crypta*)

This uniquely named member of the perch family, found only in the Chattahoochee River and Flint River basins, sports black bands along its flanks against a yellow, amber, and orange background. It grows to lengths of 5 inches and is found in shallow, swift-moving water associated with shoals. Its distribution demonstrates how dams fragment fish habitat. They have been found in the Upper Chattahoo-chee and Chestatee Rivers of the Blue Ridge as well as the Flint and streams feeding the Lower Chattahoochee in South Georgia. The fish once likely ranged up and down the river basin, but dams have permanently isolated populations, making their continued survival more tenuous. They are listed by the state as a threatened species.

Shinyrayed Pocketbook (*Hamiota subangulata*)

Listed as federally endangered, this is the beauty queen of Georgia's mussels. Reaching lengths up to 3 inches, the yellow shells of this mussel are marked with bright emerald green rays. It is found only in portions of the Chattahoochee, Flint, and Ochlocknee Rivers in Georgia and the Apalachicola River in Florida. It is one of six federally protected mussels found in the Apalachicola-Chattahoochee-Flint River system.

Gulf Moccasinshell (*Medionidus penicillatus*)

Listed as federally endangered, the Gulf moccasinshell grows no larger that 2.5 inches in length. Its shell is yellow to greenish brown and is marked with fine, interrupted green rays. The inner shell is dark purple or green. Though it once ranged throughout the Apalachicola-Chattahoochee-Flint River system, it is now believed to only be found in portions of the Flint and Chattahoochee systems and is considered one of the rarest of the river's native mussel fauna.

Oval Pigtoe (*Pleurobema pyriforme*)

Once one of the most common mussels in the Apalachicola-Chattahoochee-Flint River system, today it is listed as federally endangered due to habitat degradation, pollution, and dam construction. It is believed to have been eliminated from two-thirds of its historic  range and can now be found only in small sections of the Chattahoochee, Flint, and Ochlocknee Rivers. They grow to about 2 inches in length and are difficult to identify because the shape and color of the shell vary greatly.

Purple Bankclimber (*Elliptoideus sloatianus*)

Listed as federally threatened, this mussel is among the largest found in the Chattahoochee River. Its shell can reach lengths of up to 8 inches, but most specimens are about 4 inches long. Dark-gray to black with many bumps and ridges on the outside, on the inside the shell is smooth and white with deep purple coloration along the edges. Archaeological evidence suggests that it was a staple in the diet of Native Americans.

Protecting the Chattahoochee

If you have put this book to use by exploring the Chattahoochee, you can cite dozens of reasons to protect the river and its tributaries.

Unfortunately, just a small portion of Georgia's population is as lucky as you are, but even those who have never set foot or paddled in this river need do little more than look around them to find a million reasons to protect it—the more than 4 million residents who depend on the Chattahoochee for all, or a portion, of their drinking-water supply.

Dams, pollution, and water diversions all threaten Georgia's longest and most important river, which is the lifeblood for communities that lie along its banks.

You can protect the Chattahoochee by getting involved in one of the organizations listed below. Make a contribution to support their efforts, volunteer as a water monitor, get involved in a river cleanup, learn about Georgia's laws protecting our rivers, report problems when you see them, engage elected officials in supporting laws that protect our rivers, and tell your friends and neighbors about the treasure that is the Chattahoochee.

Can one person make a difference? You bet, and the river teaches us how. The spring that begins the Chattahoochee, in and of itself, is but a trickle of water—enough to fill the canteen of a backpacker, yet by the time the young Chattahoochee has traveled less than a mile, it has been joined by dozens of other trickles. The combined force of these waters has carved and etched a path out of the mountains. As other tributaries join the flow, a mighty movement forms—an unstoppable force that nourishes about 40 percent of Georgia's population.

Likewise, the lives we lead and the choices we make can create a mighty movement—one that cherishes and protects the Chattahoochee River.

Chattahoochee Riverkeeper
3 Puritan Mill
916 Joseph E. Lowery Blvd. NW
Atlanta GA 30318
404-352-9828
www.chattahoochee.org

Chattahoochee River Warden
P.O. Box 985
Columbus GA 31902
706-649-2326
www.chattahoocheriverwarden
.com

Georgia River Network
126 S. Milledge Ave.
Suite E3
Athens GA 30605
706-549-4508
www.garivers.org

Georgia Water Coalition
www.garivers.org/gawater

The Georgia Conservancy
817 W. Peachtree St.
Suite 200
Atlanta GA 30308
404-876-2900
www.georgiaconservancy.org

Georgia Sierra Club
743 E. College Ave., Suite B
Decatur GA 30030
404-607-1262
www.georgia.sierraclub.org

Georgia Wildlife Federation
11600 Hazelbrand Rd.
Covington GA 30014
770-787-7887
www.gwf.org

The Nature Conservancy
1330 W. Peachtree St. NW
Suite 410
Atlanta GA 30309
404-873-6946
www.nature.org

The Trust for Public Land
600 W. Peachtree St. NW
Suite 1840
Atlanta GA 30308
404-873-7306
www.tpl.org

Photo Credits

All photos are by Joe Cook except the following, for which the author thanks the photographers:

Brett Albanese, Georgia DNR: 234 bottom; 258 top, middle, and bottom; 259 top

R. D. Bartlett: 236 bottom

Steven J. Baskauf, http://bioimages. vanderbilt.edu: 242 left and right; 243 left and right; 244 left and right; 245 right; 246 right; 247 left and right; 248 left and right; 249 bottom right; 251 top and bottom right

Giff Beaton: 231 bottom; 232 top and middle; 241 top and middle

Alan Cressler: 257 top

EIC, used under Creative Commons license 3.0: 228 middle

Kevin Enge: 237 bottom

Arlyn W. Evans: 257 bottom

Cris Hagen: 238

Ty Ivey: 232 bottom

John Jensen: 229 bottom

Steven G. Johnson, used under Creative Commons license 3.0: 235 middle

Phillip Jordan: 228 bottom; 229 top; 230 bottom; 233 middle and bottom; 234 top; 245 left

Thomas Luhring: 236 top

Linda May, Georgia DNR: 249 top and bottom left

James H. Miller: 253 bottom

James H. Miller and Ted Bodner: 250

top, middle, and bottom; 252 bottom; 254; 256 top and bottom

Hugh and Carol Nourse: 252 top left, center, and right; 253 top; 255 top; 257 middle

Richard Orr: 240 middle; 241 bottom

Robert Potts, © California Academy of Siences: 227 top

Todd Schneider, Georgia DNR, Wildlife Resources Division: 246 left; 251 bottom left; 255 middle and bottom

David E. Scott: 235 top and bottom

Terry Spivey, USDA Forest Service, Bugwood.org: 229 middle

David Stone: 240 bottom

Robert Wayne Van Devender: 237 top and middle

Jess Van Dyke: 239 top

Daniel F. Vickers: 227 bottom; 228 top; 231 top left and top right; 233 top

Jason Wisniewski, Georgia DNR, Wildlife Resources Division: 259 middle and bottom; 260

Whatcom County Noxious Weed Board: 239 bottom

Tom Wilson: 230 top and middle

Jason Wisniewski: 239 middle

Robert T. Zappalorti: 236 middle